Routledge Revivals

RATIONAL EVOLUTION
(THE MAKING OF HUMANITY)

RATIONAL EVOLUTION
(THE MAKING OF HUMANITY)

BY

ROBERT BRIFFAULT

Routledge
Taylor & Francis Group

First published in 1930 by The Macmillan Company

This edition first published in 2018 by Routledge
2 Park Square, Milton Park, Abingdon, Oxon, OX14 4RN
and by Routledge
52 Vanderbilt Avenue, New York, NY 10017, USA

Routledge is an imprint of the Taylor & Francis Group, an informa business

Publisher's Note
The publisher has gone to great lengths to ensure the quality of this reprint but points out that some imperfections in the original copies may be apparent.

Disclaimer
The publisher has made every effort to trace copyright holders and welcomes correspondence from those they have been unable to contact.

A Library of Congress record exists under ISBN:

ISBN 13: 978-0-367-18072-0 (hbk)
ISBN 13: 978-0-367-18075-1 (pbk)
ISBN 13: 978-0-429-05942-1 (ebk)

RATIONAL EVOLUTION
(*THE MAKING OF HUMANITY*)

RATIONAL EVOLUTION

(THE MAKING OF HUMANITY)

BY

ROBERT BRIFFAULT

NEW YORK

THE MACMILLAN COMPANY

1930

Set up and printed. Published October, 1930.

SET UP BY BROWN BROTHERS LINOTYPERS
PRINTED IN THE UNITED STATES OF AMERICA
BY THE CORNWALL PRESS

PUBLISHER'S NOTE

Rational Evolution is a completely rewritten edition of a book by the same author published originally in 1919 under the title *The Making of Humanity*. In its first editions it enjoyed wide reading, provoked considerable discussion, and brought much commendation to its author. Its publishers have pleasure in presenting this new edition, printed for the first time in the United States from new plates.

CONTENTS

RATIONAL EVOLUTION
(*THE MAKING OF HUMANITY*)

I

MAN THE CREATOR

THE intellectual revolution of the nineteenth century has transformed the conception of history in much the same manner as the intellectual revolution of the seventeenth century changed that of the cosmic universe. Like the pre-Copernican world, encased in crystalline domes adorned on their outermost layer with adherent stars, the notions that were entertained less than one hundred years ago concerning the career of the human race were dingy, stunted, and mean. History was, like the primitive epic whence it evolved, exclusively concerned with racial, dynastic, and religious edification. The date 4004 B.C. was gravely accepted as the boundary of its retrospect, and long before reaching back to it, the conventional fable faded into pure legend and mythology.

As when awakening science crashed through the tinsel vaults of puerile cosmologies, discovering the sun-strewn infinities through which speeds our quivering earth-mote, so have the mists of legend lifted, and it is given unto us to view the panorama of man's long and wonderful career in something of its natural perspective and proportions. Those ages that were once peopled with the myths and monsters of fable now show a world of teeming nations. Peering down the vista of Time we may perceive our own civilisation in the making, Europa that is to be, borne on forked-prowed Kretan galleys that seam, from the Nileland and the Aegean shores of Italy and Spain, the midland sea; jingling donkey-caravans which bear from the Twin Rivers, through the realm of the pig-tailed Hittite, to the Euxine and Phrygia the freight of a culture that reaches farther back than Archbishop Usher's date of the creation of the world. Ten thousand years before, the Magdalenians of the Pyrenean foothills are seen decking with strange frescoes their temple-caves, and weirdly dancing their rites accoutred in the masks of beasts—prototypes of those which Attic maidens shall don at the shrine of Artemis Brauronia, and of those through whose brazen mouths shall be chanted the lapidary lines of Aeschylean choruses. Yet even that savage culture of the last Ice Age is a mature fruit, the culmination of successive eras of human growth computed by hundreds of thousands of years. Beyond stretch æons of time as unseizable to our imagination as are the distances of sidereal space.

Transferred to the open vastness of those expanses the whole perspective, the meaning itself, of history is changed. As in the geocentric theory of the universe, the view which obtained was not merely untrue; it was an exact inversion of the truth. The career of mankind was conceived as one of continuous degeneration. It was held to have had its beginning in the perfection of a divinely endowed humanity, to have run a downward course into deeper and deeper corruption, sinking to the level of modern humanity, the debased and decrepit progeny of the mighty men of old. Savage races found in remote lands were held to be the descendants of once noble and civilised ancestors. Degeneration was the law of history. The Past was the repository of virtue and lost wisdom. It stood exalted above the puny Present in proportion to its antiquity. The revelation of the eternal standards of truth and good were to be sought in what were deemed the most ancient human records. Learning and scholarship consisted in the study of the ancients, not on account of paramount interest attaching to historical enquiry, but because culture was to be obtained only by drawing from its undefiled source in the Past. The function of historical studies was to hold up the excellences of our forebears as a paradigm to a waning age.

Those views are not the quaint fancies of the Middle Ages. It is only a matter of a generation or two since they were generally approved, and the dust of the last rear-guard battles is hardly laid. In his great work on *Primitive Culture,* Edward Tylor had occasion to devote a lengthy chapter to the considerate refutation of 'the theory of degeneration,' and he cites long passages from distinguished contemporaries in hot defence of that theory. Tylor's book was published in 1871. Delusions which have held sway for centuries trail their shadows after them, and although the theory of degeneration is heard of no longer, it is still customary to set down every evil to 'corruption,' and theorists win applause by representing every nastiness of uncultured humanity as the effect of corruption on a pristine state of virtue.

It is now currently known that the human world has risen out of savagery and animality, that its dawn-light shines on no heroic or golden ages, but on nightmares to make us scream in our sleep. During an incalculable period of time our ancestors were ruder and more brutal than the primitive races whose fast-dying remnants survive. Man's life was, as Hobbes surmised, "poor, nasty, brutish, short." Throughout a tale of ages compared to which the name-and-date period of history is of negligible amplitude, mankind has roamed the wild earth among other animal herds, differing little from them in its mode of life, in its mentality, driven by the same exigencies, by cold, famine, drought, urged by the same impulses as all other animality which it was but imperceptibly transcending.

Our imagination, corrupted by creation-myths, still fails to function in terms of less crude conceptions. It is still asked: 'When did man first appear?' To which enquiry the proper answer is that he never did. So imperceptible was man's emergence out of animal conditions that nowhere in the age-long transition can a line other than an arbitrary one be drawn to mark the event. Scores of animal races have probably hovered for millenniums on the brink of the transition. Fossil remains are for the most part those of animals which have been drowned; apes are too alert to be drowned and not sufficiently imaginative to bury their dead companions. But for those circumstances the earth would probably be strewn with 'missing links.' The proto-human races stood higher than any anthropoid race, yet fell short in many respects of human characters. The power of speech, for instance, was slow in developing; it was lacking in races that may otherwise be accounted human. If possessed at all by the Piltdown and the Pekin races, it can have been only miserably rudimentary. It cannot have been much more highly developed in Neanderthal man.

The first tottering advances of human culture have been crowded in a few hundred thousand years. Fire, pottery, horse-taming, weaving, tillage, cattle-herding, and the going down to the sea in ships were world-shaking discoveries and adventures which, at millenniums of interval, commoved a bewildered humanity which found itself raised one giddy step above the brute.

Man has not 'appeared,' he has grown.

The blunt disclosure of human origins was, like the discovery of the starry heavens, accounted an intolerable affront to human dignity. Feudalism still runs in our tradition; birth is of more account than worth. To be descended from a baron puts pride into a blackguard. Victorian wits gloried in claiming descent from ineffectual angels, and in proving themselves insufficiently intelligent to apprehend the revelations which graced their age.

In sober truth, no myth of miraculous creation is so marvellous as the fact of man's evolution. The elevation of the progeny of the ape by the sole operation of powers and qualities inherent within him, in the face of the buffets of hostile nature, of the intractabilities of his own character, into MAN, the thinker, the deviser, the aspirer after truth and justice, greater in his achievements and his endeavours than all the gods he has been capable of conceiving—if there is in the universe of known facts one apt beyond all others to inspire wonder, it is the grotesque fact in which Victorian wits could perceive only a theme for hilarity. Man, whom Hebrew ignorance had made a fallen angel, was revealed by nineteenth-century science as the creator of whatever is godlike within him.

To turn for a while to the contemplation of that wonder is well. The vileness, the baseness, the imbecility of humanity are only too vividly thrust upon our notice. It is well to remind ourselves that in spite of them humanity has created whatsoever is of worth within our ken, and that the wonder of that creation is all the greater because it has been achieved in the teeth of that vileness and imbecility. The marvel of man, the transcendency of Pascal's "thinking reed," over all the patible qualities of what he contemplates, is one of the cheap commonplaces of meditative thought. But that prodigy is removed to a far loftier plane when no longer viewed as a privileged endowment, a residual relic of pristine divinity, an illapse from some other sphere of being, but as the fruit of his own slow and toilsome effort. Man was not created; he, on the contrary, has been the creator. His transcendency is not his privilege, but his achievement. Those qualities and powers, those enthusiasms, those heroisms, those aspirations, that creative spirit which has brought forth art, poetry, eloquence, Parthenons, Odysseys, Giocondas, Hamlets, that masterful intellect which sits over the world, harnesses its forces and transforms it, that sacred flame which rises above life and defies death, defies wrong, defies falsehood, wills right, is loyal to truth—all that man is, has been, and aspires to be, is the accumulated product of a power which has pursued from the dimmest rudiments "the gradual paths of an aspiring change," built up that dignity which sets him on an equal plane with all the sublimities of the universe. The human world is man-made. Everything which we call precious and divine is the product of human power. It has been wrested by human effort from the dark chaos of brutality and nescience.

It is common for passionate and sensitive natures to be filled with boundless disgust for the human world about them, its ugliness, its vulgarity, its shams, its falsehoods, its obstinate ignorance, its triumphant injustice, its brutality; their souls are racked by the seeming hopelessness of its prejudices and coarse instincts. They long to fly from its besmirching contact, to seek refuge in solitude in the midst of uncontaminated nature, to possess in freedom their soul, their thought-world, unsullied and unexasperated by the meanness, the iniquity, and the ignorance of the world of man. But they do not know, or do not reflect, that those very aspirations, those impulses and delights of the mind, that very sensitiveness to the faults of the human world, that very protest and revolt which fills them with denunciation, those ideals with which they would dwell alone, are products of that same human world from which they recoil as from a thing unclean. It is in such a world that the very substance of their own souls was conceived and formed; it is that same humanity which has through the strifes and struggles of its long evolution brought into being those ideals which lift them upwards. In the course of millions of years, more ugly and more horrible than the world which surrounds them, humanity itself has fashioned every one of those thoughts and feelings in which they would proudly withdraw themselves.

The human world is at once the most venerable fact in the universe and a thing to make angels weep, a glory and an abomination, an inspiration and a stumbling-block, a thing sacred and vile, sublime and grotesque, a fit object of worship and of contempt, of pride and shame, of hope and despair. According as it is viewed with an eye to the portent of its growth from crudest origins, or in the light of the knowledge that is in us of what should, could, and ought to be, we have cause to be filled with a sense of reverence or of disgust. But our revolt against what is, and our knowledge of what should be are as much a part of the forces of the living world as the evil against which they rise. It is by such revolt and such knowledge that humanity has achieved the miracle of its creation.

The power which created man out of the brute did not stop there. It has never ceased to be at work. The prodigy of mankind's emergence is repeated in every step of the age-long process whereby the human world has been wrested from brutality and savagery. The wonder of it is no less in one part of the creative process than in another. That the brute-ape should be the father of thinking man, that is a prodigy; that the gibbering savage should be the father of the Periklean Greek, that also is a prodigy; that the tenth century should be the father of the twentieth, that is no less a prodigy.

The conception of human progress, which inspired the faith of a Condorcet under the very knife of the guillotine, never, perhaps, stood in less credit than at the present day. Its main connotation in recent times has been the expression of complacent satisfaction with the existing order, the blatant glorification of industrial civilisation.

The existing order is not an object of complacency to modern intelligence.

In point of fact the revolt and protest of modern intelligence, its questioning of the concept of progress as the mere designation of the process which has led up to the existing order of the human world, are far more direct tokens of the forces which have determined the progressive development of mankind than were the complacent apotheoses of the nineteenth century.

More urgent than ever in a world which is in the travail of divine discontent is the need of apprehending clearly the nature of the process that has shaped its course. Setting aside for the present any estimate of the intrinsic quality of that process, we shall best be enabled to form such an estimate if, taking it at its face value, we concern ourselves with the means by which it has been achieved. What is the nature of the power which has enabled brute-born humanity to raise itself from the level of savagery and barbarism to one which, for all the survivals of savagery and barbarism in its midst, is yet higher than any vapid angelical plane whence it once claimed to have fallen?

II

MAN'S MEANS OF EVOLUTION

THE answer to that question, well-nigh the most momentous to which thought can apply itself, is simple and obvious. Yet—and the difficulties which the operation of that power has been called upon to surmount are thereby conspicuously illustrated—the plain answer has been studiously eluded. In its stead 'philosophies of history,' abstract and mystical adumbrations, have been set forth exhibiting the unfolding of providential plans, or of Hegelian 'Ideas' floating down in the rarefied atmosphere of German metaphysics towards the mistlands of the Unconditioned. Or human advance has been elucidated by the Development of the Ego, the shaping of Superindividuality, and other vaporous psychological unsubstantialities. What man has achieved has been set down to his religion, to his morals, to his innate benevolence, to everything, in fact, except to his intelligence.

The development of humanity has taken place, like that of every form of life, amid the conditioning factors of its environment. Every phase of it and every aspect have been subject, as is organic evolution, to the determining influence of geographical and economic conditions. But geography and economics are the conditions, not the means, of development. No geographical or economic conditions can bring about evolutionary development in the absence of progressive powers of adaptation. In human history, as in organic history, the material geographical conditions and the economic conditions and interests are the determining factors of every act and form of adaptation, and afford therefore, as after much resistance is now universally recognised, the key to every interpretation of its phenomena. But that interpretation postulates the other term of the reaction, the adaptive powers of the organism upon which material and economic conditions operate. It is with the latter that we are concerned. That adaptive power is not supplied by external conditions. The power by which man has extended his control over the conditions of his life has not been drawn, as he has drawn mechanical power out of coal or water, from his environment. It is by means of a power inherent in himself that he has been enabled to employ the sources of power afforded by the conditions of his environment. If any progressive quality marks the course of his career, it is in the means of adaptation of which he has disposed, and not in the conditions to which he has applied them, that such a quality is to be sought.

A presumptive clue to the nature of that quality is obviously afforded by first answering the antecedent question: 'By what means did man in the first instance become exalted above animality?' It is plausible to suppose that the adaptive powers which have determined the advance of the human race in its subsequent career are related to those which brought about its first emergence. There is here no place for fine metaphysical theories and subtle 'philosophies of history.' Ape-man was not exalted above himself by virtue of his religion, or of his morals, or of the transcendentalism of his ego. The human animal transcended other animals because he was more intelligent.

Progress in organic evolution consists in increased power to cope with the environment by means of greater efficiency in the organs of sensation and of action. Sensation serves to direct the means of action. The power of claw and fang, of limb and wing, is extended in scope by the keenness of eye and ear. The function of the senses depends upon experience. The sight of a menacing foe or of an attractive prey, being interpreted in the light of experience, forestalls the more urgent sensations of closer contact. Intelligence is but an extension of the same method of inference from immediate to prospective experience. Its efficiency depends upon the correspondence between the two. An animal so stupid as to mistake a ravening lion for a sucking-pig would get itself into serious difficulties. Intellectual honesty is of the essence of the biological mechanism. Doubtless an animal of refined taste would much prefer to come upon a plump sucking-pig than to encounter a hungry lion, but should its preference for pig so far prejudice its judgment as to vitiate the evidence of its senses, and it should persuade itself that the lion's roar is the squeaking of a prospective meal, the consequences to the animal with idealistic propensities would be disastrous. Animal intelligence, rude as it may be, seldom plays such tricks. Only human intelligence does. Its much more complex methods of prognosticating the future from the present, the unknown from the known, have, like all complex and delicate mechanisms, the disadvantage of being liable to perverted use. By virtue of his godlike reason man is the only animal that enjoys the privilege of persuading himself that things are not as they are, but as he would like them to be.

Emergent humanity, fortunately for it and for us, was at first insufficiently human to abuse to any dangerous extent that privilege. It was as yet untroubled by the thought whether its conclusions were in accordance with what is taught at Oxford or what might offend the Non-Conformist conscience. Like all other animal races, the human race was concerned only that the conclusion of its intelligence should agree with immediate experience. It is by virtue of such rudimentary intelligence that some brainy races of apes established their title to the lordship of creation.

That *homo sapiens* owes his biological supremacy to his brain is an anatomical truism which goes undisputed. It is, perhaps, not quite so simple, or even so true, as it appears. Brain development is, of course, the outstanding anatomical mark of the evolutionary approach to humanity. The ape's brain foreshadows it. The extinct apes which left one of their babies at Taungs, in Bechuanaland, considerably excelled any living ape in brain growth. Pithecanthropus, in Java, proceeds farther along the same path of cerebral increase. The brute-man of Chou Kou Tien and the Piltdown woman take us apparently a little way across the indefinite border. But human emergence was not simply and solely a matter of brain growth. A big brain is not necessarily human. Some birds and rodents, as well as some of the lower monkeys, have a bigger brain, proportionally to their bodies, than man. Man is not the result of an hypertrophic growth of brain-substance, but of the circumstances which led to that growth. Brainy animals are slow-growing. Their brain growth is the effect of prolonged babyhood. It is consequently no mere congenital hypertrophy, but development organised under the direct control of actual experience. Brain-matter which is not laid down under the direct influence of that control, but is turned out ready-made by heredity, is of inferior quality; it is not intelligent, but instinctive. The intelligence to which man owes his specific advantage is not the result of his having a big brain, but of his having a brain slowly matured during an abnormally long infancy through the immediate action of experience. The ape's brain is the result of a babyhood more prolonged than that of any other brute animal, man's brain of a babyhood about twice as long as that of any living ape.

Prolonged infancy gives rise not only to an intelligent

brain, but also to a persistent sense of dependence upon the assistance and goodwill of other individuals. It results not only in intelligence, but in social dispositions. Apes tend to hang about in troops. In infant humanity that tendency, and the disposition to look to others for protection, assistance, and guidance, to require their approval and sympathy, were at least twice as strongly implanted. Man was not only intelligent, but social. His emergence out of animality was not only a biological phenomenon marked by the growth of a big brain. It was also an entirely new kind of phenomenon: it was a social event.

Not the individual animal is thenceforth the theme of the story, but society; not natural history, but history. The whole method of operation of evolutionary forces had itself to be adapted to the new phenomenon, and modified in its scope. These forces no longer operated upon the individual, but upon the social organism. Their medium was no longer mainly anatomical, but predominantly psychological and social.

It is not infrequently enquired whether the form of man may be expected to undergo startling changes, whether he is not likely, by the transforming operation of organic evolution, to put forth wings or to grow eyes in the back of his head. There is little likelihood of any such interesting developments. Except for modifications of almost negligible importance, man's bodily form is, to all intents and purposes, withdrawn from the action of those causes which have brought about the transformations of organic forms. And the reason is that, as a consequence of the specific conditions of human society, the operation of those causes has become transferred from the individual to the social organism. The products of human evolution are not physiological organs, but ideas, habits, opinions, devices, social institutions, organisations, relations, traditions. It is upon these, and not upon the bodily form of the individual that the conditions which impose adaptation and efficiency, conformity to facts, operate. It is upon these that natural selection exercises its eliminative action. In a social organism, the weakness of the individual, his inadaptation, are to a large extent shielded from the penalties of natural inadaptation. The penalty is paid by society; it is the society, not the individual, which is penalised for defying facts. Individual dishonesty may command success; social dishonesty dooms itself.

The products of human evolution are not transmitted by the method of physiological reproduction. Each successive generation acquires them anew from the social environment in which it develops. They are not located in germ-cells, but in social tradition. The individual organism, its glands and plasms, and physiological mechanisms, are not the bearers of human heredity, but the race as a whole. A man's place in the scale of human evolution is not determined by the anatomical structure of his body, but by the social structure in which he develops. It is not determined by the fact that he belongs to the nine hundred and sixty-second generation since his ancestor danced painted with woad, but by the fact that he belongs to the twentieth century; it is not determined by biological, but by historical conditions. Not the loins of man, but the cultural tradition of humanity is the bearer of human evolutionary characters.

As a consequence of that unique biological situation, not only has social man not developed by any physiological process those wings he has so intensely desired, but having become provided with a brain equal to the demands of social existence, he has not even proceeded farther in the matter of brain development. Rather to the embarrassment and perplexity of the older evolutionists, and to the gratification of the fundamentalists, the brain of fossil man is found to be not conspicuously inferior in size to that of modern man. Normal human brains range roughly from 1200 to 1900 cubic centimetres in capacity. The Piltdown woman, who scarcely possessed the anatomical means of articulate speech, had a brain capacity of no less than 1200 c.c., and possibly of as much as 1300 c.c. The Gibraltar woman, the smallest-brained individual known of the Neanderthal race, had 1200 cubic centimetres of brain, an allowance which suffices many a modern man going about his business in a normal and satisfactory manner. Other Neanderthal people, such as the La Chapelle man, with a horribly missing-link-like form of countenance, had a brain of 1600 c.c., which many a professor might envy. An Australian savage goes about performing his incantations and mummeries with a brain which falls only by a trifle of some 100 c.c. below the average of a Londoner, and which might quite well serve all the purposes of an Archbishop of Canterbury.

The lack of progressive development in man's brain, perplexing to thought hemmed in by the time-honoured notion that man is a self-contained 'ego,' is due to the fact that the operation of natural laws does not proceed on that assumption. As an individual animal organism, man has not appreciably evolved since he was a roaming savage; modern man is not markedly, if at all, more intelligent than his ancestor of the Stone Age. He is in a position to make an immeasurably greater use of his intelligence for the same reason that a schoolboy of the present day is in a position to instruct Archimedes and Aristotle.

Hence, incidentally, the utter futility of the goose chase after causes of human evolution in processes taking place within the individual, in the growth of his 'ego,' whatever that may mean, or in intellectual, moral, or humanitarian refinement of his natural disposition. The individual cannot be made more intelligent, or more moral, or more just and less cruel, unless those improvements are effected in the social organism from which he derives his mental constitution.

One of the floundering notions endemic in historical philosophising is the fallacy that "history is the biography of great men." Great men are, like other men, the products of their environment. If by virtue of the character of that environment they are enabled to go a little beyond it in clearness of vision, they can influence their age only by appealing to qualities and tendencies—far more complex than any of which individual evolution is capable—already present and ripe in the medium which brought them forth. A much more important question, it has been realised for some time, than 'Who was the originator of that idea, of that device?' is 'How came that idea to grow? by what steps was that invention, that discovery evolved?' The men whose names are associated with the most revolutionary changes in human history and ideas, such as Gautama, Muhâmmad, Luther, Columbus, Copernicus, Newton, Darwin, hark back to so long and farspreading a mental genealogy of precursory ideas, and their influence so thoroughly harmonises with the tendencies and ideas ripening in the mental atmosphere and conditions of their age, that it is often difficult to say which is their individual contribution and which that of the collective agencies of the times; and that we may in many instances doubt whether those revolutions would not have taken place in much the same manner had the particular individuals with whose names they are associated been absent from the stage. A society gets not only the government it deserves, but the thought, the art, the science it deserves and determines. The thought, the art, the science for which it is not fit, it takes good care to eliminate by ignoring them.

Even the 'supermen' whose colossal figures traditionally loom as the very embodiment of overpowering individualism, violating fate, diverting with their strong hand the course of history, seizing mankind by the hair and curbing the age to their own strong will, a Cæsar, a Napoleon,[1] can on a closer scrutiny be seen to have been called forth, evoked, created by the operation and natural selection of circumstances, to have been drawn into the current of events and carried away breathlessly in a stream in which they struggled, gasping and fearful, and in their boldest hour to have been driven by the necessity of an environment whose awful pressure they were powerless to withstand.

The progress of human intelligence is not due to the almost negligible, and as often as not neglected, contributions of this or that individual, but to the fact that its fruits accumulate through all time at compound interest. Every advance it achieves extends the field of subsequent achievement, and every element of the human world which is subject to its operation is thus subject to a process of progressive development.

Not only is the operation of intelligence progressive because it enlarges the foundations of knowledge and experience in geometrical ratio, it is also progressive because its logical operation cannot stop short of ultimate conclusions. A new principle, an idea, does not proceed at once to its last consequences. Its beginnings are in most instances timid and inconsistent. Yet once it has been formulated, nothing is more inevitable than the unfolding of its remotest implications. It is a logical process, and logic cannot stop halfway. That development may be wholly unforeseen at the origin of the process. The most direct and obvious implications of the new principle may be not only foreign to the thought of those who have

[1] See Ferrero, *Giulio Cesare,* and A. Vandal, *L'avènement de Bonaparte.*

advanced it, but wholly abhorrent to them. The reformers, the revolutionists, the innovators, the heretics, the iconoclasts of former days would stand aghast before the consequences of their own work, and would in many instances occupy today the ranks of the opponents of those principles which they themselves devoted their lives and energies to establishing. Yet nothing can arrest the process. As the consequences follow in the order of logical thought, so do they as inevitably follow in the order of human development. Compromise and moderation constantly recommend themselves as adaptations to provisional conditions, halfway houses are built in the confident delusion that they can serve as permanent abodes. But logic knows no halfway houses, and the logic of facts is identical with the logic of thought. Both mental development and the development of human relations are governed, in the end, by that logic. It takes its course, though the deduction may require centuries to take effect.

The means of adaptation which ensured the biological supremacy of the human race was, thus, not only more effective than any developed in the antecedent course of organic evolution, it was also intrinsically progressive in its operation. Man's adaptive variation, his intelligence, has not only raised him above animality, but has supplied him with the means of extending continuously his control over the conditions of life. Its operation is progressive. And it is the only specific character of the human species which, from its very nature, possesses that quality. There is no manifest reason why good taste, or humane dispositions, or the appreciation of beauty, or moral ideals, or creative imagination, should exhibit in their development a progressive advance. And in point of fact, they do not, except in so far as they are subject to the influence of progressive intelligence. If moral ideals, if social justice, if humanitarian sentiments have shown a continuous tendency to improve, it is because their development has been conditioned by the action of rational thought.

Human intelligence is, like every character which has bestowed upon an animal race more efficient means of control over the conditions of life, a method of adaptation to those conditions. It is a means of securing the conformity of man's behaviour, of his thoughts and ideas, with the relation which actually obtains between him and his environment. Upon that correspondence, as upon the correspondence between the vision of the senses and the experience which it forestalls, depends the efficiency of man's adaptive faculty. The human environment has grown to infinite complexity. It not only includes the physical universe, the material necessities of life, but likewise the even vaster and more varied world of human relations. That world which has grown out of the comparatively simple environment of the savage, the world which man has made, is the outthrow of his mind. The stones of his cities and the steel of his engines are fashioned out of his thought. The appetites, the passions, the emotions, the interests, the prejudices, the loves and hates, amid which he moves are the outcome of social edifices and structures built, like his cities and his engines, of thought. The degree in which he is able to exercise his control over that complex environment depends upon the measure in which his thought accords with existing facts. It depends upon the accuracy of his perception of those facts. He will fail in the measure that the perception is false, succeed in the measure that it is true. Progress depends upon truth.

III

PRIMAL STUPIDITY

AND truth depends upon intellectual honesty.

The tasks of man's intelligence are beset with difficulties incomparably greater than are the limited operations of animal intelligence. While the latter is controlled by the stern discipline of immediate experience, man's thought escapes by its extended range from that ruthless supervision. Its errors are not instantly penalised; fallacy can flourish without calling down immediate retribution. Reason is fallible. To palliate its natural imbecility, to extend its secure foundations, has been the long and laborious task of philosophical discipline and science.

But to assume, as is commonly done, that human folly and failure are effects of the fallibility of human intelligence, of its natural inadequacy, its imbecility, its impotence, is itself a pernicious fallacy. The function of intelligent thought is to operate rationally. But there are two senses in which thought may be said to be rational. It may be effectively rational by successfully achieving what it intends to do. Or it may, even while failing to achieve its purpose, yet be rational in intention. Falsehood and folly in the human world are only to an infinitesimal degree due to the failure of intentionally rational thought, and in an overwhelming degree to thought which is irrational in purpose and intention. Great as are the natural disabilities of intelligence and the difficulties of its tasks, they are as nothing beside the obstacles which man has deliberately set in the way of using his intelligence.

What progress he has achieved has not been won by remedying the fallibility of his intelligence, but as a result of an age-long strife against desires and interests which have deliberately sought to oppose its operation.

Man is anxious not to know the truth. He uses his intelligence, as no other animal is permitted to use its means of guidance, to suppress what he accounts unpleasant facts, and to establish belief in what harmonises not with his experience, but with his wishes.

African hunters, when they chance unexpectedly upon a lion, endeavour to ward off the animal by asserting emphatically that "it is not there." Bechuana warriors, when they desire that their presence shall be undetected by the enemy, avail themselves of the services of a priest who loudly assures them that they are not seen. The Akamba of East Africa, when they wish to bring a roaming elephant to a standstill, declare that it is not an elephant, but a stone. That Coué method which, were it employed by any other animal to defeat the function of what intelligence it might possess, would ruthlessly bring about its suppression by the stern logic of natural selection, has been habitually used at all times by the human race, and is applied by primitive humanity to all occasions.

It is found in full use at the dawn of human culture. The race of African hunters which swarmed over into Europe as its climate became more temperate and the Saharan country more desiccated, and exterminated the gorilla-browed Neanderthal men, not only excelled them in flint-knapping and in the neatness of their bone-tipped assagais, but employed the same methods as the African hunters of the present day. It was not for art's sake that the Aurignacians painted those wonderfully realistic bison, horses, and deer on the walls of their cave-galleries in Dordogne and northern Spain, but in order that their confidence in the abundance of their food-supply and in the cunning of their right arm might be confirmed. They slaughtered the painted bison by transfixing them, sometimes in the very heart, with painted spears. At Tuc d'Audoubert, among the northern foothills of the Pyrenees and the upper waters of the Garonne, where the men of the last Ice Age have left their actual footprints in the loam of the long passages that wind into the bowels of the earth, there stand in the inmost recess of the stalactite sanctuary two clay statues representing a bull and a cow bison. They are riddled with the thrusts of the hunters' javelins. To enact their wish, to affirm its fulfilment was their adjuvant to the use of their skill and intelligence. To the former method much rather than to the latter did they pin their faith.

The Magdalenian method of killing bison has not only persisted down to modern ages as the most familiar procedure of malignant magic, it pertains to the essence of those substitutes for rational thought which have been ever since in favour, and were destined to play the most prominent part in human culture. Their purpose has been to control the conditions of human life, not through the operation of that intelligence which first enabled man to do so more effectively than any other animal, but by the aid of supernatural, that is to say, irrational means. In the life and activities of primitive humanity the endeavour to apply rational thought to the control of existing conditions has been small, the endeavour to exercise that control by irrational means much greater. Savage humanity has chiefly relied on what Dr. Preuss has pleasantly called *Urdummheit*—'primal stupidity,' which is usually denoted by the terms 'superstition' and 'magic,' and to which in more recent times the name 'religion' has been applied.

The irrationality, or 'primal stupidity' of the savage has been represented as an endeavour to solve the philosophical problems of the nature of the universe and of life. But that suggestion is only another form of primal stupidity. Nothing is more remote from the mind of savage humanity than any interest in or apprehension of such problems. Savage magic has reference to the chief interests of humanity, savage and civilised, namely, food and generation. Primitive man connected his interest in food with the animals which provided it, and which were his 'totems.' He connected the unintelligible, and therefore magic, process of generation with the moon, which appears to control the generative faculties of women.

The faltering intelligence of savage humanity, far from speculating, as has been imagined, upon philosophical questions, and meditating upon life and death, was not even capable of apprehending the nature of death. Animals are, of course, in the same case. Monkey mothers carry about the putrefying corpses of their dead babies, not being able to comprehend what has happened, and expecting the visible form to wake up from sleep. Savage women in Australia do the same thing. All primitive peoples believe that something of man survives as long as visible portions of his body remain. The semi-articulate Mousterians sometimes buried their dead relatives in the caves which they occupied while alive, as do most savages in order to prevent dead men from wandering about and troubling the survivors. It is generally supposed by savages that the immortal portion of a man consists of his bones, which endure longer than other aspects of human nature. Teeth and the bones of the skull are observed to possess the faculty of immortality in a higher degree than other portions of the skeleton. It is accordingly a widespread practice to preserve those portions and to pay honour to them. In the Azilian Age the savages of southern Germany observed the same rites as do those of Uganda and of New Guinea at the present day. In the cave of

Ofnet, in Bavaria, the skulls of men and women, the latter adorned with coronets of shells and stag's teeth, and all abundantly painted with red ochre, are carefully laid in rows facing west. Those palæolithic Germans had evidently already developed quite a fund of irrational ideas.

The transference of the evolutionary process from the individual to social tradition, while it enables the dwarf to stand upon the shoulders of the giant and makes the individual heir to all the ages, has disadvantages. Social tradition not only transmits as a permanent legacy the accumulated experience and knowledge, the achievements of intelligence, it likewise transmits as a no less persistent constituent of that legacy of the ages the fruits of human effort to outreach intelligence by irrational means. It transmits superstitions, that is to say, in a literal etymological sense, survivals. The traditional heritage is not only a precious storehouse of accumulated experience and power; it is also a cesspool of superstition.

It is, to say the least, extremely doubtful whether the mind of modern man would be naturally disposed to place any reliance upon the methods of primitive irrationalism which the savage used as a substitute for the methods of reason, had that savage irrationalism not been handed down by cultural tradition. It is difficult to imagine the independent development, to any considerable extent, of a faith in magic in the modern world. Irrationalism can flourish by the side of critical and scientific thought, and commingle with all the resources of modern intelligence, because the savage's 'primal stupidity' is embedded in human tradition, and tradition has imposed itself upon every generation by the intrinsic sanctity of its authority.

From the earliest stages of its growth, human intelligence has been checked by that authority. The incubus of established custom, of traditional opinion, heavily though its weight presses upon the mind of civilised humanity, is but a fraction of the load which holds down the mind of the savage. The direst despotism of a Dominican censorship was lax compared to the unrelenting grip of the tyranny to which, throughout its earliest stages of development, the human mind has been bond. Savage society is ruled by custom. To innovate is worse than rash, it is impious. Behaviour proceeds, in the ritualism of the lower stages of culture, by conformity with formulas which do not owe their sanction to tried efficiency, but to an established authority which it were dangerous, unlucky, and treasonable to question.

To that inertia of established custom, far more than to any incapacity of primitive intelligence, the fact is due that throughout the savage ages of tribal humanity cultural growth has never proceeded within a self-contained community beyond a narrow limit. The backward tribal cultures which have remained in a primitive condition owe their arrest of development, not to inferior racial intelligence, but to the absence of cultural contacts by whose shock alone the force of a petrified social tradition might have been broken. The Melanesian islands and Australia have been cut off from all other cultures since pleistocene times. Africa, south of the Sahara, America, where no native pastoral society has been possible, have known no sharp contrasts, no successive crops of cultural contacts and combinations. They have accordingly settled down in a stagnant state maintained by cultural tradition.

The peculiar mode of transmission of the products of evolution in social humanity render sporadic and isolated evolution impossible. Nothing short of the coördinated growth of the race as a whole can satisfy the conditions of the process. The evolution of tribal communities is rigidly limited; it can only take place up to a sharply defined level which constitutes an impassable boundary.

Why has the basin of the Mediterranean been the cradleland of human civilisation? It is not because it has been the home of superior races, it is not because it has afforded superior material advantages, because its shores were richer and more fertile. It is because its land-bridges supplied easy paths to migrant swarms, its inland waters a safe open highway to primitive navigators, and cultures developed on its shores under a great diversity of conditions, in the sun of Africa and in the mists of the Alps and Pyrenees, in the loam of Asiatic rivers and on the tundras of high grasslands. It is because those varied cultures have time and again come together in the sweep of migrations and the clash of conquests, and their heterogeneous products and traditions have commingled. Not one of those cultures could, probably, have risen, self-contained and isolated, above savagery. Western culture, Europe, is not the product of any one people, but of the fertilising contacts of scores of diverse cultures.

Of its earlier elements none perhaps was native to Europe. Those predestined lands which were to be the focus of civilisation were for countless ages the home of a sluggish Caliban-like race whom the passing of century after century taught nothing beyond some trifling improvement in the rude knapping of flints, forced upon their females by the need of scraping the pelts of beasts to protect themselves against the rigour of the frost. The ungainly Mousterians remained unchangingly brutish until, like the savages of Tasmania, they faded out of existence at the advent of more alert invaders. As in much later times, when Europe lay under another spell of Dark Ages, and was roused into activity by the Spanish Moors, so the beginnings of cultural life came to her across the isthmus of Gibraltar in successive waves from Africa. Thence, besides the Aurignacian races which exterminated the Mousterians, came the agile Capsian bowmen adorned with feathers; the Grimaldi race of tall, dark warriors, superstitiously excited by the witchcraft of their steatopygous women; and later the dolmen-builders who ranged over Western Europe to Ireland and Scotland; and another race following close on their heels, but pushing farther east, beyond the Danube, whose men were great archers and whose women were great basket-makers and potters, and have left their bell-beakered pitchers from Bohemia to Scandinavia, as the mark of a cultural revolution—for these are the 'round-barrows' people, and no longer dwell in caves, but in huts, and theirs is not the culture of the Old Stone Age, but the rich neolithic culture.

In the very midst of the Old Stone Age there appeared in France a strange race, which withdrew eastward again after slaughtering hundreds of thousands of horses in the Rhone valley, at Solutré, and is surmised to have come from the horse-country in the steppes of Little Russia. Like their descendants, whom the Greeks called Scyths, they made drinking-cups from the skulls of their slain enemies. If the surmise is correct, they are representatives of branches of humanity which had a long continuous development under special conditions, in relative seclusion from the rest of the world, but in close intercourse between their component tribes, an intercourse which led, in the western section of those tribes, to the linguistic uniformity noted in the so-called 'Aryan' languages. Both that western section of the dwellers on the high plains and the probably older eastern section lived in complete dependence upon the teeming herds of horses that swarmed over the grasslands, the animal being accordingly the sacred source of their existence, whose solemn sacrifice, the Asvamedha of Vedic religion, constitutes to this day the outstanding observance of their magic rites. But while the western horsemen hunted, and eventually tamed the horse, eastern Asiatic humanity appears to have long existed in an even more parasitic relation to the animal, living on the milk sucked from the mares' udders. The more active western horsemen remained also more adaptable, and not only built what may have been the first mud cities in the Anau district of Turkestan, and overflowed into the Iranian plateau and down to Mesopotamia and India, but spread again and again over Europe.

Besides the men from Africa and the men from the steppes, are found, chiefly in the highland regions of neolithic Europe, those lake-dwellers who were already there in Azilian times, at the end of the Old Stone Age, and remained till Roman times, leading industrious lives in their pile-villages on the lakes of Switzerland, Savoy, Italy, and Hungary, raising varied crops on the mainland, and tending flocks of sheep, goats, and an abundance of domestic pigs. Their women were skilful potters, and they were superstitious moon-worshippers, scarcely any object or dwelling being deemed safe without the protection of the magic crescent. Those industrious people had, it seems, wandered all the way from Syria, driving before them their flocks of sheep and their pigs.

From its remotest beginnings Europe has owed its cultural fertility and vitality to the commingling, not of races, but of cultures. And what was true in prehistoric ages holds good of every phase. The evolution of human society in segregated isolation is scarcely less possible than the evolution of the isolated human individual. No isolated human society, however civilised, has ever proceeded through its own isolated resources beyond a given limit. Its growth becomes choked by its own cultural tradition till complete arrest and stagnation take place.

In proportion as a civilisation is shut off by a wall of national pride and complacency within the fatal boundaries of its cultural tradition, its growth is stunted and its existence condemned. In proportion as it lives in free intercourse with other cultures, and its own tradition is broken by their impact, will that culture thrive and continue to live and grow. As an inexorable consequence of the peculiar character of human evolution, the ideal of an independent and segregated culture, of a society developing by itself and for itself, of a national civilisation, a self-contained empire, a sovereign state, is not only a factitious 'cold monster'; it is an unrealisable impossibility.

IV

CIVILISATION AND IRRATIONALISM

CULTURAL tradition may not only be segregated within an isolated society and its power of development become paralysed by the fixation of custom, it can also be segregated and sterilised by being confined to a class within the social aggregate. That is a feature common to all civilised societies that have existed hitherto, and constitutes the cause of their inevitable decay.

Primitive tribal humanity is equalitarian. That condition is not a principle of social organisation, but a character of primitive psychology, which is not readily intelligible to civilised man, whose social psychology rests upon the opposite principle of individualism. The conception of authority or of privileged claims to possession is equally unintelligible to primitive tribal humanity. Leaders, headmen, chiefs, which the feudal imagination of the European postulates as natural constituents of social organisation, are unknown in the sense in which he interprets them throughout the primitive phases of humanity. There is much conflict of interests between tribes, between clans, but there is none between members of the same social group, and what opposition of individual interests may exist is obliterated by the overshadowing sense of social cohesion. No personal quality, neither age, nor wisdom, nor valour, nor even the far more important claim to magic power, establishes in uncivilised society a title to privilege, or subordinates the social status of an individual not possessed of those qualities. Primitive equalitarianism is maintained by the complete inability of the primitive human mind to conceive its opposite.

Even between the sexes no differentiation of status exists. Hence the women who are the natural builders of the home are the chief contributors to material culture. In a Mousterian cave in Jersey it has been noticed that the *coups de poing* flints, the men's weapons, lie at the entrance. In the interior are to be found the scraping tools used by the women to prepare hides and the hacked bones left over from their preparation of food.

All uncultured societies are communistic. Every item of food, were it a sprat, is scrupulously divided. Private property is not forbidden; it is not understood. Darwin, observing that among the natives of Tierra del Fuego "even a piece of cloth given to one is torn into shreds and distributed, and no one individual becomes richer than another," was distressed to think that, holding as they do such detestable principles, "the perfect equality among the individuals composing the Fuegian tribes, must for a long time retard their civilisation, until some chief shall arise with power sufficient to secure any acquired advantage. On the other hand, it is difficult to understand how a chief can arise till there is property of some sort by which he might manifest his superiority and increase his power."

Darwin was right. Primitive equalitarianism precludes civilisation. The rough distinction of phases of culture into savagery and civilisation is not so arbitrary and superficial as might be supposed. It represents two forms of social organisation which are contrasted not only in their outward appearance, but are even more sharply distinguished by the principles upon which they are founded. Civilisation is commonly thought of as an advanced state of culture differing merely in degree from one which is more backward. But civilisation is only secondarily thus characterised. If it were the mere advance of culture beyond a given stage, constant uncertainty would arise in drawing the line of demarcation, whereas there is in fact seldom occasion for hesitation. Civilisation literally means living in cities. The permanency, the resources, the wealth, the organisation, the culture of cities are the outward signs of civilisation. But those resources and that wealth are the effect of a particular social configuration, to wit, the power of a ruling class. Civilisation is the fact of that distribution of power, which is non-existent in lower phases of social development. It consists not only in power to control natural resources, but in power to control men and to dispose of their labour.

Civilisation, it is considered, is marked by wealth, power, prosperity. But it is just as true that civilisation is marked by poverty, slavery, and misery. The latter, like the former features, are not found at stages of culture below the level of civilisation. The development of civilisation is not, accordingly, a gradual transition out of lower forms of culture, but a revolution from a state of social equality to one of social inequality.

Power wielded by man over his fellow-men furnishes means of controlling the conditions of life more potent, beyond comparison, than all the forces at the disposal of individual man. To have one's dinner served is vastly more satisfactory than to go out on the moors and catch it. Useful as are flint-axes, bone needles, weapons and tools, hand and brain, to get other people to use them for you is an enormous improvement on using them yourself. Not tools and weapons, but men, become the instruments of the holder of power. With that discovery a gigantic new force was introduced into the human world. The advantages of human instruments over mere tools and weapons are so enormous that from the moment the practical possibilities of the discovery are realised, to maintain and extend that power becomes the consideration which takes precedence over all others. Not, thenceforth, to use the natural endowments which secured the victory of the creature man over his environment was the aim of his thought, not to control the conditions of life by means of rational intelligence, but to use and control men.

How is that control brought about and maintained, how is power wielded over men? Innumerable as are the forms and degrees of that power, the superiority of the leader, his wisdom, his valour, knowledge, rank, authority, the power of physical force, of divine authority, of wealth and economic control, of delegated office, that power ultimately rests upon ideas which sanction its validity and justify its authority. Like every other product of human evolution, established power is the manifestation of ideas.

Established power thus not only introduces a new structure in social organisation, it also introduces a new mechanism into the operation of the human mind. Over and above the primitive irrationalism which seeks to circumvent inacceptable facts by self-suggestion, over and above the despotism of tradition which imposes conformity, the human means of adaptation by rational intelligence are deflected from their function by an even more potent force. The interests of the holders of power require to be upheld by the operation of human thought. Since it is upon men and men's minds that power is wielded, the primary purpose of thought is no longer to correspond with facts as they are, but with the ideas upon which constituted authority is founded. The criterion of every mental process is no longer its intrinsic validity, but its favourable or unfavourable bearing upon the sanctions of authority. That becomes the touchstone by which every judgment, every value, every thought is tested. All that tends to undermine established power is bad and therefore false, all that tends to confirm it is good and therefore true. The purpose of intelligence is no longer to fulfil, but to frustrate, its function.

That perversion of the purpose of intelligent thought is independent of any dishonesty in the intentions of the holders of power. The most conscientious is more keenly concerned than the most unscrupulous that the authority he wields should rest upon a just sanction. He is more passionately intent upon that justification than any tyrannical usurper. The falsification of thought in the interests of power is to an enormous extent sincere and well-intentioned. But we are probably too prone, in our tolerant, euphemistic way—euphemism and tolerance, the courtesies and charities of judgment striving to be dispassionate, are themselves ruses of self-protective power-thought—we are too prone to minimize the part played by intentional and deliberate fraud. Wherever access is afforded to detailed evidence deliberate deception is found. From the tricks of the witch-doctor and the Pompeiian priest's speaking-trumpet down to the 'political intelligence' and the education of public opinion of our newspapers, there is a vast amount of fraud which cannot be wholly euphemised away by charitable interpretations. The old 'imposture theory' has perhaps been unduly discredited—it was an unpleasant theory, and therefore it was only proper to dwell upon its superficiality.

It is however not easy, in general, and it is unessential, to draw a sharp demarcation between conscious and subconscious intellectual dishonesty. Opinions have an ingenious tendency to flow in the channel of vested interest. The priestly class is favourably disposed towards mythology, the landowning class towards feudal principles, and stock-jobbers are particularly acute to perceive the dangers of communism. The adaptation of rational intelligence to the interests of power has little difficulty in justifying itself as a virtue and a duty. The necessity of sound principles, the principles upon which the existing order rests, is manifest. Subversive facts are a danger to society, and the social order must be protected even against itself. To abet dangerous tendencies of thought, to dwell unduly upon facts which, to the unsound judgment of many, might prove misleading, would be clearly culpable. It would be a betrayal of their welfare, for which the holders of power, who enjoy the privilege of sounder culture, must account themselves responsible. The duty laid upon them demands that they should discountenance the dissemination of poison. Nay, it were culpable to permit their own minds to dwell upon facts calculated to sap the principles which make for general security and stability. And if a slight modification in the complexion, in the presentation and nomenclature of facts conduces to a more wholesome attitude of the mind, so much the better. Do not our most reputed philosophers offer us, as the modest conclusion of their meditations, the cogent argument that, since we have to live under existing conditions, we should believe anything that will help us to do so?

Like most biological processes the falsification of thought, however deliberate in its inception, becomes automatic. Intellectual fraud never can endure as such; it rapidly assumes the form of honest and sincere conviction. With the fullest sense of rectitude, and of freedom from prejudice, the falsification of human thought proceeds to carry out the astute mendacity of its operations in a medium of stainless candour and integrity. The mind itself becomes twisted into a posture which refracts every fact, deforms every perspective, and prejudices every issue in a predetermined sense. The falsification of human thought brought about by the interests of constituted power is by no means confined to any given order of principles or formulas bearing directly and obviously upon the sanction of that power. Power-thought is not equivalent to authority or tradition. The whole world of human knowledge and thought is reflected in the distorting mirror of the established interests under the domination of which it has been fashioned. The structure comprises every value, every field of science, of art, of literature; it embraces "the choir of heaven and furniture of earth." In every sphere the intellectual counters are counterfeit; men think by means of ideas stamped with spurious values; their vocabulary, the import of the words they use is part of the falsified mental world in which they move and have their being.

Within that environment takes place the mental growth of the multitudes over whom the power of the few is exercised. The primary object of cultural tradition is to influence the minds of those who are used as instruments of power. They must be made to see the advantages, the justice, the reasonableness, the necessity of the arrangements by virtue of which power is exercised over them, the harmony of those arrangements with the order of the universe, the falsity, the wickedness of any view out of harmony with that beneficent authority. And the adaptation of human thought and intelligence to the interests of the holders of power is brilliantly justified by the sincerity, the conviction, the enthusiasm, with which its interpretations are accepted and honoured by the servants of power, by the devotion and loyalty with which they are prepared to die in their defence. The holders of power have been the civilisers of mankind, its teachers, its educators. The cultural tradition of humanity, handed down from generation to generation, from savagery to civilisation, from ages of feudalism to ages of democracy, has been their creation.

The evolution which has raised the power of human intelligence from the level of savagery and barbarism to ever-extended control over the conditions of life has not been a growth of its intrinsic effectiveness, a struggle against its own natural fallibility. Human evolution presents indeed the spectacle of a long and arduous battle, but against quite other forces. Not the infirmities of reason, not the difficulties of the problems with which it has been confronted have been the obstacles that have stood in its path. In the conflict by which humanity has won the degree of adaptation to the conditions of existence to which it can lay claim, the antagonist against which its powers have been pitted has been the authority of social tradition falsified by the interests of holders of privilege power.

That conflict is the theme of history. From the dawn of culture until this day, under innumerable aspects and names, in every field of human endeavour, the wavering battle has been waged. Politics, religion, industry and commerce, science, art, literature, life and its complex relations have been moulded in the vicissitudes of the ceaseless contest. It is not between Error and Truth that the secular strife has been waged. What human intelligence has won, it has wrested from the power of irrationalism.

V

THE SECRET OF THE EAST

WHEN nomadic humanity in search of pastures came upon the alluvial plains of the great Asiatic water-courses, and discovered that, with but little labour, bounteous nature yielded abundant winter food for cattle—and, it soon occurred, for men also—it ceased to wander, became agricultural and settled into permanent abodes. From the slime of the Jaxartes, the Oxus, the Yang-tse, the Euphrates, and the Nile, civilisation was born. Nature afforded leisure, relieved man from the hand-to-mouth struggle for food; leisure gave opportunity for thought and device.

But the conditions which gave permanent abode and secure sustenance, furnished likewise the occasion of new struggles. In a community that lives on fish or game no decided advantage can accrue to any individual or group from domination over the rest; under purely pastoral conditions the cattle are the common property of the tribe, and, while one tribe may steal another's herds, there is neither inducement nor facility for individual appropriation from the common flock. But where the land itself, permanently occupied, is the source of sustenance and wealth, where the needful work can be performed as well by the labourer working for another as for himself, where leisure renders surplus production possible, the advantages to be derived from power wielded over man, and from individual possession, are obvious and substantial. The claim to ownership of the soil, if it can be made good, places the owner in possession of men also and their labour.

Even the armed warrior's strong hand is powerless alone to break the primitive equalitarian constitution of the tribe. The war leader is but the foremost among equals. He cannot act without the assent of his peers, and the beardless youth that bears the spear claims right to call him to account. Warlike pastoralists flourished in Arabia, in the uplands of Central Asia, on the plains of the Danube and the Dnieper for thousands of years before civilisation dawned. Amorite Bedâwin, led by their patriarchs or 'judges,' drove their flocks into Syria and Palestine; semi-nomadic Turanians were beating copper swords in Turkestan, while the savages of Spain were still dancing their buffalo-dance, and before the land of Shinar had risen out of the waters of the Persian sea. Yet the tribesmen remained, in no mere rhetorical sense, free and equal. Not the warrior, not the owner of cattle enslaved the human herd, but the priest.

The power of the medicine-man, the magician, on whose incantations, more than on human care and industry, the fertility of the soil is understood to depend, assumes with agricultural peoples enormous proportions. The bountiful alluvial soil is a gift of the god; "the earth is the Lord's," the Lord is the landlord. And rent, accordingly, first-fruits and tithes, must be paid to him. Payment of rent is one of the most effective propitiatory rites. The priests, the family of the god, collect the rents due to him, and pay rent to themselves. Hence one inevitable genesis of landed ownership.

The representative of the god was not backward in using his advantage: he bled the people white. Here, for example, is a little memorandum which we happen to have picked up of fees due to a Sumerian priest for reading the burial service over one of his flock and consigning him to mother earth: "Seven urns of wine, four hundred and twenty loaves of bread, one hundred and twenty measures of corn, a garment, a kid, a bed, and a seat." Chaldæan priests helped themselves to first-fruits and death duties, that is to say, they plundered the farmer and left the widow naked. Urukagina of Girsu expresses the pious hope that the day may come when the priest "shall no longer come into the garden of a poor mother and take wood therefrom, nor gather tax in fruit therefrom."

The gods of the savage tribesman are undignified and are treated with naïve and good-natured familiarity. They are but magnified magicians, and the magician is, for all his dreaded lore, but a fellow-tribesman. Not until the power of the god has been made manifest in that of the priest, are his greatness and his majesty apprehended. The oppressed and plundered people are filled with the fear of the Lord, for is he not all-powerful, can he not send flood and storm to destroy them, them and their fields? They may not resist his awful power, even should he slay them. His wrath must be appeased by greater gifts; to him are brought not only their corn and kine, but their sons and daughters to go through the fire, or be his servants and concubines. The contrite heart alone can hope for divine favour. The Asiatic and Nilotic river-lands, the gift of the god and ruled by his vice-gerent, have accordingly been notable for their 'genius for religion,' and their alluvial plains have been the brewing-vats of religious fervour whence every religion, save one, that has counted in the world is issued. The fact that has most impressed the diggers and decipherers of that earliest civilisation, the form of which has but lately been emerging from the mounds of Mesopotamia, is the magnitude of its all-pervading piety. Its life cannot escape from the orbit of magico-religious thought. Not a step is taken in that magic circle, not a word spoken, not a brick made, not a mouthful eaten, without bringing man into contact with the supernatural. In that charmed atmosphere of mystery has the Oriental mind been formed.

Between agricultural communities scattered along the banks of the great rivers and the adjoining marshes disputes inevitably arise, chiefly in regard to grazing grounds, which remain communal, and as more land is brought under tillage, extend farther and farther afield. Provision must be made for protection and refuge; that afforded by the sanctuary of the god is wisely supplemented by an enclosure of strong walls. The home of the community becomes a walled city.

Of such kind are the settlements dotted at the dawn of recorded time over the plains of Eastern lands, where civilisation had its birth. Adjoining city-states tend in the course of tribal warfare to fuse under the sway of the strongest, paying tribute to the dominant chief-priest, the steward of the god, the *patesi,* as he is called; and little kingdoms arise with varying fortunes around Erech and Eridu, Lagash, and Ur of the Chaldees. The priest is the ruler. He becomes almost identified with the god whom his own power and splendour have manifested. The walled temple, raised on high, in memory of the high places whence the savage shaman of old invoked the moon, is his palace, and within its storehouses is gathered the treasure of the nation. When he dies he shall, like the fabled Sardanapallos, be accompanied by his slaves, his women, and his treasure, and distant posterity shall gasp before the golden and jewelled shambles of the graves of Ur.

Eventually the fate of the temple-cities of the plain, undelimitated by natural frontiers, is to form mighty empires stretching from the rising to the going down of the sun, witnessing to the glory of the priest-king, the offspring of the high gods. Thus did Eannatum of Lagash and Sargon of Agade "pour forth their glory over the world," and Sumu-Abu, the Amorite, who built near Kish his capital of Bab-Ilu, the 'Gate of the Gods,' and Hammurabi weld Sumer and Semitic Akkad into the first Babylonian Empire.

So in Egypt the Horus-Lords of Abydos absorb adjoining tribes and extend the sway of their gods to the Fayum, till Narmer, subduing the Delta people, unites the Nile Valley under his rule, assuming the title of 'High priest of Hininsu (Herakleopolis) and Qubti (Koptos).' But the priests of On in the Delta country, whose culture is, owing to closer Asiatic and Mediterranean contacts, more advanced, shall wrest the throne from the pyramid-builders, the dynasts of Abydos, and shall set up their new god, Ra, above the old moon-gods and totems of the land, and annex the cults of the holy city of Osiris. The priest is jealous of his power and his ambition is cunning; the devices of his brain are mightier than the sword of the conqueror.

The civilisation of the Sumerian temple-cities is the oldest that has stamped its tradition upon human records. The impress has remained indelible. Semites supplanted Sumerians; Akkadian and Amorite absorbed the culture of the land of Shinar; the gods, rites, myths, laws of the priests of Sumer passed with little added or changed into those of Babylon and Asshùr. For the Semitic people have ever had the gift of assimilation; seldom have they created. Semi-nomadic Aramæans, Moabites, Jebusites, Canaanites wall in their temples and set up theocratic city-states, often mere fortified mounds—some, such as Jericho, measure but a dozen acres in all—after the model of the god-protected cities of the river-land. The wealth of Babylonian traders linked together the whole world of western Asia by a network of caravans, and spread abroad the culture of the priestly cities. For not only is the land of Shinar "so bountiful in its yield of grain that it returns on an average two-hundred-fold, and the ears of wheat and barley are four fingers in size," (Herodotos, i, 193), but it is also the trade-centre of three continents. The priests were merchant-princes, and even the temple-prostitutes held shares in far-flung commercial enterprises. Before the dawn of history, Ur already sent its caravans for copper to Oman and to Ararat, for silver to the Kilikian hills, for gold to Elam and Cappadocia, and the plain of Antioch, for lapis-lazuli to Persia, where wild fur-clad Mongols brought it from the Pamirs. The trade of Babylon scattered its wealth and its culture over hither Asia. Even the bands of wild Khabru, or Hebrew, bandits from the desert who infest the hills of Canaan wax rich, and set up diminutive kingdoms which ape the pomp of Babel. The old Amorite fortress of Jerusalem, which has become their chief lair, is situated at the junction of the caravan routes from east and north, which bring the spices, incense, and myrrh of Hadramut and Sheba to the marts of Gaza, and ply from the Orient to Egypt; and the Jew bandits, trading the cedars of Lebanon for the wealth of the Yemen and of Tyre, find barter as profitable as plunder, turn traffickers and money-lenders, and fill their temple-treasury with shekels.

The military empire of Assyria, whose fierce hosts washed off the blood from their swords in the waters of the Pontus and the Nile, hung the skins of flayed chieftains on the walls of Samaria, Susa, and Memphis, and filled the harems of Nineveh with deep-bosomed daughters of Israel, trampled in the seed sown by the trader. And when Kurrush (Cyrus), King of Anshan, created the Persian Empire, the successor of Nineveh, the culture of that world-empire, which stretched from India to Ionia, and was the great political fact of the ancient world, was the civilisation of Sumer and of Babylon writ large. The

Persian satrapies of India, which supplied in gold-dust one-third of the revenues of the treasury of Ecbatana, and whose archers fought at Plataea, planted the Babylonian civilisation of Persia in the Magadhan kingdom of the upper Ganges; and when, after Alexander's raid, Chandragupta overthrew the Nandas, the first great Indian Empire of Maurya, which rose to its height under King Asoka, was modelled upon that of Persia, and its capital, Pataliputra (the modern Patna), was a copy of Persepolis.

The cupidity of warlike desert and hill tribes, excited by the wealth of the cities of the plain, brings swarm after swarm sweeping down over the motherland of civilisation, highlanders from Elam and the Zagros hills, Kassite horsemen from the snow-capped mountains of Pusht-i-Kuh, the terrible Hittites from Cappadocia, Cimmerian northerners from the Crimea, wielding monstrous swords, and with whose horses run packs of fierce hounds. But all those inroads have little other effect than to spread abroad her influence. The conditions remain unchanged. In vain are the gods of Babylon carried away to the hills and to Khana; their power remains with the rivers and their priests.

When the warrior attempts to shake off the spell, to take power into his own strong hand, when the Shalmanesers and Asshurnarsipals, and Sennacheribs, the lords of Calah and Nineveh, try, like mediæval emperors, to shake off the dominance of the arrogant priests of Asshùr and Babylon, to oppose their privileges, to question their immemorial claim to exemption from taxes, and dare to lay hands on the temple-lands, they find themselves in the end worsted. Till at last the Assyrian Empire, excommunicated and abandoned by all, goes down before the Mede amid the curse of the nations. And when in another age, the Greek Xenophon marches astonished through the ruins of Nineveh, his guides are unable to tell him the name which they once bore. The empire of the warrior, built by the sword, perishes by the sword. The dominion of the priest, established over the minds of men, endures.

The despotic power of theocratic absolutism in the Morning-lands, that unresisted tyranny which was founded in the very heart of the slave, in mental prostration before the power of the gods, that fearful, willing abjection of subjugated human herds, was the foundation, the indispensable foundation of civilisation. Without it Greece, Europe would have been impossible. It would be fine to be able to say that civilisation is the child of freedom, that it is incompatible with tyranny and slavery. In point of fact men never bethought themselves of building decent homes until they had seen gorgeous palaces and temples built with the tears and blood of thousands; they never bethought themselves of living in reasonable comfort until they had witnessed the opulence and the luxurious orgies of satraps and kings; they never bethought themselves of controlling the forces of nature until herds of human chattels had, under the kurbash of their slave-drivers, dug canals and artificial lakes, embanked rivers, and quarried mountains; they never knew scientific curiosity, the powers of the mind, the greatness and might of knowledge, the glories of the intellect, before leisured parasite-priests created culture. Totally emancipated for the first time from the material organic struggle, commanding the resources of the land, commanding inexhaustible supplies of forced labour, ready at hand to carry out their will, the priests of Sumer and Babylon and Egypt devised, contemplated, thought, discovered. They brought forth architectural and pictorial arts, crafts, industries, taught men to quarry and chisel stone, to hammer and inlay metals, glaze pottery and tiles, blow glass, weave rich fabrics and impart to them gorgeous dyes. They laid the foundation of mathematical and mechanical knowledge; they measured the land, mapped out the heavens, gave the planets and constellations the names which they still bear, and traced the courses of the moon and sun through the zodiacal belt of the 'Houses of the Moon.' They invented writing, the mighty weapon that shall multiply a hundredfold the powers of man's intelligence.

Ever glorious and venerable must be those first outbursts of that culture and civilisation which impressed their mould not upon the dim ancient Orient only, but upon all ages to come. Its conquests, greater than those of any king, its achievements greater than those of any builder of cities, are embedded in the foundations of that tradition which has borne the edifice of civilised culture long after Babylon and Persepolis had crumbled to dust, and is the heritage of modern man. But that heritage is, like that of all human tradition, a mixed one, bearing great good mingled with great evil. The Sumerian priests who were the creators of culture were the witch-doctors who, among the savage tribesmen of old, had muttered their spells and incantations, read omens from the livers of pigs, exorcised demons, and drawn charms from the moon. Amid the opulence of the civilisation they had built, they continued to discharge the selfsame functions. 'Chaldæan' means 'moon-worshipper,' and in Roman times was the synonym for sorcerer, as our term 'magician' is the name of the priests of Iran. The gods, the myths, the spells, the incantations, the tabus of the temple-cities, of Babylon, were the irrationalism of the primal savage, supersisting unchanged. Grown to power and wealth, the shaman had become a theologian and a scribe. He set down, elaborated, and systematised the old moon-myths, the savage fables of the origin of death and the Fall of Man, of the creation of the world. He set down how the Serpent-god tempted man to disobey the tabus, and thus brought sin and death into the world; how the Son of God, whom the scribe called 'the Anointed,' or 'Christ,' sought to save mankind, and interceded with the Father that man should have eternal life by partaking of the miraculous sacrament of Bread and Wine. The Chaldæan witch-doctor scratched on his clay tablet, and what he scratched there shall hold the intelligence of humanity, and its life, and its very social structure, for sixty centuries under its spell. He scratched his tablet of clay, and Rome, and Oxford, and Tennessee shall seek, six thousand years later, to put down science. The spell which he wrought was mightier than he knew, more potent than all his other exorcisms and enchantments.

Among the offthrows of Chaldæan culture was the Jew Bible which Hebraic slaves, liberated by Cyrus, brought back with them from Babylon, and which their *cohen,* Ezra, published at the inauguration of their restored temple. When Sargon of Nineveh had blotted out the tribes of the Ben-Israel, the priests of Jerusalem, rid of their northern rivals, had conceived the astounding plan of putting down all religious worship in Judah itself except in their own temple. The 'Torah,' or Law of Moses, founded on the laws of Sumer and Babylon, had been 'found' in the temple by the priest Hilkiah to give divine sanction to that ingenious monotheism which secured for Jerusalem the monopoly of religious taxes and revenue. A reign of terror was instituted by the fanatical priest-king Josiah to carry out the religious *coup d'état.* The temples of Yahu at Bethel and Nob were destroyed, the seven-horned images of the god and those of his goddess broken up, and the faith of Judah was founded on the rock of Zion. One likes to think of the poetic justice of fate which assigned to Greeks, Greek soldiers from Ionia in the service of Pharaoh Necho, whose path Josiah attempted to stop at Megiddo (Armageddon), the privilege of cutting the throat of the old Jew who founded Judaism. The Egyptian monarch sent a silver breastplate to the temple of Apollo Didymeos at Miletos in commemoration of their good service. The maddened impotence of frustrated ambition, the vindictive hatred of all peoples, by turn cruel and cringing, sanguinary and slinking, murderous and maudlin, which had always made the Jews the most abominable race in the sight of all nations, could during centuries of humiliation and subjection to contemptuous masters, Assyrian, Egyptian, Babylonian, Persian, find no other outlet for their powerless arrogance than vituperation and curses, and delirious claims to be the 'chosen people,' their temple the only temple, their law the only moral law, their chief god Yahu, a divine name of Amorite, Babylonian, and Canaanite gods from earliest times, the only god. The lyric hate of the prophet-bards of Judah ushered for the first time fanaticism and intolerance into this stricken world.

Not only on generations to come was the paralysing spell of Oriental theocracy founded upon savage irrationalism laid. It recoiled, as inevitably and invariably do all irrational and unjust foundations of power, upon the culture which it created. The dead hand of religious authority which was to strive to strangle human intelligence in the seventeenth, in the twentieth century, did no less effectually stifle it at the very dawn of historical time. Behold a phenomenon even more strange than the swift emergence of those first civilisations out of the night of savagery. From their very infancy they are smitten with a hidden malady. They shoot up with astonishing rapidity in a dim distant age, full of light and promise, and forthwith a spell is cast upon them. They stand still, petrified. They do not die; they live on and on, century after century, from one millennium to another, a charmed, weird, sepulchral life, in a trance, unchanging, as if under some awful curse.

In Babylonia all native culture has produced its best, its all—but for what the fastuous splendour of an Asshurbanipal can impart to it of opulence—long before the first Babylonian Empire had come into existence. "So far as we know," says Mr. Woolley, "the fourth millennium B.C. saw Sumerian art at its zenith. By the Ist Dynasty of Ur if there is any change it is in the nature of a decadence, and from later ages we have nothing to parallel the treasures of the prehistoric tombs. The principles of architecture understood by the early tomb builders were not forgotten, but for the rest the evidence that we have would seem to show a steady decline both in imagination and in craftsmanship. The conventions already fixed in the time of A-anni-padda gradually crushed all originality, and with lack of interest the worker lost his skill also, so that when Babylon inherited the art of Sumer we are brought up against the stereotyped and lifeless figures, smothered with meaningless ornament of Hammurabi and the Kassite kings." Babylonian science, which has supplied the germ of all science to the world, was exactly as far advanced in the nebulous dawn of Sumerian culture as it was nearly four thousand years later when the Greeks came to gather up its crumbs. Not a single aspect or feature of Babylonian civilisation shows in the course of the thousands of years of its supremacy the slightest indication of advance or development. As the legend transmitted by Berossos has it, "Oannes," the serpent-god, "taught people all things that make up civilisation, and nothing new was invented after that any more."

In the isolation of Egypt the spectacle is no less striking. Culture is actually more advanced under the pyramid builders of the IVth dynasty than at any time in the three-and-a-half millenniums during which twenty-five dynasties succeeded them. Not even the brief freedom of development under the heretic pharaoh Akhenaten, or the cultural contacts which under the XIIth dynasty produced Beni-Hassan and the jewellery and scarabs of the period, can recapture the first fine rapture of the art of the Old Empire. The civilisation of the Theban Empire at its height, though immeasurably more wealthy and commanding vastly greater resources, falls conspicuously below that of the Memphitic Empire, two thousand years older. Compare, for instance, the statue of Princess Nefert or the Sheikh al-Balàd with, say, the Rameses statues of Luxor. Compare the king's chamber of the Great Pyramid, the huge cementless ashlars between the joints of which it is impossible to introduce the blade of a penknife, masonry, as Flinders Petrie says, "only comparable to watchmakers' work," with the jerry-building of Karnak and its patchwork pillars held together by stucco. If the artists of Thebes cannot match the realism of those of Memphis, and still draw their figures in that curious way, trunk and eyes front view, limbs and head in profile, it is not that they know no better and are clumsy—the artist who decorated Seti's temple at Abydos and his tomb at Thebes, is, one can see, a fine draughtsman—but the convention is too sacred to be broken.

Our engineering and mechanical skill is the lineal successor of that of Egypt and of Babylon; yet to this day the fellah and Kurdish peasant plough with the same wooden share as their forefathers at the dawn of time; the Nile air reverberates to the sounds of creaking shadoofs and sakyahs as it did five thousand years ago, and the snapshot of the modern tourist reproduces the same scene as the mastabas of Sakkâra; the peasants of the Tigris Valley sail down-stream in those curious round leather tubs which carry two men and a donkey, and return home with the leather boat packed on the donkey's back, just as Herodotos saw them, and as they had done long before the official 'creation of the world.'

Theocracy in the East has not been intellectually tyrannical or coercive. The obscurantism, the holding down of thought, the perpetual warfare against intellectual revolt, which are a familiar feature of the European world, are not found in the Orient. And that for a simple reason: there has been no intellectual revolt. The true intellectual impulse never arose. The West has a rationalistic tradition at its back, the tradition of Greece and Rome. Oriental civilisation has had from the first a purely religious tradition only. Every civilisation, every nation has at one time or at another, suffered the incubus of theocracy; but Western civilisation did not arise, as did that of the Orient, out of theocracy. The East has had no other tradition, no other antecedent, no precedent to set against religious thought. The only changes which the East has known have been religious changes, the supplanting of one theocratic tradition by another. Revolt against religious tradition means there a 'new religion.' (The pietist, when his religious tradition is attacked, invariably asks: 'What new religion, then, do you propose to set up?') Revolt against Magian Mazdaism by Zarathustra became Zoroastrianism, revolt against Brahminism by Gautama and by Mahavira constituted Buddhism and Jainism; revolt against Pharisaic Judaism became Christianity.

Of secular, clear-cut, sharply focussed thought, the Oriental mind is not capable. The very languages of the East are structurally unfitted for the expression of precision and accuracy of thought; they have no terms for mental facts, they can be expressed only by material images. To the Oriental, Greek poetry is unintelligibly frigid because the motions and states of the mind are expressed by words, not by strings of metaphors; they do not know the use of inversion, they mark emphasis by repeating a thing three times over; they have no syntax, no means of expressing the varying relations and connections between thoughts; propositions are strung together like beads, and the only conjunction is 'and . . . and . . . and' reiterated to infinity. The human mind had to break through the gyves of such a mental conformation ere it could apply rational thought to the higher problems of its situation and destiny. And that mental constitution, that incapacity which is the central fact of Eastern culture, is the inevitable product of the mode of birth of that culture. It is the fruit of the lordly leisure and boundless domination of a small class holding multitudes in mental submission by virtue of the religious sanction of their power. The mental world which they created was itself inexorably dominated by their position. Their power, their wealth, their leisure, their opportunity of intellectual achievement, their very life and being, depended upon the sanctity attaching to that mental world, to established convention and tradition, upon the mystic prestige of its divine and consecrated character. They were neither wicked nor unintelligent men, those genial priests. On the contrary they were the most admirable men of their day. They were filled with a profound sense of the sacredness and worth of their mission; they were conscious of being what in fact they were, the civilisers and teachers of mankind. It was with a genuine zest and love, that they followed their intellectual pursuits, studied the heavens from the top of their *ziggurat,* or temple-towers, sought to assist the practical operation of agriculture, of land reclamation, of irrigation. And what is more, they were uplifted by a strong feeling of responsibility, of moral duty. They desired the welfare of the people. It is quite evident from the elaborate codes of laws they devised, that they were zealously anxious that righteousness should prevail. No Christian priest today is filled with a more exalted ideal of his functions, with a loftier endeavour, than were the priests, the *patesi* of Babylonia.

Yet all those aspirations were involuntarily perverted and paralysed. The momentum of thought, the whole interests of the thinker were enlisted in the cause of a tradition; and all the knowledge and wisdom they acquired were pressed into its service. The most intimate thought was hemmed and deformed under the pressure of those conditions: was crumpled, distorted and withered. The priests' science was magic, their astronomy, astrology. Their art was stifled by traditionalism. All the products of their mind were inextricably entangled in fantastic Oriental metaphor, in uncouth, misshapen dreams, swayed in grotesque mythological chimeras. Their moral aspirations resulted in a world which presented but one relation, that of lord and slave; their superhuman world reflected the same relation. We look in vain in all their achievements for a clear ray of thought that can strike a responsive spark in our own minds, and allow us to forget for a moment the difference between Eastern and Western thought. And that desiccated, aborted world has gone on living its sacred, devotional, mystic, and mummified life through the ages, in senile infancy, for ever incapable of growth. That is the Kismet of the culture brought into being by the medicine-man, the priest; that is the Secret of the East.

VI

THE HELLENIC LIBERATION

A TIME came when the fruits of Oriental culture, disseminated among varied populations, reached certain active and intelligent tribes of pirates. Scattered over islands and sinuous cliff-shores, they could not become welded into large empires of slaves and theocratic despots, but retained unchanged the primal tribal organisation. Each individual had to bear to a smaller or larger extent a share of the cares, fortunes, and perils of the tribe. Hence no ruling power amongst them was under the necessity of upholding its authority by means of a sacred tradition. Thus arose Greek thought, thus was laid the foundation of the Western world.

In the midst of the magic, dreaming, cataleptic Orient, at once infantile and senile, which must needs remain alien and exotic to the European mind, Greece appears to rise panoplied and full-grown, like her goddess Athene, and, almost without a transition, we find ourselves transported, as if by the stroke of her spear, into a world which is actually closer to our own than are the ten centuries which intervene between the passing of Hellenism and the rebirth of Europe, a world which is not Oriental, but Western.

It is not merely because our intellectual heritage is Grecian, because the structure of our ideas, of our outlooks, of our modes of expression, the forms of our literature, of our metaphysics, of our logic, the structure of our thought, are the progeny of Greek thought, that as we pass from Egypt, Babylon, Judæa, into Greece, we step from an exotic world into one which is Western and modern. It is because the qualities which make Greek thought European are those qualities which enable European thought, to this day, to stand up against the irrationalisms of tradition and authority. Not only is the Hellenic spirit with us today; it is one with everything which, in our own world, is most alive, most free, most replete with promise of growth and life. The forces which oppress the modern world, the obscurantisms in our midsts, the forces of reaction which cling to the past, the tyrannous dead hands which arrest the growth of intelligence, those have no kinship with the Hellenic spirit. Their affiliation is with the empires of divine vice-gerents and abject herds, with the savage irrationalism of the uncivilised, with the Orient and with Judæa, not with Greece. Greece owed its life, as we ours, to the liberation of the human mind from the shackles and gyves which weighed it down in the theocratic East. Greece created the Western mind. She brought it into being by breaking the spell, by exorcising the fatal charm which had fallen upon human evolution.

When we turn to the history of the Greek peoples, we are not merely inquiring into the annals of some very minute city-states in the Levant. Greece is not a chapter in historical annals, it is a turning-point in the evolution of humanity. Speaking as an anthropologist, Dr. R. R. Marett remarks: "To break through custom by the sheer force of reflection, and to make rational progress possible, was the intellectual feat of one people, the ancient Greeks; and it is at least highly doubtful if, without their leadership, a progressive civilisation would have existed today."

The ingenuity of historians has been puzzled to account for the 'miracle of Greece,' as it has been called. Between an age of dim fable and the height of Athenian intellectual splendour, scarcely two hundred years have elapsed, though in reality the growth of Hellas has been silently proceeding for some eight centuries. And in the two or three centuries of Greek activity the course of human evolution appears rather to have taken a sudden leap than followed the slow path of a process of growth. Within that short space of time the Greek mind has blazed the tracks which all human thought and creation has subsequently followed, in philosophy, in criticism, in literature, in politics; so that every path which the human mind has trod leads, traced backwards, to Greek thought.

Many have been satisfied to fall back on the old method of explanation of Molière's doctor, and to say that the Greeks were endowed with a wonderfully gifted natural disposition. "We have to take that character for granted," says Professor Bury. Some have thought that the charmed words 'Aryan' and 'northern races' shed light over the problem. But the racial dispositions of social humanity are the outcome of social factors.

The gifts of the Hellenic mind did not, moreover, come with any particular race, but developed in an heterogeneous enough commingling of racial stocks. The invaders who descended from the Balkans and the Danube, and whom alone Herodotos calls 'Hellenes,' have as a race contributed little to the spirit of Hellenism; the protagonists of that spirit have been peoples whom Achaioi and Dorians found already established in the Aegean, the 'People of the Sea.' Athens and Ionia were Pelasgian; the Dorians were represented by the semi-barbarous hill-community of Sparta.

The Greeks acquired the products of Oriental theocratic cultures without paying the price. Sufficiently separated by distance and natural obstacles from those cultures to make their own absorption into Eastern empires impracticable, and too poor to make it desirable, they yet came into constant and close contact with them. They reaped the fruits while remaining immune to the malady of the civilisations of the East.

The material culture of Neolithic and Bronze Age Europe had reached as high a pitch of development as it is possible for the culture of tribal communities to attain. It had been stimulated by innumerable tribal contacts, and the great river trade-routes which were to last down to modern times were already opened up. The copper, the manufactured bronze of Spain, of France, of Italy were being exchanged for British tin and Baltic amber. In the Aegean itself had arisen the most highly developed of those cultures, and by far the most effectual means of intercourse and trade. Born of seafaring enterprise, and of the contacts of the strong Kretan despots' far-flung fleets with every Mediterranean shore, that brilliant material culture, whose labyrinthine palaces, with their monumental throne-rooms, staircases, and bull-rings, their stuccos and their cameos, their frescoes picturing the pomp of the gay Minoan court, with its flounce-skirted ladies and feathered page-boys, astonish us, transmitted to Greece the command of the wine-coloured sea.

Borne upon its waves over a sea-way made easy by countless stepping-stones, and which brought him at the end of every radius of his course in touch with some new culture, the Greek became a sea-rover, and, like his hero Odysseus, "many men's cities he saw and learned their minds." He mixed and competed with the merchants of Tyre and Sidon; he met Babylonian caravans in the bazaars of Lydia and Synope; he went as trader or as mercenary to Syria and to Egypt, fought in the armies of Nebuchadressar and sacked Jerusalem, in the armies of Pharaoh, and scratched his name on the colossi of Abu-Simbel; met Phrygian and Assyrian and Ethiopian; roamed the Ionian and the Tyrrhenian seas, traded in

Sicily and Italy and with the Gauls of Massalia. And when Persian power gathered up all the old civilisations of the Orient, the Greek was in daily, and by no means always unfriendly, relation with the great cosmopolitan empire. He absorbed every culture of the Eastern world. The first book of history published in Greece was not a history of Greece, but of all the 'barbarians' whom the Greek found so interesting. And in a later age, Plutarch wrote a pamphlet to vent his patriotic indignation against Herodotos, who was a shameless 'pro-barbarian,' who had found his spiritual home in Egypt and whose interest in foreigners had led him to criticise and belittle his own people in a shockingly unpatriotic manner.

How different is his manner from that of the Jew who vowed curses and perdition upon all Gentiles and proclaimed himself the Chosen People! How different too the outcome of those cultural contacts upon the Greek! Instead of striking him with the paralysis of a petrified tradition, they served but as the raw material of restless creation and renewal. For no sacredness attached in the eyes of the Greek tribesman to the culture of the Persian, of the Phœnician, of Babylon or Egypt, none to that which he took over from Minoan and Mykenean. They were approached with curiosity, interest, acquisitiveness, but with no pious reverence. They were not sacred nor divine.

When the Greek tribes came under those influences their social organisation was that of all barbarians before the establishment of large fixed communities and of fully developed agriculture; it was that tribal organisation of warlike bands which is much the same wherever it is met with, whether among Germanic tribes or American Indians, or Central African, or Polynesian communities. The older writers, such as Robertson and Guizot, were struck with the resemblance between the social condition and character of the ancient Germans and the Red Indians, and someone even wrote a book to prove that the Redskins were Germans. Only our elegant pseudo-classic tradition has prevented the same likeness from being sooner perceived in the Homeric Greeks, and the pictures of the Iliad from being recognised as obviously taken from Fenimore Cooper's novels.

Their clans, *genoi,* phrateries, were not, as Grote and Maine imagined, groups of families, but family-groups, which retained the primitive equality of the savage clan. Constituted interests, class privileges, traditions of authority and absolutism were unknown to them. Their *basileis* were never, either then or later, 'kings' in the sense which the title has acquired, in the Oriental sense of divine vicegerents, of priestly sacred kings, but war-leaders subject to the authority of the tribe and liable to be rebuked and have their beard pulled by the least of their fellow-warriors in the ekklesia of the tribe, in which the people did not prostrate themselves before the awful majesty of the representative of the gods, but signified their approval or dissent by shouts and murmurs and the rattling of their spears on their shields. Our old 'histories of Greece' were rendered thoroughly unintelligible by the notion that the Greek states began with 'monarchies' and invented democracy. The measure of authority acquired by war-chiefs was that which the leader of a band of pirates holds over his men. That power tended continuously to dwindle and to become restricted; the *basileus* became *archon,* at first elected for life, then decennially, finally annually. While in the riparian civilisations of the East the priest became king, his magic functions developing into the autocracy of divine absolutism, among the Greek tribes the kingly office of the war-leader sank into the insignificant office of the priest, the second *archon,* as in Rome he became the *rex sacrificulus.* The Greeks did not invent democracy, as our school histories supposed; they had never occasion to abandon their original condition of tribal democracy. What they did was to endeavour to maintain that primal democratic state under the civilised condition of the City, to maintain it in spite of all factors which amid growing wealth and corporate power make for class privileges and usurpation.

There were plenty of attempts to establish privilege and oppression in Greece, Eupatrid claims, 'tyrannoi.' The earlier—and much of the later—history of Greek cities is taken up with struggles against the desperate efforts of various powers to establish themselves, with the checkmating of their attempts. But those very struggles testify to the untamed force of the primitive equalitarian spirit. The constitution of Solon was necessitated by the most terrible condition of plutocratic ascendancy. The Athenian merchants, enriched by the Eastern trade, held the whole agricultural land and the farmers themselves in the grip of their mortgages. But the force of old-established democracy was too strong: all debts had to be cancelled. (Imagine Capital and Labour agreeing to submit to the decision of a Professor Solon, and capitalists tamely submitting to expropriation!) The conditions under which the Greek people had developed did not permit of any attempt at usurpation achieving lasting success. Usurpation had no power of tradition at its back; it was not 'divine' and sacred, it never had the means of getting itself sanctified and venerated: it had to fight under its own undisguised banner. The Greek tribesmen had never occasion to prostrate themselves before a vice-gerent of the god. The 'tyrannoi' were no more tyrants than the basileis and archons were kings; they usurped the administrative and executive power by popular support and armed force, but none dared or had the power to alter the actual constitution, to claim to be 'legitimate' rulers.

Peisistratos enforced the laws of Solon, and even made them more liberal; the only means of power which those usurpers had was to please the people. In passing from barbaric communism to civilisation, the Greeks never lost the spirit of their equalitarian condition. And the height of the intellectual growth of Athens coincides with a form of absolute democracy, which is, and will probably remain, without parallel. The 'democratic jealousy' with which the Kleisthenean constitution is almost fanatically obsessed, was bent upon prophylactic insurance against the remotest opportunity of individual or class dominance.

That superlative democracy rested, it is true, upon slavery. When Attic imperialism was at its height a hundred thousand citizens were surrounded by three hundred and sixty-five thousand slaves. But at a time when slavery was a universal institution the condition of Attic slaves was so mild, except in the silver mines (the lot of miners is always bad), that they never once revolted. The agricultural slave was rather a farmer than a slave, and, having paid a certain fixed proportion of produce to the landlord, could do what he liked with the rest. The industrial slave assisted his master, who worked as hard as himself; and Demosthenes could claim that slaves in Attica enjoyed greater freedom than citizens in many another land. Hence slavery in Athens never affected her intellectual development through any anxiety about the maintenance of power. That it did not affect it by producing idleness is attested by the fact that in the time of Perikles the number of citizens who could not afford to lose a day's work to serve on the juries was so great that he introduced the payment of jurymen. As a matter of fact most of the crafts and industries of Athens were carried on by free labour, not by slaves, the former being cheaper and better. No slave labour was employed in the building of the Akropolis. Slavery did exercise a profoundly pernicious effect upon Greek culture, and ultimately contributed to its downfall. But neither in Greece nor in Rome did it ever seriously affect the complexion of social and political thought, compel it, as in the East, to adapt itself to the interests of oppression. The slaves were imported foreigners, a fluctuating population lying outside the social community, not oppressed citizens, not the people themselves reduced to subjection. The social and intellectual questions developed in Greece between citizens and citizens, not between masters and slaves.

No form of power or privilege in Greece ever moulded itself on the pattern of a superhuman ruler, of a god. The primitive magico-religious beliefs and rites of the Greek peoples were exactly similar to those of all other peoples. There is not a theological conception or superstition of irrationalism, of 'primal stupidity,' there is not a weird, magical practice of savage man, which cannot be abundantly illustrated from the records of the Greek states. Indeed not a few of the divine personages of Greek myth and of the symbolisms and rituals attaching to them appear to have been, for some reason which is not as yet clear, transplanted there from the Semitic lands of Western Asia—Aphrodite, for instance, the goddess of Ephesos identified with the Artemis of Delos, and the Kretan goddess, are but forms of the Semitic Ishtar; Herakles is no other than Shamash. Even names are sometimes identical, as, for example, Melikerta at Korinth, who is no other but the Tyrian dying god Melqart. The fund of magico-religious tradition was, in fact, the same in Greece as in Sumer, Babylon, or Judæa. But what a universe of difference in the ultimate outcome! That immeasurable difference rests upon the circumstance that primal irrationalism in Greece never served as the foundation for constituted power, that authority was never founded upon it. It was never edited, sanctified, 'spiritualised' in the service and in the interests of the rule of a priest. The task of reducing the crude, inchoate medley of local irrational traditions to some semblance of formulated order did not fall to an 'inspired' priest, but to the poets. They "made the generations of the gods for the Greeks, and gave them their names and distinguished their offices and crafts and portrayed their shapes" (Herodotos, 2.53.) They accomplished their theological task in the bungling fashion of inexpert amateurs. The Olympian gods of the city-states, of the poets' mythologies, of the matchless craft of the artists, were, from the religious point of view, pitiable and admitted failures. They were utterly unconvincing. At once coldly abstract and grossly anthropomorphic, they were, in fact, not really believed in. Olympian religion was not a religious faith. The Greek was scrupulous and punctilious concerning the official rites of the City's cult, about the honour and service of the City's gods. They were, much as the Roman's *Dea Roma,* the symbols, the banner of the *Polis*. Impiety towards the City gods was, by good citizens, felt to be horribly offensive in the same manner as an insult to the statue of Cæsar was offensive to a Roman, or an insult to the Union Jack is offensive to an Englishman. Therein consisted the piety of the ordinary Greek citizen; but he was not religious in the sense which the epithet bears in our Oriental tradition. He was not reverent in his attitude towards the gods. No tribal society is reverent. The savage tribesman, for all his superstitious irrationalism, is hail-fellow-well-met with his gods, tells amusing stories about their mishaps, and beats and kicks them when they prove obdurate and intractable. The Greek poets told amusing stories about the Olympians, how, for instance, the cripple Hephaistos caught his wife, Aphrodite, in a net with Ares, her paramour, and exhibited the guilty pair before the whole Olympian assembly, which made Olympos rock with their laughter; or how the jealous shrew, Hera, yelled with pain when young Herakles squeezed her pap. It appears that the secret of religious reverence is only known to people who have been accustomed to grovel and kiss the dust in the throne-room of a divine priest-king, with the more ponderous parts of their persons converted towards heaven. Mental reverence towards sacred things would seem to be in some manner correlated with that anatomical attitude, with an acquired weakness of the knee-joints. The priest never became a king in Greece; he was a minor public servant. The City-state was not an enclosure built round the temple of the priest's god; it was the successor and representative of the primitive tribe.

Religion, accordingly, while resting upon the selfsame primal conceptions and myths in Greece as in Babylon or Jerusalem, stood with the Greeks, as with the Norse, the Germans, or the Latins, for something wholly different as regards the place it occupied in human life from the religions of the Eastern river-lands. And the difference depends upon the circumstance that in the latter the whole sphere of the supernatural was from the first bound up with the power and privilege of a theocracy. As the all in all of human life, engrossing man's thought and activities, excluding every other attitude of the mind, religion, as the term is still understood, is a product of the East. In the Orient every act of conduct is subject to divine sanction. In Greece no inevitable connection was even apprehended between morality and religion. There were rites due to the gods and to the dead, but relations with the living were a matter of justice, not of divine commandments. The Jews bound every scrap of their literature, their chronicles, their proverbs, their romances, even their erotic poems and love-songs with the Torah, the Law of God. The Greeks regarded the Homeric poems as the canon of their tradition, but it no more occurred to them to regard them as the consecrated word of God than to account the poems of Anakreon or the comedies of Aristophanes sacred. It has been said that Homer was their Bible. That is precisely what it never was. They had no word of God, and therefore the word of man and the thought of man grew in power unfettered. The Greeks were probably no more ingenious or of more penetrating intelligence than the priests of Chaldæa; their ingenuity and their intelligence were merely free from the obligation of being religious. For the Oriental that was impossible. The priests of Ur and Babylon had laid the foundations of science and culture. The Greeks had little patience with scientific details; but when it came to using and interpreting facts, the Greek was scientific and the Oriental was incapable of being so. When someone brought to Perikles a ram's head with a single horn curiously growing in the middle of its brow, a soothsayer was prompt with his interpretations, drawing omens and prophecies from the circumstance. But Anaxagoras, who happened to be present, split the skull in two and showed how the monstrosity was the natural effect of maldevelopment in the bones of the skull. It was in Greece that the human mind could for the first time move freely outside the charmed circle of supernatural tradition. Thus it was that when the Greek tribes culled the fruits of the old civilisations, the civilisations of the Oriental priests, they transformed them into a new power, a new phase in human evolution.

It was not in Greece that the Hellenic mind was formed. The 'miracle of Greece' took place in Asia. There already the sagas and 'chansons de geste' of the Achaean tribes' heroes, and of their battles in Thessaly and round Kadmaean Thebes, had collected around the story of the fight for Troy, which came in a later age to be symbolic of the opposition between Europe and Asia—the name given in Homer to a meadowland in Lydia. There Greek tribes had settled on the Anatolian seaboard and the adjoining islands as far south as Knidos and Halikarnassos, and been held up in Kilikia by the Assyrian troops of Sennacherib. It was among migrants from Attica driven by a Dorian wave that the Greek spirit actually came to birth and full power. Ionia lay on the fringe of the rich, Oriental Lydian kingdom, whence the youth of Kolophon came back, Xenophanes complained, flaunting Eastern dresses in the agora and reeking with perfumes; where at the court of Sardis, the Athenian Solon, like a country yokel, mistook each gorgeously clad courtier with his train of attendants for the king; and when the king took him round his treasure-houses and sought to dazzle him with the wealth of vases, and tripods of gold and electron, and jewels, golden clasps, and chains, and pectorals, and golden sand from Tmolos, and the new device of coined money beautifully designed to his order by Ionian artists, and Babylonian carpets, and carved cedar chests full of rich embroidered garments, the Greek refused to be impressed, to the annoyance of the king who expected the usual hyperbolic, Oriental compliments—how characteristic the whole anecdote is of the Greek attitude! It was that semi-Asiatic Ionia, grown to wealth through intercourse with the Orient, which was the cradle of Greek culture, whence it harked back with trade to the Attic mainland, as also did sea-love and sea-power. While Anakreon of Teos, and Alkaios of Lesbos, whose brother served in the army of king Nebuchadressar of Babylon and had an ivory-handled sword given him for distinguished service, and 'burning Sappho' loved and sang, and Mimnermus of Smyrna composed his elegies, Greek intellect rose in the harbour-cities of Ionia to the first splendour—and was it not also the best and soundest?—of its creative power. From Miletos, the sea queen at the mouth of the Menander, whose fleets plied regularly to Egyptian Naukratis, and Abydos, and Byzantium, and the Crimea, and the rest of her sixty daughter colonies, and where the caravans from Susa and Babylon ended their journey, came Thales fully equipped with the lore of Egypt and Chaldæa, and first introduced mathematics and astronomy, and philosophical speculation to Greek lands; and Anaximenes who thought all land animals, including man, were descended from fishes; and Hekataios who travelled all Oriental lands and wrote a description of the world half a century before Herodotos of Halikarnassos followed in his footsteps; and Anaximander who first drew maps, like that 'brass table' with which his countryman Aristagoras astonished the Spartans when he sought to induce them to attack Lydia, "with all the seas and all the rivers set down upon it." He was said, too, to have invented the gnomon, but that had been in use for ages in Babylon. It was customary to credit the first Greek who introduced an Egyptian or Babylonian invention with its discovery, just as in the Middle Ages every Arabian invention was set down to the first European who happened to mention or use it. From 'piney' Kolophon came Xenophanes railing at the gods whom Homer and Hesiod had pictured immoral, and whom oxen and horses would have pictured bovine or equine, and taught Parmenides of Elea from whom Plato learned. From Klazomenai came the great Anaxagoras who "brought Ionian science to Athens," and taught his friends Perikles and Euripides 'atheism.' From Ephesos came Herakleitos, that Ionian Nietzsche who in proud scorn denounced the vulgar instincts of the herd who, like asses, preferred chaff to gold, and the man-made values which it mistook for eternal realities, while Nature and her unswerving forces of perpetual change and becoming wrought beyond good and evil. From the Milesian colony of Abdera came Demokritos who conceived matter to be composed of atoms; and from Samos Pythagoras, half scientific genius, half crank, whom tradition, perhaps too lightly dismissed, made the pupil, not only of Chaldæan and Egyptian priests, but of Persian and Indian teachers.

Thus was the old wine of the Orient put into the new bottles of Greek criticism and rationalism. It was that exceptional concourse of favourable conditions which moulded the Greek mind and liberated the forces which were to create Western culture.

It is sometimes said that Greece saved Europe, saved it from being swallowed up by the East. But it was not so much at Marathon, at Salamis, at Plataea, at Mykale that Greece overcame the Orient. Before saving Europe, Greece had to create it, to create the Western mind. And that too was a battle scarcely less desperate and even more glorious in its issue than her struggle against the hosts of Persia. That also was a struggle against the Orient and against all the forces upon which the Oriental mind was founded. And the East was beaten ere a single soldier-slave of the Great King had set foot across the Hellespont.

The many-nationed hosts of Persia and her Tyrian fleets were by no means the sole, nor the chief menace which Greece had to encounter. At one time the fate of Europe, the fate of human evolution had been in even more grievous peril than when Xerxes stood, with the smoking ruins of the old Akropolis behind him, "on the rocky brow which looks o'er sea-born Salamis." A century earlier the destinies of the world had, for a moment, even more fearfully and momentously trembled in the balance. And it was not the hoplites and seamen of Greece that saved them then, but a handful of gruff old men in Ionia solitarily thinking and revolving in their minds unpractical things.

The formal official cults of the City gods had robbed the products of primitive irrationalism, the magico-religious traditions of the land, of their power over life and mind. Olympian religion was, religiously, a failure, and for that very reason it had, without intending it, been a victory over irrationalism, had drawn the fangs and clipped the claws of irrational tradition. Translated into cold symbols of the state, into abstract departmental gods, into allegories, the aboriginal deities, the primitive magical moon-gods, the mysterious Great Mothers, the undefined, Protæan forms of supernatural powers harking back to savage magic, had shed all trace of mystery and had sunk to the level of popular folklore. They had lost all 'spiritual' life and power.

In the world before Greece was, in the Oriental world, only one thing could, in the circumstances, have happened. Some new, some 'higher,' more 'spiritual,' religion would have evolved and taken its place at the helm of the mind and life of the race. Had that come about there would have been no Hellenic mind as we know it, no Western civilisation built upon the foundation of an extra-religious development. And it was in fact by the narrowest margin that for two centuries that catastrophe was averted, and Europe made possible. Continual contact with Oriental religion awakened the ever-present craving for the magic, the supernatural control of life. The Olympian pantheon appeared, as it appeared later to the Christian, but a bald and cold fiction of symbolic idols beside the rich, mysterious values of the Oriental's theocratic cults. The Greek mystic, the Greek populace, recognised in their own traditions, in their own ancient cult those same qualities, those same elements, now disguised and effaced in the formal official cults, which, among the barbarians, were so fruitful of mystic exaltations, of mysterious promises, of magic transcendences above cold reason. From the dark recesses of the older shrines, from Thessaly, the land of witches, from Boeotia, the home of oracles, rose the veiled, phantasmal forms of the 'chthonic' deities, Demeter and Persephone, Hades, Hekate, and Hermes psychopompos, the lords of the resurrection and the life everlasting. The cults of the old primitive gods who had been gathered together by the perplexed poetical makers of theogonies under the name of Dionysos, and who had never succeeded in finding a place in the court of the official Olympos, the dithyrambic, orgiastic, miracle-working god of mystic enthusiasms acquired an importance more vital than any Olympian cult. The mystic Dionysos was freely identified with Oriental gods, with Attis-Men, Osiris, Adonis, and the god of the Jews. At Eleusis the old agricultural rites of fertility assumed new, more exalted significances. The Telesterion had been rebuilt after the model of an Egyptian hypostyle hall, and the elect, cleansed of all impurities by ritual waters, were admitted to the mystic meal; the hierophant, successor of Tryptolemos, raised the holy symbol of the bread of life, the body of the dying and resurrecting god. All Athens set forth on the night of the winter solstice to celebrate by torchlight the feast of the Nativity.

Another god of the nether-world, Orpheus, was given out to be the prophet of the new religion. The rustic population, the women in particular, became possessed with a wild religious frenzy, and had ecstatic visions; the dancing madness spread like an epidemic through the Greek world.

In the enthusiasm of that revival the temple priests came forth out of their obscurity and neglect, and began to speak with authority. New elaborate, esoteric systems of theology were promulgated. Proselytising missionaries and preachers, metragyrtes, orpheotelestes, theophorites, went abroad teaching and announcing the god in the market places, healing the sick, claiming "a power derived from Heaven that enables them by agreeable ceremonies and rites to atone for any sin committed by the individual or his forefathers. They produce many books from which their rituals are drawn, and persuade not only single persons, but entire cities, that they may be purified and absolved from sin, both in this life and after death, by the performance of certain ceremonies which they call 'Mysteries,' and which are supposed to save us from the torments of Hades, which neglect of them is punished by an awful doom." (Plato, *Rep.* ii, 364-5.) One of those prophets, Onomakritos, gained considerable influence and favour at the Athenian court of Peisistratos, and was employed in the preparation of the new edition of the Homeric poems, into which he managed to slip some 'Orphic' passages. He had, however, the misfortune to be caught red-handed at the old religious game of forging documents—some poems which he sought to father upon Musæos. In the Orient such a procedure was taken as a matter of course; every priestly writing in Jerusalem was set down to Moses, or to David, or to Isaiah, and the Jews fell down and worshipped the holy word of God. But such was the difference between East and West that, instead of regarding the pious fraud in a broad-minded, sympathetic way, the Athenians had the bad taste to denounce Onomakritos as a liar and a scamp, and the prophet was discredited and disgraced.

So indeed, after a brief suspense, was the whole Orphic religious movement—for one or two precious centuries at any rate. It had seemed as though Greece were on the point of being submerged under a flood of religious irrationalism, as if the dead hand of a theocracy were about to be laid upon the cradle of Western thought, and the liberation of the world be indefinitely prorogued. The names of the heroes who saved Europe then were not Miltiades, Themistokles, Pausanias, but Thales, Xenophanes, Herakleitos, Anaxagoras. The thinkers of Ionia had not thought and spoken in vain; they had revealed to man a new dignity and a new power. Against the new madness in particular, against the ignorant exploiters of ignorance, the preaching god-bearers, "the most pestilent brood I wot of," as Athenæus, a gleaner of old texts, calls them, "save, perhaps, those who go round collecting subscriptions for the Demeter"; against all the hosts of unreason, their voice was raised in hot and indignant protest.

And Greece, the better instinct of Greece, heard the summons and rallied round its thinkers. Even before the people of Kroton summarily put an end to the Pythagorean mystic brotherhood, Orpheus had slunk away out of sight, and Greece had peremptorily given to all mystagogues notice to quit and cease from fooling. 'Of uncertainty and mystery there is, by Zeus, enough in this strange, rich life, and to spare. But how shall the myths and mummeries of a barbarian priest help it, or make it less or otherwise? What can be known we shall seek to know with all the might of the honest means of knowledge whereof we dispose; and what we cannot know we shall face fearlessly with no less honest ignorance. But while power remains to the mind of Hellas, the thought of man shall at least be free, and to the generations to come, so long as they can hear her voice, Hellas shall bequeath that heritage of freedom.'

When with languid, half-condescending curiosity we seek to gather from the surviving fragments and mutilated relics collected in Diels's book some notion of the ideas and conceptions, often to us somewhat naïve and crude, of the early thinkers of Ionia, how many of us realize clearly, or at all, that if it is given us today to face the world and its problems with open eyes, with some small measure of adequate power of clear judgment, and some armoury of accumulated knowledge and understanding, it is to those men, who to most are little more than empty names, to *them* in the first place and beyond all others who have subsequently utilized the freedom they won, that we owe it?

The Greeks were the first rationalists, and they were the most rationalistic people that have ever lived. They were so to a far greater extent than we are, for our own thought is brought up at every turn against the tradition of the priest and the pietist, and cannot move without being conscious of the dead weight of fierce, obstinate prejudice, subtly insinuating itself under all disguises. Greece in the period of her vitality never once allowed that weight to be laid upon her shoulders. Therein lies the achievement of Greece. Therein lies also the perennial charm which pervades Greek thought. In perusing the literature of Greece we come upon much that is crude and naïve, much that is absurd, much that from the vantage point of our knowledge is hopelessly fallacious and puerile. But we never once meet with obdurate, blind and fanatical, consecrated prejudice. We breathe freely because we feel that we are in the presence of open minds, in which the operation and growth of thought is never choked by hardened traditional formulas, by the jealous monopoly of a dogma, by blinding preconceptions. The freedom of human thought was not, as with us, a revolt. Thought in Greece was never otherwise than free. And in a world where all thought had hitherto been sacred, the mind of Greece acted for the first time outside the orbit of religious interest. Compare, for example, old Herodotos, who is not by a long way a Xenophanic sceptic or even a thinker, but on the contrary a typically commonplace and rather pious person, according to Greek standards—compare him with the turgid, bombastic annalists of India, of Assyria, Egypt, or Judæa, who invariably wrote thousands for hundreds, and millions for thousands, and in whom we have to excavate every fact from under an impenetrable mound of miracle-mongering and nauseating panegyric! Whenever Herodotos meets with the miraculous and supernatural, or even with patriotic exaggeration, he is filled with distrust and determined scepticism. "How could a dove speak with human voice?" he asks when told the legend of the priestess of Dodona; the ravine Peneios was caused by Poseidon striking the earth with his trident, he was told, "but it appears evident to me that it is the effect of an earthquake"; the Persian fleet was tossed about for three days until the Magi quelled the storm by offering prayers and sacrifices, "or else it slackened of its own accord." Even when he recounts the most glowing moments in the glories of his own people he jibs at any improbability. When, for instance, he relates the story of Skyllies of Skione, the famous diver, who was said to have swum eighty stadia to give the Athenian fleet at Artemision warning of the coming Persians, he adds simply, "If, however, I may offer an opinion in the matter, it is, that he came in a boat." It is not that his intelligence was abnormally acute—was it really more acute than that of those genial and learned Egyptian and Babylonian priests with whom he conversed?—but because there were no influences in the Greek world which branded disbelief in the miraculous or in adulatory exaggerations as 'wicked.' The Greek mind developed not because it had essentially more power, but because that power was not crippled.

A passion for rationalism became its supreme characteristic. To reason, to argue, to discuss, was the Greeks' delight. Politics, government had with them always meant discussion, conflicts of arguments, not ukases; and they extended the habit to every phase of life. They were the first to rationalise (in the theological sense), to criticise, and to reject their own religious traditions. They constructed formal logic; they reduced dialectics to a science; eloquence with them meant argument, and they worshipped eloquence above all things; their drama ever tended towards a pendulum swing of pros and cons. Art itself, the art which produced the Parthenon—that 'syllogism in marble,' as Boutmy calls it—and Greek sculpture, was obsessed with 'canons,' modules, standards, with a desire to penetrate to the rationale of the artistic effect. Iktinos, who raised on the Attic rock the beauty pure and perennial of the 'Maiden's Chamber,' wrote a treatise expounding the logical principles upon which he wrought. And the spirit of their art manifested itself in ordered regularity and symmetry, corresponding as it were to the balanced and orderly disposition of logical thought; in Olympian calm expressive of the composed serenity of detached judgment.

They carried the passion for conscious, deliberate ratiocination—paradoxical as it may seem—to excess. To the Greek the very form of ratiocination had a captivating and irresistible fascination. No entertainment held the populace like a display of argumentative acuteness. They came to delight in dialectics for their own sake. A favourite exercise of their orators was to establish a position by argument one day, and to demolish it the next. They were ratiocinative even to the neglect of the foundations of rational thought, of investigation and experience, of the practical methods of trial and error. And thus, as we shall see more fully, they missed science and remained pre-scientific. It is worth while noticing that the Greeks had not in any very high degree what we call the passion for truth; the frenzy for getting to the very root of facts, to explain, the ideal of the supreme sanctity of truth. They were rather impatient of nonsense, of pseudo-explanations which are an insult to intelligence, than possessed with any high passion for truth for its own sake. Cleverness, beauty, and moral beauty, they admired rather than truth; a clever plausibility would satisfy them without any too severe enquiry as to whether it was true.

Such as it was, the efflorescence of the human mind in Greece, which has created *homo sapiens* anew, which has initiated and made possible the whole subsequent evolution of humanity, has been, it has seemed to many, the high-water mark of human development. That is to a large extent an illusion. But the illusion is excusable, for never since has the human mind had the opportunity to develop free from the incubus of consecrated irrationalism.

It need cause no wonder that the career of Greece was brief; the wonder is not that the greatness of Greece failed to maintain itself longer, but that it succeeded in maintaining itself at all. It was a premature birth, only rendered possible by an exceptionally propitious concourse of circumstances. Human experience was utterly insufficient to serve as an adequate basis for such a purely rational attitude as that of the Greeks. Politically they had managed to preserve the essential spirit of primitive tribal democracy throughout all the altered conditions of advanced civilisation, in spite of the numberless agencies which in the ordinary course of human circumstances necessarily put an end to it. They had withstood and overcome the encroachments of war chiefs, the pretensions of nobles, the almost irresistible despotism of money-power, the corruption of foreign gold, the armed power of the Persian. They had by radical and elaborate contrivances endeavoured to adapt democracy to the changed conditions.

But that achievement was almost a paradox, a state of unstable equilibrium which could not in the nature of things be kept up indefinitely.

With some peoples decadence sets in insidiously through the operation of inherent faults which slowly creep and extend and eat them up; others lose their balance at the very height of their success, and through those very virtues and qualities that made it possible. The latter was the case with Greece, or what is for us the same thing, Athens. After the repulse of the Persians the Athenians grew intensely self-conscious of their greatness and glory and became infected with the toxæmia of jingo-patriotism. Patriotism is an altruistic virtue; it means the subordination of individual self-interest to that of the community. But then all depends upon what is understood by 'the community.' Savages manifest in the highest degree all the social virtues with reference to the tribe, and all social iniquities, barbarisms, and cruelties with reference to every other tribe. Patriotism is a virtue, but it is also a vice. Patriotism towards the City-state was the supreme moral idea of the Greek, his religion. And the City-state was merely the substitute for the tribe of the savage. Athens was patriotic towards Athens and unpatriotic towards Greece. That incurable separatism, those wanton, fatal bickerings of half a dozen trumpery villages, appear to us unspeakably foolish and absurd, and only to be explained by some peculiar 'individualistic' twist of the Greek character. But that separatism and interstate anarchy were as wanton and foolish as European separatism and anarchy, no more and no less. Size is merely relative; the City-state was the political unit of the Greek world as the nation-state is of the European, and even in his Utopia Plato could not conceive of any other political unit. A league of Greek nations, such as the Cynic and

Cyrenaic philosophers advocated, was all very well before the instant menace of Persian aggression, but as a permanent order it was an unpractical dream outside the sphere of political realities. It would, for one thing, mean the giving up of the command of the sea, and that, of course, was not to be thought of. So Athenians stuck to 'the empire,' and stood up for Athens first, Athens right or wrong. The nemesis came sharp and swift in the quarries of Syracuse and on the sands of Aegospotami; and when the traitor Alkibiades brazenly asked the Athenians whether it would pay them better to accept Persian gold as the price of democracy, or perish utterly, they hung their heads in silence. And when the Spartan Agesilaos actually went forth in one last attack against Persia, he was driven back, he said, "by thirty thousand bowmen," meaning the golden darics stamped with the figure of the Great King as an archer, with which the Greeks at home had been bribed and bought, and his recall secured.

Hellas, torn and exhausted by incurable petty patriotisms and jealousies and strifes, and all the nameless corruption and ignoble selfishness and lying which such contests breed, was, it was clear to everyone, fast sinking lower and lower; and the 'Peace of Antalkidas' made her virtually a subject-state of the Great King, from whom the Greek states abjectly took their orders. The blossom was drooping and wilting on its stem. How long would it be before the closing tides of barbarism, which were already strangling the Greek colonies in Italy, and the irresistible power of Persia, before which, like a shivering bird hypnotized by a serpent, Hellas lay a doomed and helpless prey, would make an end of Hellenic civilisation? How much of it, if anything at all, would survive? Those seemed the obvious questions. When, behold, a strange thing happened: instead of dying, Hellenic civilisation conquered the world.

There were some Greek tribes—probably as purely Greek, notwithstanding Peonian and Illyrian admixtures, as the Athenians and Milesians—who had remained in the backwaters of the Southern Balkans, cut off from the operation of the influences which produced Ionia and Hellas. Note the true relative values of race and environment: they remained insignificant barbarians in the same condition as the early Greek tribes. Their mediocre little barbaric kingdom was of no account until one of their kings sought to introduce Greek culture and drew to his court artists and poets from the south, Zeuxis the famous painter, Hippokrates the physician, possibly Thucydides the historian, Timotheos of Miletos the poet and musician, Agathon the tragic poet, and another far greater and more tragic poet also, Euripides by name, a very sad and very weary old man, with his faith in humanity sorely bruised and shaken, who went thither to die, and, before dying, wrote there his swan-song, the *Bacchae*. The successor of King Archelaos, who was brought up at Thebes, perceived the possibilities presented by the disintegration of the Greek city-states, systematically trained an army and, after defeating Athens and Thebes at Chaironea, established a kind of 'sphere of influence' over all Greece, getting himself appointed archistrategos, or, as one might say in Latin, imperator of the Hellenes. His son even more carefully educated—his chief tutor was Aristotle—landed a very efficiently trained and equipped little army, the equivalent of some four modern divisions, on the plain of Troy, by the heroön of Achilles, scattering the satrapic armies before him at the Granikos, liberated both the willing and unwilling cities of Ionia, and after a couple of pitched battles the whole 'ramshackle empire' of Persia, the whole known world of the Near East, Asia Minor, Phœnicia, Babylon, Palestine, Egypt, lay at his feet. He pushed on beyond the limits of the known world, meeting with Chinese in Baktria, founding Kandahar in the Afghan tableland, and did not stop till he had entered Lahore and Hyderabad. When he returned to rest awhile in Babylon, the old first metropolis of all civilisation, and prepare for the conquest of the West, submissive embassies came to the young new Dionysos to offer him the homage of the whole world, Arabs, Ethiopians, Scythians, Carthaginians, Iberians, Gauls, Etruscans, Italians from Brutium, Samnites—whether also from a little village called Rome, history does not mention. The whole world was Hellenised.

The fertilising spirit of Hellas was spread over the whole earth for all peoples and for all times. But not in its purity. The Orient had, after all, its revenge, its terrible and fatal revenge. The conquering young Greek hero had offered sacrifice to Artemis at Ephesos, to Melqart at Tyre, to Ahura Mazda at Ecbatana, to Ptah at Memphis, to Ammon at Sîwa, to Yahu at Jerusalem. And the Gods of the East smiled.

The ghosts of primitive, savage irrationalism, which had been laid by Greek thought in the vigour of her prime, now rose on every side from the conquered Orient. And this time there was no Ionian thought, no 'Seven Sages' to resist them. Greek thought had slowly succumbed. The forces of mysticism, will-to-believe, substitutes for reason, the excitations of magic visions and dim emotions, had been battering at the gate like Persian hosts round the Thermopylai. Lacking the armoury of scientific data, the Greek mind was incapable of offering effectual resistance to the Oriental hordes of nebulous dreams which steadily crept over the ground reclaimed by rational thought. Plato shines with a splendour which is already in a large measure phosphoric. In his old age he had become 'converted.' From Platonism to Neo-Platonism was but a step. As Greece had transmuted the barbaric tinsels of the Orient into rich gold, so the East once more seized upon the jewels of Hellas, and wove them into mystic, cabalistic webs, into its gnosticisms and theologies.

VII

PAX ROMANA

SUPERFICIALLY the origin of Rome resembles that of Greece—small tribes *(gentes)* in whom a jealous spirit of independence is inveterate. Here the *patres familias,* not the tribal war-chiefs, are the natural rulers wielding stern familial authority, and will become the *patres conscripti* and the ruling patrician aristocracy. As in Greece, phases of 'kingship' were swept away by the insubordinate forces of tribal democracy. As in Greece, violent struggles and conflicts took place between patrician and plebeian, and here again the forces of self-defence proved too powerful to allow of any complete triumph on the part of encroaching privilege. As Athens had its Solonian and Kleisthenean revolutions, so Rome had its Secessions to the Sacred Hill, and its Licinian laws.

But under that superficial similarity lay differences which could scarcely be more profound. While the Greek of poverty-stricken Hellas was perforce a sea-rover, a pirate, an adventurer, tasting of all the rich fruits of the Eastern world, the Romans were a tribe of stay-at-home farmers, with all the peasant's limitation of outlook, conservatism, stolid abstemiousness, plodding stubbornness, his close-fistedness and keen eye for the main chance. The necessity of defending their crops and of settling boundary disputes with neighbouring tribes, made it a routine of their lives to be periodically called out on *commando*. But they were not temperamentally bellicose nor did they particularly like war for its own sake. They waged it with cool business-like method and calculation, and early learnt to attain their ends by negotiation, alliances and hard-driven bargains. They intensely distrusted and disliked adventure.

It was a freakish paradox of fate which thrust upon those cautious, unimaginative Italian Boers the part of world-conquerors. When first drawn into wide foreign embroilments after the first Punic War, they proclaimed a policy of no annexations (and large indemnities). Scipio expressed the general and deep traditional feeling when he advocated a Monroe Doctrine deprecating all expansion beyond the Tuscan Apennine and the peninsula; and we find the same caution recurring even so late as the political testament of Augustus, and in Hadrian's renouncement of the conquests of Trajan. Only when the peasants were set agape at the sight of the undreamed-of wealth brought from Pontus and Syria by Lucullus and Pompey, did they lose their heads and become infected with the get-rich-quick fever.

What drove them to go empire-building was not any romantic ambition or love of glory, or vanity, such as might actuate an Oriental despot, or any hollow ideal of empire and passion for ruling, but purely and simply the desire to make money, to make money quickly. The conquests, as they soon saw, offered plenty of opportunities; the farming of taxes, army contracts, the financing of political aspirants, money-lending at exorbitant rates, and, richest prize of all, the government of a province, when the raising of the tribute was left to the proconsul, and no questions asked. Those were the chief ways of making large fortunes. There were no great industrial enterprises then, no railways or oil-wells, no great commercial organisations. The money had to be invested and the only possible form of permanent investment was land. They invested their money in land. The original small farmer being more and more frequently absent on active service, his farm, left to the care of some elderly relatives and a few slaves, went to rack and ruin. He was easily mortgaged or bought out. Italy was thus soon divided into vast estates which were productively and economically worked by means of slave-labour supplied in abundance by the wars. After Italy the foreign provinces followed. In the famous impeachment of Verres, Cicero brought out the fact that in one district of Sicily there were, when Verres went there as propraetor, 773 landed proprietors, and three years later only 318. Half the province of Africa was at the time of the early Cæsars owned by six landlords.

There is no harm in making money and investing it. But what was to become of the dispossessed farmer? There were no factories or other employment for him to go to, he had perforce to go back to the army or to lounge in Rome at the expense of the state. He had nothing left. "Your generals," said Tiberius Gracchus, "urge their men in battle, telling them to fight for their hearths and homes and the graves of their dear ones. They lie; not one of all those Romans possesses a hearth or a home, or even a family grave. That others may enjoy riches and pleasures, that is what they are fighting and dying for, those Romans who are called 'masters of the world,' while they have not so much as a sod of earth that they can call their own." (Plutarch, *Tib. Gracchus.*) The wars of Lucullus, of Pompey, of Cæsar had brought in hundreds of thousands of slaves who worked on the large estates. But thereafter the supply abruptly dwindled. Slaves did not breed, they had no families, there were few women. Instead of being cheap, they became expensive; the labour supply failed. The freemen had to be employed; they were employed as *coloni;* they became bound more and more to the soil. At first they paid rent, then a proportion of the produce, beside sundry customary 'gifts,' or *xenia,* then had to contribute a certain amount of labour to the working of the villa, to supply transport, etc., and finally, under Diocletian, they were completely bound to the soil, forbidden to move. They too became slaves, predial serfs in all but in name. And they too dwindled. The whole population decreased until it became an ever more serious problem how to keep up the strength of the armies, even for purely defensive purposes. In the early empire those vast frontiers, far more extensive than the battle-line on all fronts in the Great War, were defended by garrisons amounting to the absurd number of about 300,000 men.

Greek culture, which they at first fiercely resisted, did not sufficiently transform the enriched peasants to enable them to continue it, or use it as the starting-point of original development. The influx of civilisation tended with them in general to coarseness, to the vulgarity and megalomania of the *nouveau riche.* In the pictorial arts they remained sterile, save for the production of the realistic portrait-bust—the idealising Greek never carved a real portrait. In architecture, while carrying to high development the engineering aspect of construction, as in the arch and the dome, they perpetrated—and unfortunately perpetuated—as regards the purely artistic and decorative aspect, the most appalling horrors of bad taste, such as the pilaster and the use of mixed orders. Greek drama bored them, they preferred mimes, buffoons and acrobats.

To the end a stodgy pedestrianism remained the mark of their mentality. The sacred fire, the divine folly was never theirs. The very brief and evanescent *grand siècle* of their literature did not contribute a single creator to the Olympus of world inspirers, scarcely a work of genuine inspiration—Lucretius, the exponent of Epicurus, and Catullus, the lover of Claudia Metella, are the nearest approach to exceptions. The first brief outgush of imitative production was followed by an almost unbroken sterility. Roman intellect tended forthwith to settle into a rut of cultural traditionalism; it lived under the oppressive weight of 'the great models,' who had set the standard of attainable excellence. The goal of literature was to approximate as closely as possible to the form and language of those consecrated great ones who had fixed the ideal for all time. In what is called the 'silver age,' the rococo renaissance of Quintillian and Pliny, literary art consisted in imitating Cicero, whose language was as 'dead' then as during the Italian Renaissance. Other writers, like Fronto and Apuleius, harked back to still older archaisms. *"Multi ex alieno sæculo petunt verba: duodecim tabulas loquuntur"* (Seneca, *Ep.* 114, 13). In the last stages of the empire the surviving cultural elements exhibit the same spirit and attitude which centuries later will be found in the grammarian-humanist, the antiquity-worshipper of the Renaissance. Like him they lived upon the past. Symmachus, Ausonius, and their contemporary belles-lettrists might be transferred without a single mental change from the fourth to the fifteenth century; the ideal of refined culture was the same in the two periods, the same which still lingers on in the academic tradition of classical scholarship—to indite correctly Ciceronian periods, to compose a sweet thing in the way of well-turned Virgilian hexameters, or Horatian verses clothed in frowsy mythological language, to elaborate the obvious in elegant conversation on 'polite literature,' to take a childish delight in parading one's familiarity with *the* authors by a plentiful besprinkling of quotations, to rehearse with beatific mental vacuity the consecrated phrases, to 'look down from the heights of scholarship upon the common herd.' Literature, thought, life itself, became a kind of ritual, a round of prescribed formulas and duties, serenely detached from the throbbing actualities of the world, a breviary of 'correct things' to be said, thought, and done correctly.

But side by side with the fossilisation of an imitative intellectual culture, there went on a process of genuine growth, one which, apart from the political legacy of Rome, and not altogether distinct even from that, constitutes her most momentous contribution to the world, and the most fundamental and distinctive feature of her mental development. That continuous process which runs unbroken from the first naturalisation of culture down to the final submersion of its last lingering remnants, is one of moral development. In Greece with the first onset of symptoms of weariness in the metaphysical effort, philosophical thought had shown a tendency to concentrate upon the purely human problems of life and conduct. But it was chiefly in Rome that the tendency developed and matured. That ethical aspect was the only one which appealed to the Romans; of metaphysics they took no account. A love of solemn moralising, a Polonius-like sententiousness was always a trait of their peasant psychology. The creed of Stoicism, so congenial in its affinity to the old austere Latin spirit, became their lay religion, the dominant vein of Roman thought. Its identification with the chief intellectual occupation of the cultivated classes, the sphere of law, the development of jurisprudence, led to the greatest and most permanent concrete achievement of Rome. All Roman thinkers were lawyers. The ultimate goal and practical application of their education, their literary, their rhetorical, their philosophic training, was the law-courts. This was a natural consequence of the administrative tasks and problems thrust upon them by the expanding empire. It was the great discovery of their cautious, matter-of-fact minds—"*omnium virtutum et utilitatum rapacissimi*" [1]—that the only really effective way to manage and rule men is by a certain amount of fairness and justice, that honesty is an asset in business, even if that business be the most atrociously immoral exploitation. They had long recognised that the principle of freedom and justice to conquered populations was the most practically efficient, as well as fiscally the most profitable. In those circumstances the old code of the Twelve Tables required constant adaptation and supplementing by means of case law; heterogeneous populations had to be dealt with under the principles of the *jus gentium,* that is, legal norms common to all nations; and this in time gave rise and place to the conception of a *jus naturale,* natural principles of equity, a notion which, although vaguely supposed to refer to some ideal 'state of nature,' simply amounted to this, that all privilege and social distinctions, all arbitrary traditional usages, must be regarded as artificial conventions, and that justice rests therefore upon the necessary postulate of unsophisticated equality. Fifteen centuries before Rousseau and the American Declaration, Ulpian laid down the principle that "All men are born free and equal." From that noble growth of Roman law which went on broadening out continuously in its spirit of humanity and justice almost down to the last breath of Roman power, abolishing the fierce patriarchal tradition of parental tyranny, protecting the widow and the orphan, attenuating slavery almost to the verge of abolition—from that highest achievement of the Roman mind, philosophic thought, the rational theory of life, was from the first recognised to be inseparable. The philosophers of Rome were her lawyers

[1] Plin. *Hist. Nat.* 25, 3, 4.

and legislators; the juridic and philosophic thought were one.

The growth of Roman law was, indeed, but an expression of an ethical evolution, of the development of a particular ideal, which went on throughout the career of the Roman mind, and which—though I shall not stop just now to judge of its absolute validity—represented, and is still commonly held to represent, the supreme standard of moral excellence. Of that stream of ethical development the literature of Tacitean diatribes and homiletical tracts on ideal Germans and Agricola, the fierce denunciations of satirists, which furnish the materials for the old conventional myth of 'growing moral corruption,' are manifestations. So in a more direct way is the long series of moral and devotional manuals, and 'consolations,' from Cicero to Seneca, Epictetus, Marcus Aurelius, and Plutarch. A whole set of informal institutions attended the establishment of that lay religion of morality. The moral sermon became part of the regular routine of life, and large congregations crowded under the pulpits of the fashionable preachers. From the days of Paulus Æmilius it became customary in the homes of the aristocracy to keep a household chaplain, or philosopher. The exhortations and consolations of the most reputed spiritual directors were eagerly sought after in all times of affliction and distress; and auricular confession was constantly enjoined and practised. Nor was the movement confined to the cultured and aristocratic. The capital and the countryside swarmed with itinerant preachers, and the populace were exhorted in their own rough speech to the higher life by the mendicant brothers whose rules and tenets have been described to us by Epictetus. They were vowed to poverty and celibacy, they were fathers to all, men being their spiritual sons and women their daughters in God, they preached as messengers from God the gospel of renunciation and repentance, they were to suffer calmly scoffs, insults and blows, and to love them that did them wrong and persecuted them.

In the closing centuries of the Western Empire the moralising spirit tended, like the literary, to settle into an established vein of consecrated sentiment, growing somewhat frowsy and conventional. The typical Roman gentleman of the decadence, especially in the provinces—the life of large and wealthy cities is always 'immoral'—was a confirmed puritan, the model of staid bourgeois virtues, and as morally correct in his sentiments as in his literary tastes. He and his womenfolk were quite early-Victorian in their stodgy beseemingness, strait-laced propriety, and serious earnestness on the subject of moral platitudes. He subscribed to charities, and read family prayers to the servants. If he did not adopt Christianity, it was because his settled toryism was somewhat shy of new-fangled labels; he was not quite sure that the chapel people were quite 'the thing,' and he disapproved of the undignified excesses of his friends who took to monasticism and hair-shirts. But in moral sentiment he was quintessentially Christian, or rather his Christian neighbour's moral sentiments were nought else than his own pagan righteousness linked with extraneous mystic and dogmatic elements.

The intellectual culture of the ancient world, even at its best, suffered from a fundamental disability and weakness. It lacked a solid anchor-hold in concrete knowledge. It was pre-scientific.

The power of rational thought depends upon two elements, its method and its data. Without adequate data, without experience, consistency and rationality are of small avail. The patient investigation of details, toilsome enquiry and research, the slow accumulation of facts, on the one hand, and the broad judgments of generalising thought, on the other, are unfortunately the attributes of two different types of mind. The specialist who dwells in a little world of little details grows to be satisfied and to take pleasure in those minutiæ; one little fact exactly ascertained is the prize towards which his mental activities tend; it suffices him, he is not drawn towards broad and new horizons, he is not at home in the thinner atmosphere of generalisations. The thinker, on the other hand, chafes at trifles and details; he who is accustomed to fly on the pinions of thought cannot suffer to be confined and to crawl among the dust of isolated facts. To number the hairs on the appendages of a new species of shrimp is a task belonging to an order of mind distinct from that which is drawn towards the great problems of life and of the universe; an inferior, if you will, humdrum, myopic, round-shouldered order of mind. Only when the multiplicity of facts and details becomes illuminated by a generalising theory, when each small fact and each small detail are transformed into a witness to a great and universal significance, do they acquire value and interest to the higher type of intellect.

In the exultant confidence of its dialectic freedom and suppleness, the Greek mind never developed any consciousness of the sacredness of observed fact. It was abstract. Accuracy of thought meant for it accuracy in the operation of discursive reason, logic; but it never formed any conception of accuracy in the basis of the reasoning process, in the materials and data of thought in ascertained experience. It was ready to disport itself in the dialectical game on any given theme, on any given premises; but so long as those premises were logically defined it did not trouble very much as to their intrinsic validity. It had curiosity, but not the thirst for hoarding up the coins of knowledge, not the preoccupation for submitting their value to crucial test. The intellect of the Greeks was concentrated upon the intellectual process itself, to the almost entire neglect of the materials upon which that process operates. It navigated adventurously the seas of speculation, but with neither compass nor loadstar; it set out in search of strange lands, but without the means of taking its bearings.

In the whole of classical literature we cannot find above two doubtful mentions of a scientific experiment; that of Pythagoras on the vibration of a cord, and that of Ptolemy on refraction. In his encyclopedia on the natural knowledge of his day, Pliny, among a host of grotesque hearsays, does not once use the word 'experiment' in our sense. In the most methodical thinkers of Greece, in Aristotle for instance, we meet with the most astounding carelessness in matters of easiest verification. He states, for instance, that there is only one bone in a lion's neck, that man has eight ribs, that men have more teeth than women, that men only have a beating heart, that female skulls, unlike those of males, have a circular suture, that eggs float on sea-water, that if sea-water be collected in a wax vessel it becomes drinkable. The Greeks, in short, had no science, and no scientific spirit. It is science and the scientific spirit which constitutes the distinction between the ancient and the modern world.

It was, indeed, on the foundation of the few facts and methods gathered by Chaldæan and Egyptian science that Greek thought first arose; and the early Ionian thinkers came nearer to the scientific spirit than almost any Greek in subsequent times. But even with them the chief interest lay with the final synthesis, the generalisation; and, with brilliant divination, they used that faculty of inspired guesswork which is one of the most valuable instruments of science and its crowning triumph, but which has little place in its beginnings. Thereafter, the only form of science which was cultivated by the Greeks was mathematics, which is a form of logic, and in which they were interested as logic and 'music,' not as an instrument of research. Plato would have none but 'mathematicians' among his pupils, but the meaning he attached to the word may be gauged from his attitude towards Archytas and Menaichmus who had devised some sliding-rules and compasses as aids to mathematical study. "Plato," says Plutarch, "inveighed against them with great indignation and persistence as destroying and perverting all the good there is in geometry; for the method absconds from incorporeal and intellectual to sensible things, and besides employs again such bodies as require much vulgar handicraft: in this way mechanics was dissimilated and expelled from geometry, and, being for a long time looked down upon by philosophy, became one of the arts of war." The man whom, by the influence which his surviving works have exercised, we are accustomed to regard as the most scientific genius of the ancient world, Archimedes, was of exactly the same opinion as Plato; and it was only under loud protest that he consented to degrade mathematics by putting his knowledge to practical application. The Greeks not only ignored the actual groundwork of science, experimental research, observation, they persistently decried, depreciated it, and despised it. Aristophanes ridiculed astronomy and geometry. The Athenian Nikias at Syracuse was, when there was an eclipse of the moon, as helplessly a prey to the soothsayers as the merest savage, although Thales and Anaxagoras were acquainted with the Babylonian method of predicting eclipses.

Sokrates "brought down philosophy from heaven to earth," as the fact was usually expressed. 'Why,' asked he—how constantly do we hear around us the argument!—'Why spend our time and thought in studying the heavens, in measuring the distance of the stars, in fretting about the constitution of matter, of the universe, in studying birds and beasts and trees? The thing which it is of importance to us to study is life, this human life wherein our business lies; not the distant stars, but the human world we live in; not animals and insects and plants, but men. Before seeking to know about the stars, and shells, and trees, it behooves us to seek to know something which lies much closer at hand—ourselves. The proper study of mankind is man.' How wise and sensible it all sounds! And how that straightforward common sense has always captured the approval of the plain man. And yet it is an utter and pernicious fallacy. It is through that star-gazing that man has first been placed in a position to measure at all his own stature, the proportion and significance of his life in the universe. That 'natural history,' as it used to be called, that harmless, somewhat childish hobby of collecting moths, of studying birds and trees, of botanising and bird-nesting, that somewhat absurd, trifling pastime has, lo, and behold! developed into a science of biology; and the whole conception, the whole significance of man, of his life, of his being, of his world has been utterly transfigured. Man went about for centuries with Γνῶθι σαυτόν on his signet-ring, studying himself, studying humanity, pleasantly talking and talking round and round in old circles, to no purpose. And, behold, the only real knowledge, the only illumination, the only revelation which has come about himself, has come from that unpractical star-gazing and studying of beasts and plants. He thought to begin at the beginning by attending to what lay closest at hand, his own self; and he was in reality in vain and futile effort trying to begin at the top. He could not rightly understand himself without first trying to understand the world he lived in. Through that remote, irrelevant enquiry lay in fact the main road to self-knowledge.

As all their scientific notions had by the roaming

Ionians been derived from Egypt and Chaldæa, so the only organised scientific movement in classical antiquity, that of the Ptolemaic University of Alexandria, took place on the foundations, under the influence, on the very soil of Egypt. With only one or two notable exceptions Alexandrian science occupied itself with systematisation and compilation rather than with original discovery and development of method. The first occupant of the chair of mathematics, Euklid, did little more than order and gather together the scattered geometrical theorems of his Ionian predecessors, Hippokrates of Chios in particular and Eudoxos of Knidos, the friend of the priests of Heliopolis, whose mantle the Apis bull had licked. The only mechanical device which we actually know to have been used by Archimedes, the pupil of Euklid's successor, Konon, the Archimedean screw, had been in use on the Nile before Greece existed. The greatest systematiser of astronomical knowledge was Hipparchos, whose work we only know through the clumsy compilation of Claudius Ptolemæus, a work full of astrological fancies, which perpetuated for centuries the unwieldy methods and doctrines of epicycles. Aristarchos of Samos, who first suggested the simplification of all astronomy on the theory of a central sun and moving earth, could not get a hearing.

It is a notable and striking fact that Greece and Rome, who so completely transformed the world and opened up a new universe of civilisation, did not produce a single practical invention or industrial discovery of any importance. Almost all the crafts and industries of the ancient world, textile fabrics, dyes, papyrus, glass, glazed porcelain, were Oriental discoveries and remained essentially Oriental products. From the early days of Babylon and Egypt there is no new material discovery of importance to record until the introduction of paper, gunpowder, and the mariner's compass into Europe by the Arabs. The genius which could create a new world of intellect, differing from that of the Orient as noonday from midnight, appeared incapable of extending in any way the material powers and resources of life. So far as material processes are concerned, the Romans excelled the Greeks: they did excel in engineering and the building arts, in road-making, drainage, mining: the Greeks never got so far as making a road or building an aqueduct. The practical and realistic Roman mind was really more disposed towards observation and research than the Greek, but it was entirely governed by the influence of Greek tradition; and when Cæsar wished to reform the calendar, mathematicians and astronomers had to be fetched from Egypt. The Græco-Roman civilisation remained pre-scientific.

Failing that necessary ingredient no real progress in the powers of the human intellect beyond a set limit was possible. A dozen successive Athens could not have carried it any farther. It could wander this way and that way, circle round to its starting-point, but it could never establish its advance by any permanent occupation of the conquered territory. And it remained, in spite of all the splendid rationalism of Greece and Rome, essentially destitute of solid protection or security against the impinging tides of irrationalism. Modern experience has shown time and again the insecurity and powerlessness of the most brilliant abstract intellectual achievement, until it is grounded in the solid basis of demonstration and unshakable evidence. It has become a commonplace of science that the true discoverer is not the man who formulates, but he who substantiates, not the brilliant thinker who first glimpses the vision of truth, but the humdrum plodder who accumulates such a foundation of facts that all the world cannot shake it.

Besides that fundamental limitation ancient culture was inadequately diffused. Although it had no esoteric spirit

—the ruling class did not owe their power to tradition, but to wealth—although its circulation was free; the circle of men in the Roman Empire who were at all abreast of the mental resources of the age, was in reality extremely restricted. Even among the wealthy a large proportion were new and vulgar rich, idlers, *ingenui,* self-made men, who cared for none of these things. There was no organised provision for general education, and no agency, like the printing-press, to make up for the deficiency. In a small, compact community like Athens, every citizen came more or less under the influence of existing culture. In the teeming, heterogeneous, shifting population of a vast empire, the case was different. Those swarming masses of humanity were not mere herds of crushed Oriental slaves, with child-like mind patiently slumbering in a twilight of tradition; but, as so many are in our own civilisation with its infinitely greater opportunities, restless barbarians outwardly clothed in a thin veneer of cultural contacts, sufficient to conceal their own ignorance and barbarism from themselves. Their undisciplined mentality weltered in a flood of superstitions and mysticisms, the usual disease of minds stimulated by the external influences of civilisation, yet entirely unequipped and defenceless.

Life was complex, accelerated, restless, full of sudden changes, full of sorrows, of struggles, of desires stimulated and thwarted, of disappointments and disillusions. To that troubled humanity the religions of the dreaming East, offering their substitutes for thought, came as a light and a revelation, supplying that for which they yearned. The Orient came to their rescue as a saviour.

Rome had fought for her existence in a death struggle with the East, and, like Greece, had finally subdued it. But the Orient had its revenge; and it was far more glaring and complete than in the case of Greece. The same year which was signalised by the definite triumph of Rome over Hannibal, saw the advanced guard of eastern theocracy established within the walls of Rome, called there by the senate itself in compliance with some oracle which associated the step with certain vague promises of world empire. As the triumphal procession of Scipio, more magnificent than any yet witnessed, with its caparisoned elephants and quaint figures of Semitic captives, wound its way to the Capitol amid the acclamations of a people who were henceforth marked as the masters of the world, the strange monotonous strains of an exotic psalmody might have been heard from a chapel on the Palatine, on the side of the old, humble Roma Quadrata. The Oriental priests who were chanting those psalms were also members of an army which, like that of Rome, was to march from that spot to the conquest of the world.

From that day, amid swarms of Asiatics, astrologers from Chaldæa, wonder-workers from Egypt, Hebrew cabalists, Persian magicians, Syrian sorcerers, Indian fakirs, the Orient poured legion after legion of grave, stealthy, tonsured and mitred priests, sent religion after religion to take possession of the world-city.

To the philosophic moralists of Rome, who eschewed metaphysics, their ethical convictions, aspirations and endeavours needed no external dogmatic or emotional support, sought no other religion than 'the divinity within their own breast.' The kingdom of God was within them. They looked with disgust and abhorrence on those barbaric and effeminate superstitions, and strove long to put them down and exclude them. But the minds of the ignorant and troubled masses, and above all the women, found that for which they thirsted in the mystery of those Eastern cults. A marvellous peace fell upon them in the extramundane atmosphere of the dim sanctuaries, sounding with solemn music, now wafted as from a distant sphere, now weeping with the tenderness of human sorrow, presently bursting forth into transfigured ecstasies of triumphant hope. The grave rituals, the chanted hymns and litanies, the solemn intonation of the Mithraic clergy, as they called upon the "Lamb of God that takest away the sins of the world," soothed their troubled passions as with a delightful balm; and they were thrilled with a strange excitement as the tinkling bell of the acolytes announced the culminating mystery of the rite, and amid clouds of incense, the officiating priest turned to the kneeling crowd and raised breast-high the sacred chalice filled with the wine of life. They were born again as the cleansing baptismal waters washed away the stains of misery and sin; and what emotion overwhelmed them when, after a stern preparation of fast and penance, they were admitted to partake of the sacramental communion, of the consecrated bread which was the very body of the God! The women found ineffable comfort in unburdening their sorrows before the Queen of Heaven who bore in her arms her Divine Son, and who seemed to mingle her tears with theirs as she mourned over the Dead God. The thought of death itself lost its sting for the votaries who received the assurance of eternal life from the Saviour and Mediator who had triumphed over the grave.

East and West have not only met again and again, they have indissolubly commingled. In the Hellenistic Orient of the Macedonian Empire the dawn-myths and hieratic rituals of the East and the dialectics and metaphysics of Greece had come together, and brought forth strange hybrid chimeras; new religions innumerable, countless illuminated and ascetic sects, Essenic and Ebionitic, Nazarene and Therapeutrid, swarmed from the ancient brewing-vat. And in Antioch and Alexandria all the mysticism, occultism, trismegistal philosophumena, and abracadabras of Jewry, magic Egypt, and Orphic pseudo-Hellas, held their Sabbath of Unreason. Platonism had become Plotinism, philosophy theosophy, metaphysics gnosis. The Word had become God.

The Isiac and Serapic cults of Rome were no more the religion of ancient Egypt, Mithraism was no more the Mazdaism of Persia, than Christianity was Judaism. Religions interchanged their symbols and rituals, became transformed into a new syncretic uniformity more homogeneous than the primitive seasonal rites whence they had sprung, and the worshipper passed from shrine to shrine as he might from one saint's chapel to the adjoining one.

As once the corrupted fragments of Hellenic thought, so likewise the ethical spirit of Rome was absorbed in the popular ferments of mysticism, and blended with the ascetic fervour of the East. The guilds and brotherhoods which were attached to each cult fostered the feelings of human fellowship and mutual help. Mithraism in particular, owing to its Avestic origin, the simplest and therefore the purest of popular cults, addressed itself to the poor, the lowly, and disinherited; the master knelt beside his slave in the mysteries, and was not infrequently called upon to regard him as his spiritual superior. That cult seemed about to absorb and supersede all others, and to become under the imperial patronage of Aurelian the official religion of the Roman world.

That position was, however, ultimately assumed by a cult that sheltered within the mystic shadows of its dense vegetation of rich allusiveness, every religious idea and every theosophic thought that the world had ever brought forth. It came, like Mithraism, from Antioch, but from the Jewish instead of from the Persian elements of the Eastern metropolis, and originally from Judæa itself, where its ideals had indeed long developed in the monastic communities of the Essenes and Nazarenes. Hence, as formerly the Jews had violently repudiated their spiritual debts to Babylon and Persia, it insisted on its exclusiveness, refused to recognise its creditors, and even denounced them. While, in an even higher degree than other cults, it gave voice to the reigning ethical spirit, and was like them an *agape,* a religion of love, it was unfortunately distinguished from them by the darkling taint, the old *delirium hebraicum,* of uncompromising intolerance. It gave expression to the seething discontent of human suffering, to the detestation of the intolerable order of the established world, to all the inarticulate forces of hostility against the Roman government; and it was that *odium generis humani* which gave it an immeasurable significance and advantage over all competitors.

The fall of the Roman Empire has ever been the grand theme of historical philosophising. The event is generally held to be accounted for by uttering the word 'corruption.' So far as political corruption goes, Roman administration was as corrupt in the days of Marius, when a petty African chief, Jugurtha, bought with gold every envoy and every general that was sent to put him down, as at any subsequent time, not excepting the fourth and fifth centuries. And as for moral corruption, since the primitive, dour austerity disappeared in large measure after the second Punic War, the society of the Roman Empire was marked, as just noted, by a continuous development in austere morality. The consecrated myth of Roman corruption traditionally cultivated as an essential part of the Christian scheme of history, is by now fit for circulation among the uninformed only. The fancy picture of the Roman world filled with Neronian orgies serving as a lurid background for the figures of Christian martyrs, might indeed be without any historical knowledge sufficiently discredited by its own inherent inconsistency. For who, pray, were those Christian martyrs, those saintly bishops, those Clements, those Laterani, those Cecilias? Were they not Romans? If Rome was 'corrupt,' then the Christian religion which it has imposed upon Europe must be accounted part of that moral corruption.

The whole notion of 'corruption' has originated with Roman writers themselves. What they meant by 'corruption' was any departure from the Spartan simplicity of life of the old peasant community. "Among the examples which they think most scandalous," says Ferrero, "are many which to us appear innocent enough; as, for instance, the importation from Pontus of certain sausages and salt fish which were, it seems, excellent to eat, the introduction from Greece into Italy of the art of battening fowl. Even the drinking of Greek wines was during many centuries considered a luxury to be indulged in only on the most solemn occasions. In 18 B.C. Augustus got a sumptuary law passed which made it illegal to spend more than two hundred sestercia (about two pounds) on a banquet on ordinary days, three hundred sestercia (three pounds) on Calend and Ide days, and one thousand sestercia (ten pounds) for wedding dinners. Even allowing for the difference in the value of money, the masters of the world feasted at a cost which we should consider absurdly moderate. . . . Silk was looked upon askance even in the most opulent periods of the empire, as a luxury of questionable taste because it showed off too prominently the lines of the body. Lollia Paulina's name has been handed down because she owned so many jewels that their value amounted to some four thousand pounds. There are so many Lollia Paulinas today that none can buy immortality at so small a cost. . . . The boon companions of Nero and Eliogabalus would be dazzled if they could come back to life in any of the large hotels of Paris, London, or New York.

They had seen more beautiful things, but never such reckless luxury. . . . Rome, even at the height of her splendour, was poor compared with our cities. There were far fewer theatres and amusements. Many vices which are widely diffused today were unknown to the ancients; they knew few wines, they had no alcohol, no tea, no coffee, no tobacco. They were ever Spartans compared to us, even when they thought they were indulging themselves. The Romans considered it quite an ordinary precaution to keep a watch on the individual citizen within the walls of his home, to see that he did not get drunk, or eat too much, or incur debts, or spend too much, or covet his neighbour's wife. In the age of Augustus exile and confiscation of a third of their property was the penalty imposed on Roman citizens, men or women, for adultery, and anyone was free to bring a charge against the delinquents. The law remained in force for centuries."

Idle, ignorant rich, and insane autocrats were in a state of moral dissolution in Imperial Rome as they have been everywhere and in all ages; but though the annals of every country can furnish Neros and Domitians in abundance, how many can parallel the figures of such rulers as Trajan or Marcus Aurelius? Roman civilisation, which by a strange and pathetic irony has been branded in the popular imagination as the example of moral corruption, was on the contrary for nothing more notable than as the period of most active ethical enthusiasm and moral development in the history of the world, and the outstanding legacy of Roman genius to humanity has been one of moral aspiration.

The gross, obvious reason why the Roman Empire fell is not, as usually stated, that it was too big, but that it was too small. It fell because there were too many barbarians outside it. Had there been no German hordes wanting 'a place in the sun,' the Roman Empire, in spite of its many deficiencies and inefficiencies, might have continued indefinitely—which would have been a great calamity. Of course if it had remained a huge military organisation, stiff with swords and military discipline, instead of being a very liberal conglomeration of free and self-ruling municipia, it might have held off the barbarians; and its survival would have been a still greater calamity.

The intrinsic cause that doomed and condemned the Roman Empire was not any *growing* corruption, but the corruption, the evil, the inadaptation to fact, in its very origin and being. No system of human organisation that is false in its very principle, in its very foundation, can save itself by any amount of cleverness and efficiency in the means by which that falsehood is carried out and maintained, by any amount of superficial adjustment and tinkering. It is doomed root and branch as long as the root remains what it is. The Roman Empire was, as we have seen, a device for the enrichment of a small class of people by the exploitation of mankind. That business enterprise was carried out with all the honesty, all the fairness and justice compatible with its nature, and with admirable judgment and ability. But all those virtues could not save the fundamental falsehood and wrong from its consequences. Their effects worked inexorably. The supply of slaves failed, the supply of soldiers failed, the supply of labour failed. And—essential fact—the exploited populations came to feel more and more as time went on that the carrying on, the maintenance of the whole thing *was no business of theirs*. They came to see, or be vaguely conscious, that they were not in the least concerned with that social machine which was run not for them, but for the benefit of a small master class. In vain official voices were raised to appeal to their 'patriotism,' to their duty of helping, and defending, and saving 'the State.' Those appeals left them cold and indifferent; they answered bluntly that they felt no patriotism whatever, that the 'cold monster,' the State might look after itself. They became Christians. They made up their own little organisations for mutual help and protection, and resistance against 'the State.' They utterly disowned it and denounced it, they refused to serve it; it might go to perdition for all they cared, it was no country, no 'patria' of theirs, their kingdom was not of this world. In Gaul, in the third century, the peasants, the *coloni,* broke out into open revolt, into anarchy and plunder, just as they did later at the time of the *Jacqueries* and of the French Revolution. Though partially put down for a time by Maximian, the *Bagaudæ* insurrection continued till the end.

When things got most desperate the Roman government had the good fortune to find a strong man of extraordinary ability and energy, Diocletian. He set to consolidating everything in the most vigorous manner, raised the army to four times its strength and reorganised it, strengthened the entire network of administration and central government and made the latter absolute. His aim was to stay all further disintegration by rigidly pinning things down with iron bonds in their existing state. When a social structure visibly threatens to topple over, rulers try to prevent it from falling by preventing it from moving. The whole of Roman society was fixed in a system of castes; no one was to change his avocation, the son must continue in the calling of his father. Sedition, discontent, disloyalty, were dealt with with a strong hand. Though partial to many Christian religious ideas and counting many personal friends in the sect, he even decided to put down Christianity. His successor, Constantine, tried the opposite policy, that of conciliation and concessions, had the ingenious idea to avail himself of the admirable network of Christian organisation, Christian trade-unions, to assist and strengthen the government.

But evils secularly developed and lying at the very root of a social order are not to be remedied at a stroke by either vigorous or ingenious political measures. Whether vigorously put down or conciliated, the exploited masses and the municipia remained indifferent and hostile. When the barbarian flood broke through, the people not only did not resist, but welcomed, them and joined with them. "The powerful decide what the poor have to pay. The poor thirst for freedom and have to endure extreme servitude," writes Salvianus in the fifth century, "I wonder only that all the poor and needy do not run away, except that they are loath to abandon their land and families. Should we Romans marvel that we cannot resist the Goths, when Roman citizens had rather live with them than with us?" With unfailing instinct, the clergy saw in the wild Barbarians a better promise of power and influence for the Church than in the officially converted Roman Empire which, in spite of Constantine and Theodosius, remained 'the Beast,' the enemy. They accordingly smiled on the invader, encouraged him, flattered him. The Roman clergy were undisguisedly pro-German. They resolutely winked at, and minimised any 'atrocities.' Had there been a massacre? Well, men had to die sooner or later. And when Alaric put Rome to the sack, looting, burning, and ravishing, St. Augustine employed himself in composing a dissertation on the question whether or no the outraged virgins would be entitled to the crown of maidenhood in the next world.

VIII

BARBARISM AND BYZANTINISM

THREE broadly distinguished stages marking the course of human evolution have been so far noted. First, the long, primitive tribal stage strictly limited in its development by the inertia of established custom which no initiative defiant of tribal solidarity can break, and which the clash of varied cultures can, now and again only, raise a step above the dead level of a sluggish life dominated by primal irrationalism. To that original phase succeeded the great Oriental civilisations founded upon the domination of the priest, whose absolutism, only occasionally and ineffectually challenged by military power, dominates all, and condemns his own creation to eternal stagnation. Thirdly comes the extraordinary felicitous accident of Greece, and at one blow the human mind is almost completely liberated and transformed. But the world contains as yet too much barbarism and Orientalism; and the Græco-Roman world succumbs at last to a gigantic tide of those elements which submerge and overwhelm it. It is eventually succeeded by a fourth phase, the one in which we live.

That phase is sharply separated from the foregoing one by the tremendous cataclysm out of which it arose. Largely owing to that circumstance the process of human advance, when estimated by the narrow parallax of ordinary historic vision, is seen in a distorted perspective. That short space of time is divided in its very middle by the catastrophe which swept away all previous achievements. Hence the whole curve is broken and disguised. Under totally new conditions, with new materials, a new development took place. Throughout the greater part of it a glaring contrast was presented between the painful struggles towards reconstruction of a world steeped in barbarism, and overwhelmed by a thousand rude and tyrannous elements, and the lucid splendour of that civilisation which lay in the dust. Men looked to the past for help, example, inspiration; they quite rightly regarded themselves as the pupils of 'the ancients,' and quite justly looked upon these as their superiors.

Yet eventually all foregoing phases of civilisation have been transcended, and the powers and potentialities of the human race magnified beyond estimation, by the civilisation which has arisen out of that melting-pot of utter ruin and destruction into which every form and every deformity of human power had been cast. It is impossible to estimate rightly and judge adequately the forces whose struggles and interaction we see before us, unless our modern civilisation is viewed in its true place in the perspective of history; unless we know in their origin and development the character of those forces, which have been brought together in the phase of civilisation which is at the present day struggling through the crisis of its development. But, although to the modern European the genesis of the civilisation in which he lives may, of all phases of historical evolution, be deemed foremost in importance, so thoroughly have traditional misconceptions and persistent misrepresentation falsified his notions on that point, that they are only a few degrees removed from the dim and fabulous conceptions which the Greeks and the Romans entertained concerning their own origins.

Although the Græco-Roman world did not sink under a catastrophic blow such as wiped out Babylon or Susa,

Asshùr or Ecbatana, and wreathed the sand-drifts of the desert over their graves; although its downfall was a process of transitional, though rapid, disintegration rather than a sudden and violent cataclysm; although the contemporaries of Alaric and of Romulus Augustulus were scarcely aware of what was happening, that a world was dropping into chaos—yet no civilisation ever suffered more complete obliteration. It is the most appalling catastrophe in history. Human civilisation, seemingly powerful and securely established, embracing the known world in one large organised, peaceful, prosperous society was completely blotted out. All that humanity had achieved seemed to be swept away and set at nought. Athens and Rome had raised mankind to a new plane; they had set it higher above the old civilisations of the East than the troglodyte of pre-history was above the ape: they had created a truly human world, mature and conscious. And now of all that growth, of all that glorious evolution, practically nothing was left. The hands of the clock had sprung back to darkness and savagery.

The depth of that ruin is not generally realised in its full horror. The records of the period are eked out with the names of barbarian chiefs and their wars, and do not dwell on the picture of the existing world. By an optical illusion the light that shines before and after tends to diffuse over the dark gap. From the fifth to the tenth century Europe lay sunk in a night of barbarism which grew darker and darker. It was a barbarism more awful and horrible than that of the primitive savage, for it was the decomposing body of what had been a great civilisation. The features and impress of that civilisation were all but completely effaced. Where its development had been fullest, in Italy and in Gaul, all was ruin, squalor, desolation. The land had dropped out of cultivation; trees and shrubs rapidly encroached upon the once cultivated land; rivers overflowed their broken and neglected banks; the forest and the malarial swamp regained their sway over vast tracts of country which had been covered with prosperous farms and waving fields. The word *eremus,* wilderness, recurs with significant frequency in mediæval land charts. Cities had practically disappeared. Where there is no trade there can be no cities. They were pulled down and used as quarries to build towers in which a bishop or a baron established himself who could afford some protection. In Nîmes, for example, the remains of the population dwelt in huts built among the ruins of the amphitheatre. Other towns were completely abandoned. Mantua was submerged by stagnant waters and deserted. The Germans, who regarded walled cities as a badge of servitude, hastened to pull them down. Of the many prosperous cities built by the Romans on the banks of the Rhine not one remained in the ninth century. Rome itself had become a wilderness of ruins. The papal city dates only from the fifteenth century. In the Middle Ages the ruins of the imperial city were completely abandoned; the mediæval population lived in hovels erected on a portion of the open space of the Campus Martius. Two horsemen could not ride abreast in its lanes, and we read of processions having to be abandoned owing to the impassable nature of the ground. The banks of the Tiber were broken and the town exposed to constant inundations. Some idea of the depopulation of Rome may be gathered from the fact that at the time of Totila's second siege (549 A.D.) sufficient corn and vegetables could be grown among the ruins to maintain the inhabitants and garrison for an indefinite time. In the provinces the ruins of the towns and the scattered settlements were visited by herds of prowling wolves, boars, and even by bears. The atria of the Roman villas, when not converted into cloisters, were filled in with hovels and dunghills, the surrounding living-rooms serving as quarries and ramparts. Clad in the skins of beasts and in coarse, sack-shaped woollen garments, the enormously reduced population lived in thatched wooden huts, huddled for protection at the foot of the barons' lairs, or round monasteries. Every such little group manufactured its own materials and clothing, and supported its miserable existence by scanty cultivation of small patches of ground round their hovels. They did not dare to go farther afield for fear of wild beasts and of marauders. Famines and plagues were chronic; there were ten devastating famines and thirteen plagues in the course of the tenth century alone. Cases of cannibalism were not uncommon; there were man-hunts, not with a view to plunder, but for food. It is on record that at Tournus, on the Saône, human flesh was publicly put up for sale. It was impossible to venture abroad without a strong armed escort; robber bands roamed everywhere. Water traffic was put a stop to by the practice of wrecking, which was actually encouraged by charters. Anarchy was absolute and unchecked; there was no law but the arbitrary will of the barons and their men-at-arms; none had power to check them. They lived in their towers in rush-strewn halls, which frequently served also as stables for their horses. They had no other occupation but brigandage, private wars, and riot.

Because out of that abyss of darkness and desolation civilisation did ultimately emerge anew, the fact is generally accepted with careless indifference as if it were quite natural. It usd to be in the popular conception of history held to be sufficiently accounted for by a reference to the 'Renaissance' and the restoration of classical literature after the fall of Constantinople. Obviously a mere begging of the question; for there is little to be explained in the fact that the Europe which had already produced Dante should proceed to bring forth Messer Petrarca and an Italian Renaissance. It has gradually become more clearly recognised that it was in the period between the end of the tenth and that of the twelfth century that Europe emerged out of the night. The old misconception and confusion is perpetuated by our current historical rubrics, which include both that period and the Dark Ages under the term 'Middle Ages,' and apply the name of 'Renaissance' to the fourteenth and fifteenth centuries, whose culture was but the ripe fruit of antecedent growth, a fruit not only ripe, but in many respects rotten. That civilisation should have grown at all out of the troglodytic Europe of the ninth century, far from being quite natural, is a very remarkable fact.

The various Germanic hordes that trod down the ancient civilisation brought with them no qualities that could help to build a new one. The panegyrical twaddle that pervades our histories about "the young, virile Teutonic races regenerating the effete and decrepit Roman world" is a brazen effrontery of racial-historical mendacity.

The cultural condition of the primitive tribal state is, as has been noted, rigorously precluded from advancing beyond a definite limit. Only in exceptionally favourable circumstances, as happened in the case of Greece suckled at the many breasts of Oriental cultures, can tribal society become an agency of progress.

The barbaric tribes of Europe were, save for possession of metals, in much the same state as the Maoris when first visited by Captain Cook. They lived in wooden huts in swamps and forest glades. They possessed a few household crafts, very little agriculture, and native poetry, which is always of considerable merit among savages. For the rest they were drunken, murderous, treacherous, licentious brutes. Their savagery was of a particularly base and bestial type. To libel them is not possible, to sound the full measure of their infamy is revolting. Gluttonous, riotous orgies, to shout, heated with strong drink, was their ideal of enjoyment. Slaughter, cruelty, obscene violence, were the natural outlets of their energies. In mind they were sluggish and heavy—*gens nec astuta nec callida* (Tac. xxii.). When not employed with bloodshed, food, and drink, they would sit for days warming themselves at their fires, while their women worked for them.

The barbaric courts were, one and all, scenes of perpetual murders, parricides, fratricides, poisonings, perjuries, bestiality, and whoredom. "It would not be easy within the same historical space to find more vice and less virtue," is Gibbon's comment, and he was not by any means emancipated from the fable of barbaric virtues. There are indeed no more utterly sickening pages in human annals than the tale of unredeemed abominations, the exploits of Clothaire, Chilpéric, Frédégonde, recorded with such inimitable unction by St. Gregory of Tours. Procopius, the Byzantine historian of the Goths, shows more delicacy; he refuses to soil his pages with the horrors exhibited by those savages, "lest I should transmit to succeeding ages a monument and example of inhumanity."

Clovis obtains the Ripuarian kingdom by inducing the king's son to murder his father, and by afterwards cracking his skull. His progress is indeed rather monotonously marked by an habitual breaking of skulls, often by way of argument or facetious repartee, but generally those of rivals decoyed to his court under treacherous safe-conducts. As St. Gregory charmingly remarks, "Thus did God every day fell down someone of his enemies by his hand, and extend the confines of his realm, because he walked with an upright heart before the Lord and did what was acceptable in His eyes." Charlemagne's son

Louis the Pious tears out the eyes of his brother Pepin's son, drawn to his court under safe-conduct. Louis's son, Lothair, vents his jealousy of his half-brother by seizing the little daughter of his guardian from a convent, fastening her up in a cask and throwing her into the river. The Lombard court of the drunken Alboin, assassinated by his wife Rosmunda, whom he had compelled to drink out of her murdered father's skull, and who afterwards married her accomplice, and in turn murdered him, presents the same vile spectacle as the Frankish court. In Burgundy the king, Gundebald, consolidated his throne by killing his three brothers. Theodoric himself, who represented more creditably than any other barbarian the effect of a Roman education, broke out after a time, as imperfectly tamed wild animals are apt to do, into primal ferocity. Each of the Gothic kings who succeeded him murdered his predecessor.

If any of the Teutonic chieftains rose at all above the lowest barbaric level, it was owing to special contact with Græco-Roman civilisation. Alaric, Odoacer, Theodoric, had been brought up in the Roman legions.

But no barbarians have ever proved themselves more refractory to all civilising influences than the 'virile Teutons.' Instead of absorbing anything of the civilisation which they overthrew, they became, with the means and opportunities of indulgence, considerably more brutal than they were before. They regarded their conquests as occasions for sottish riot and bestial tyranny. When they became Christianised they converted the monasteries into Walhallas of drunken orgy. The appalling condition of the Church and monasteries in the eighth, ninth, and tenth centuries was not due to the corruption of the Roman clergy so much as to the influx of barbarian priests and monks. The convents resounded with riot through the night. Capitularies of the Carolingian period enact among other rules that "priests shall not have more than one wife"; they lay down detailed regulations concerning incest, they forbid monks to spend their time in taverns, and ordain that "on no account shall an abbot gouge out the eyes of his monks or mutilate them, whatever fault they may have committed." [1] Legislation testifies to the universal prevalence of female drunkenness; and St. Boniface complains that, under pretext of pilgrimages, a trail of Teutonic prostitutes was left over every part of Europe.[2] Regarding as they did physical strength and combative qualities as the supreme human virtues the contempt of the barbarian invaders for the pacific population knew no bounds. They ascribed that "ignoble effeminacy" to culture and education, and consequently refused to allow their children to be educated, "for education tends to corrupt, enervate and depress the mind." [3]

Barbarian society was, like all uncivilised societies, tribal; if it was rude, it was at least equalitarian. Its so-called kings were deputed war-leaders. When, in the distribution of booty after a battle, Clovis, king of the Franks, picked out a particularly fine vase from the gathered spoils, a man stepped out of the ranks and told him he had no right to choose and had no claim to any larger share than the least of his warriors. The equalitarian character of barbarian society was abolished by the Christian Church, and the opposite conditions established. The meagre records of the process by which northern Europe was made Christian show that the agents of the Church invariably addressed themselves to the barbarian 'kings,' never to the people. The conversion never proceeded from within, but in every instance from above, by forcible imposition. The power accruing to the 'kings' from authority consecrated by the Church, wielded in her

[1] *Baluzii Capit. Reg. Franc.* Cap. Metense.

[2] *Epist.* lxxviii, ap. *Mon. Germ. Hist.*

[3] Procop. *De Bell. Goth.* 1, 4.

name, and enforced by her unremitting aid over subjected peoples, who should be taught the duty of obedience, constituted the determining argument. The Christian Church transformed the war-leaders of a free and equalitarian society into divinely appointed kings ruling by a divine dispensation over subjects. The Church has not only been the upholder of monarchic absolutism; it has been the founder of the system. Having become convinced of its advantages, the barbarian chieftains put down the usages of the heathen populations by force of arms, and caused them to be driven like cattle through the baptismal waters. Boniface boasts that he baptised a hundred thousand Germans in one year; Augustine broke the record by baptising ten thousand English in a single day. The barbarian populations resisted; they struggled during seven centuries against the loss of their independence and the destruction of their ancient cults and usages; they drove away the missionaries, murdered them. They were ruthlessly beaten into submission to the Christian religion and to the Church-appointed kings by sword and fire, by massacres, and persecution, by legislative terrorism. Boniface was 'martyred' by the Frisians while marching to their conversion at the head of the troops of Charles Martel, who completed the evangelisation of what was to become modern Belgium and Holland by slaughtering one-half of the inhabitants, while the rest fled for refuge to the islands. Clovis was originally the petty chieftain of a tribe numbering five thousand warriors all told. At the instigation of the Church and by her assistance he founded the kingdom of France and imposed Christianity upon it, not so much by means of war and butchery, as by a series of treacherous assassinations in which he was aided and abetted by the bishops. Charlemagne completed the conversion of the greater part of Germany by "spreading massacre, arson and pillage in every direction," *(Ann.*

Regni Francorum, ad. an. 782), by beheading 4,500 chiefs of the Saxons treacherously enticed to Verden under safe-conducts, and by instituting a reign of terror the monstrous atrocities of which stand recorded in his capitularies. Prussia and Livonia were converted by the knights of the 'Order of the Sword' and of the 'Teutonic Order,' created for the purpose by the Church, which assigned to them those countries in payment for the task of crushing out paganism. The people expressed their detestation of Christianity as a religion of blood and cruelty. "Far from us be such a detestable religion," protested the Pomeranians; "Christians crucify men, tear out their eyes, and commit infamies and atrocities hitherto unknown." Again and again the exasperated people rose against their oppressors and persecutors, and 'relapsed' into paganism. In Scandinavia, in Denmark, in Bohemia, king after king was overthrown in the desperate struggle against Christianity and monarchy. Could the full history of the 'conversion' of Europe to Christianity be written, it would present a tale of horror more appalling than that of the Christianisation of Spain by the Inquisition. The Christian religion has been imposed upon the people of Europe in much the same manner as it was imposed upon Mexico and Peru, in the course of whose 'conversion,' Las Casas estimates, twelve million people perished, butchered, burnt alive, and tortured.

If by imposing upon the European barbarians some relics of the administrative order of the Roman Empire, its language, its cultural traditions, the Roman Church, which was its representative, played to any extent the part of a civilising agent, it was because it was Roman, not because it was Christian.

Priests alone could read and some could write. Kings and rulers affixed to the various charters which they enacted *"signum crucis manu propria pro ignoratione lite-*

rarum." Hence we will speak of 'signing' instead of 'subscribing.' The word 'clerk' denoted indifferently a priest or a person able to read. But not even all the clergy could write; many bishops were unable to sign their names to the canons of the councils on which they sat. One of the questions put to persons who were candidates for orders was "whether they could read the gospels and epistles and explain the sense of these, at least literally." King Alfred complained that there was not a priest from the Humber to the sea who understood the liturgy in his mother-tongue, or could translate the easiest piece of Latin.

The glimmer of literacy in the monasteries isolated in woods and on the crags of savage lands did not, in general, go beyond those elementary attainments. According to Benvenuto da Imola, grass grew in most of the libraries. The literary activities of the monks consisted for the most part in scraping away the literatures of Greece and Rome in order to use the parchment for writing the legends of the saints. Of lay books there existed the manuals of Boethius and Cassiodorus; few Roman authors appear ever to have been read besides Vergil, Terence and Plautus. The wretched so-called schools established by Charlemagne, over which a grossly exaggerated fuss is made in our histories, represented an ineffectual attempt to manufacture more priests, and to produce priests that should at least be able to read and write. They only existed for a day, and offered a curriculum of which a dame's infant school would be ashamed. The 'palatine academy' never existed at all except in the imagination of historians; of contemporary evidence there is not a trace. We are liable to be impressed when we read that 'schools' were established, and that the 'seven arts,' that mathematics, astronomy among other things were taught. The impression is utterly misleading. Here, for instance, is an account of the 'founding of a school.' Charlemagne ordered the abbot of Fontenelle, one Gervold, to open a school in his monastery. He obeyed: he opened a school in which singing only was taught, for "although he knew not overmuch any other art, he was proficient in the art of singing and was not deficient in pleasantness and power of voice." [1] Alcuin of York, the organiser of those precious Carolingian schools, proclaimed "the most learned man of his time, whom no one in that age excelled in learning," thus instructs his pupils in grammar and rhetoric: he tells them to be careful to distinguish between *vellus* and *bellus*, *vel* and *fel*, *quod* and *quot*, and imparts to them the information that *hippocrita* is derived from *hippo, falsum* and *chrisis, judicium*. His 'mathematics' did not extend beyond a labourious and uncertain use of the rule of three. Here is a fair and representative specimen of it. "An accurate acquaintance with numbers teaches us that some are even, others uneven; that of the even numbers, some are perfect, others imperfect; and further, that of the imperfect numbers, some are greater, others less. . . . Take, for example, the number VI; the half of VI is III, the third is II, and the sixth part I. The perfect Creator, therefore, who made all things very good, created the world in six days in order to show that everything that he had formed was perfect of its kind. . . . When the human race after the flood replenished the earth, they originated from the number VIII; . . . thus indicating that the second race is less perfect than the first, which had been created in the number VI. . . . The sixty queens and eighty concubines (mentioned in the Song of Solomon) are the members of the Holy Church," etc., etc. Even the study of theology to which all other 'learning' was strictly subordinate must not suggest to us any subtle dialectical exercises; by theology was meant purely

[1] *Chron. Fontanell. ad a.* 787.

and simply the capacity to quote from Holy Writ and from the Fathers; the authority of a text was the sole conceivable form of argument. Of such kind was the learning which, we are told, survived and was preserved in the monasteries.

But if bare literacy existed in the Church only, it was also the dead weight of its influence which paralysed intellect and culture. It is difficult to realise the effect of that incubus in that age, the completeness with which it succeeded in snuffing out the human mind. Not only was religious dogma, the thought of hell-fire, an exclusive, constant, daily obsession; but any distraction of the attention, any deviation of the mental gaze from that one object of hypnotic contemplation, any other interest, was denounced as in itself an impiety. The Church, it is important to observe, was not then opposed to knowledge on the ground that it was 'dangerous,' that it imperilled the faith. That view was a fruit of later experience. In the simplicity of primitive dogmatic confidence the thought hardly occurred that any knowledge could be dangerous, could conflict with holy truth. Knowledge might, on the contrary, be plausibly valued as an adornment of the Church, as enhancing the dignity of its office, as contributing to the greater glory of the faith. And that notion did exist in some minds; monks like the Benedictines cultivated what knowledge they could, regarding it as a tribute to religion, as its natural appanage. But that notion was in general vigorously denounced and repressed. Secular reading was condemned not as an occupation dangerous to religion, but as an occupation *other* than religion. It was an impermissible withdrawal of the mind from its one legitimate cynosure. The attitude of the Christian mind towards culture was that of St. Jerome who, though naturally devoted to literature, renounced it by an act of self-discipline, as if casting off a temptation of Satan, and purging himself from a state of sin. Alcuin systematically discouraged secular study. In a letter to a former pupil that egregious educator takes him to task for reading Vergil; "the four Gospels," he says, "not the twelve Æneads *(sic)*, should fill your mind." The same attitude is found throughout the Dark Ages. At a much later date Edmund Rich, one of the founders of Oxford, while studying mathematical diagrams has a vision of his mother, who draws three interlaced circles representing the Trinity; "Be these," she bids him, "henceforth thy diagrams." Pope Gregory burnt all the works of Livy and of Cicero on which he could lay his hands. The rumour having reached him that Bishop Desiderius of Vienne had read some discourse on a literary subject, he writes to him with some embarrassment: "A fact has come to our ears which we cannot mention without a blush, that you, my brother, lecture on literature. I hope to hear that you are not really interested in such rubbish—*nugis et secularibus literis*." Even attention to the study of civil law was as late as the twelfth century violently denounced by St. Bernard, who bewails that the courts are busy with the laws of Justinian—the pandects of Amalfi had just been discovered—instead of confining themselves to the laws of God.

There was among the chief men of those times some sense of the terrible wreck and ruin of things. The vision, the memory of Rome and her civilised world, was too great and too near not to remain present before their eyes and impress them with a strong sense of the existing degradation. Modern historians of the Dark Ages employ themselves with describing the successive efforts that were made by barbaric rulers to introduce some rudiments of order into the weltering chaos. Theodoric did all he could, had laws codified, endeavoured to establish some kind of administration; the Lombards, the Burgundians likewise got codes written down, appointed officials, issued edicts. Charlemagne, the pious barbarian fighting missionary who converted his fellow barbarians to Christianity by fire and sword, and out of whom ecclesiastical gratitude has manufactured a legendary hero, tried in coöperation with the Roman Church to construct a Christian Holy Roman Empire. Various chieftains after him carved out little kingdoms, each making desperate efforts at organisation, law, administration.

But one net result stands out of the recital of those various political enterprises. They are all utterly futile. The laws, organisations, constitutions, as we should say, existed merely on parchment. States, kingdoms, Holy Empires, are brought into existence at the point of the sword, and with papal blessings, but they are mere card castles that come tumbling down as fast as they are set up. We may gauge the real value of the well-meaning efforts of Charlemagne, which are represented in detailed accounts as a reorganisation of the world, a 'renaissance,' by the fact that the moment he is laid in the crypt of Aachen, not a trace is to be found of it all. Under all those fictitious official titles and codes, those political shufflings which help to fill the chronicle, the actual facts of human society remain unaltered, they run their course unaffected and unchanged: brigand chiefs warring and plundering, murders and outrages, decimated populations of miserable wretches clustering round for protection.

The truth is that you cannot make laws, or organise, or do anything with masses of humanity if culture is nonexistent. You may go on devising parchment laws and kingdoms, and appointing officials with pompous titles, and signing deeds and edicts till doomsday; if humanity is in a condition of illiterate barbarism, is intellectually destitute, all your politics and organising and legislating are vain beating of the air. We shall have occasion to note later that no liberating movement can originate from the people themselves unless they are intellectually prepared for it. The reverse is equally true; no reform, no organisation, no progress can be imposed on them by well-meaning rulers, if the people are not culturally in a condition to receive it. Neither from above nor from below can civilisation be implanted upon barbarism destitute of intellectual culture.

Without intellectual light of some kind in either people or rulers it was impossible to create a new Europe. No extant elements derived either from the rigid conservative structure of the Roman Empire or from a dogmatic Church could give rise to a progressive civilisation in the Europe of the Dark Ages, any more than did those same elements in the empire of Byzantium.

Among all the kingdoms of time Byzantium stands a unique, strange, uncanny, half-understood figure of warning, like a gorgeously decked skeleton at the feast of life. Upon her as on no other empire fortune seemed to have showered every favour. Set in a site of unparalleled vantage, the cynosure of every empire-builder from the remotest time to the present day, it survived all but unscathed amid the ruin which all around it submerged the world. While Western Europe sank in headlong dissolution, it endured to all outer seeming an opulent, prosperous, dazzling civilisation. The pomp, the wealth, the flashing opulence, the stately ceremonial of its gorgeous court offered a spectacle of fastuous splendour never perhaps excelled. Its basileus, resplendent under the jeweled shower of the dalmatic, receiving in the Magnaura the homage of prostrate princes, amid the smoke of incense, the blaze of candelabra, the rustle of gold fronds, and the peals of the silver organs, surrounded by hierarchies of patricians and protospatharians, by the scholaric guards in their silver breastplates, and the excubitors with their golden shields, seemed more like a superhuman being than a man. The maze of the Sacred Palaces, with their ivory doors, rising in tiers of splendour on the enchanted shore, whence the eye roamed from marble terraces over a panorama of unmatched loveliness, the Marmora and the Prinkipo islands, the waving hills covered with parks and gardens, with palaces and villas, the Palace of Fountains, Chrysopolis on the Asiatic shore, and Bryas where stood a replica of the Kasr at-Taj of Baghdad, Blachernai on the Golden Horn, the private imperial harbour of Boukoleon, where scarlet-and-gold dromons with silken sails bearing the double-headed eagle rode at anchor; the glint of the polychromatic churches, their clusters of airy domes, "hung as if by a golden chain from heaven"; the Hippodrome decked with the obelisks of Thebes, the tripods of Delphi, and the statues of Praxiteles—that opulent spectacle needed not to be contrasted with the squalor and the desolation of the barbarous West. Byzantium was the natural emporium of the world's trade; its industries were flourishing; its dominions extended over the richest provinces of Asia; it controlled the granaries and timber-yards of the world; it possessed the only disciplined and scientifically trained armies; their officers carried the tactical manuals of Maurice and Leo the Wise in their haversacks; they were equipped with the equivalent of an artillery the dreaded Grecian fire—some kind of *Flammenwerfer,* of which they had the secret. While all the rest of Christendom were brutal savages, the princes and citizens of the Eastern Empire were marked by courtliness and polished manners, refinement in their tastes and mode of life. Byzantine culture was the sole heir and repository of the Greek and

Hellenistic world; it produced scholars, poets, mathematicians. Notwithstanding its luxurious opulence its court was, with the exception of brief outbreaks, generally free from vice, corruption and crime. It was, on the whole, a decent, orderly, well-behaved, well-intentioned society. Its elaborately organised administration, the representative of Roman law, worked smoothly. Its rulers were generally just, generally patriotic, careful of public welfare, conscientious to a scruple. How many rulers has the world since seen setting themselves to write army manuals, or compendiums of law like Basil I, or an account of their dominions, or a treatise on diplomacy and the administration of the empire like Constantine Porphyrogenitus? They invariably led their armies in person, they were their own finance ministers, personally attended to the administration of the treasury, and never once allowed the coinage to become debased.

Thus during ten long centuries the Byzantine Empire stood, the guardian of culture, the ark of civilisation, while the Christian world around it crumbled to primordial anarchy and rose again to life. It would not be possible to set forth conditions in appearance more favourable to the development of a great, glorious and mighty human society, the leader of progress, the guide of civilisation, the light of the world.

And yet that civilisation, the pampered favourite of fortune, has remained before the considered judgment of history, in spite of the attempts of some Byzantophiles to rehabilitate it, what it was to its contemporaries—an object of contempt. So insignificant that one is apt to overlook and ignore it in a purview of the development of humanity. It has contributed nothing to human growth; it lies outside the stream of mankind's evolution, a relic, a mummified survival, a failure. In those thousand years of existence it did not exhibit a spark of progress, scarcely of life. Surrounded by populations struggling out of darkness and calling for rescue and redemption, it taught them nothing, and it learnt nothing. Its fleets were swept off the seas by the Arabs; its commerce was captured, first by the Arabs, then by the Catalans, Genoese and Venetians; its army, though it did save the Empire again and again, ultimately came to be despised both by Frank and Saracen; its literature was puerile, a model of bad taste, of nauseous, euphuistic pseudo-mythologising rubbish, and grotesque miracle tales; it remains unreadable, save for the fable-distorted records of its self-contemplating history; its few scholars—there were not many—such as Leo the Grammarian, Photius, were the merest compilers, scholiasts, and pedants; the only works of any utility which they have left us are the catalogues of the libraries they knew not how to use, and the dictionary of Suidas. In the bountiful prodigality of the advantages which it enjoyed and in their utter futility, the Byzantine Empire offers, as I said, a spectacle unique in history.

If we enquire into the causes of that phenomenal sterility we find that they fall mainly under three heads. First, the real power of the Byzantine Empire was wielded by a host of ignorant and fanatical monks. They swarmed throughout every province and every town. In Constantinople whole districts were filled with rows of monasteries; there were over a hundred; that of Stoudion alone contained a thousand monks. Mount Athos, Mount Ida, Olympus, the islands of the Marmora and the Archipelago, were covered with conglomerations of monasteries. You could not go ten steps without meeting those long-haired, short-skirted, Rasputin-like figures, round whom the people crowded to kiss their hands. Every noble, every merchant, every man of wealth, every pious lady, either founded or endowed a monastery. The Emperor Nicopheros, though himself leading the life of a monk, wearing a hair-shirt and sleeping on bare boards, was so alarmed at the depopulation of the Empire, at the flow of its wealth into the monasteries, at the consequent recruiting and fiscal difficulties, that he attempted to check the evil by legislation. The long contest over the Images which appears to us so paltry, was but a vain struggle of the emperors to shake themselves free of the intolerable domination of the monks. They exercised complete control over the minds of the people, of the women, of the nobility; they fed them with wonder-tales and miracles, and lives of saints. Theology and even hell had little place in their doctrines; every event, every action was surrounded with a web of supernatural signs and portents; the Byzantine Greeks lived in a world peopled with goblins, ghosts, angels and demons. The supreme objects of their worship were miracle-working, winking images of saints, most of them painted by supernatural agencies, before which the crowds kissed the pavements of the churches, and to which they had resort for help in every circumstance of life, for success in business enterprises, the finding of lost property, the cure of rheumatism. Strong in the fanatical backing of the populace and of the women, the monks set the civil authority at defiance, bearded the emperor in his palace, in the open street, whenever they disapproved of his acts.

Secondly, that empire in spite of its priceless position of vantage was effectually isolated from the rest of the world by artificial barriers. For the Latin and Germanic Christians the Greeks had the most utter contempt; they regarded them—not, it must be admitted, without ample justification—as mere savages. The self-styled Emperor of the Holy Roman Empire was in their eyes an absurd upstart accoutred in a title which made them laugh. He appeared to them much in the same light as we should regard a savage Emperor of Dahomey aping civilised man in a frock coat and silk hat. The term 'foreigner' had for the Greek the same connotation of unbounded contempt and hatred as it had for the true-born Englishman. Those sentiments were accentuated when the crusading rabbles came and foisted themselves upon the Empire, and their boorish, swashbuckling chieftains came tramping round the imperial palaces in their ill-cut clothes, clapping the emperor on the back, plumping themselves down on his throne, like bulls in the stately china-shop of Byzantine etiquette and decorum. On the other hand that hatred and contempt were thoroughly reciprocated. The fact that a vast portion of Christendom, the wealthiest, the most outwardly brilliant remained obstinately, in spite of all efforts, outside the power of the Roman See, refusing to recognise it or acknowledge its authority in any form, was the bitterest pill which the pride, ambition and greed of the papacy had to swallow. The hardened and recalcitrant 'schismatics' were, as usually happens, regarded with more ardent hatred than even the 'pagan infidels.' Detraction of them was inculcated everywhere by the spiritual guides of Europe. The Latins and Germans looked upon the 'effeminate Griffins' with as much contempt as these did upon the Western savages. The latter constantly accused them, mostly quite unjustly —it was at best a case of pot and kettle—of perfidious treachery. While they recognised, whenever they came into direct contact with him, the Muslim as an honourable foe, and could not but be impressed with his well-nigh quixotic chivalry, they scorned the Greek as a base, sneaking fellow. The splendour, the wealth, the dazzling luxury, the civilisation of Byzantium, excited not their admiration and emulation, but their covetousness. They were always in two minds whether to redeem the Holy Land or fall upon the Greek Empire and loot it, as in the fourth Crusade they ultimately did. Thus Byzantine civilisation was as effectually insulated by a barrier of mutual contempt and hatred, as by any China wall or silver streak.

It lived—and this is the third aspect of its sterility—draped in the pride of its origin and exclusiveness. The heterogeneous medley of races which constituted its ruling classes were 'the Romans'—for they despised the name of Greek—their empire was 'the Roman Empire'; they alone had culture, good government, true religion—an exclusively national church far superior to the so-called Christianity of benighted foreigners, and owing no humiliating allegiance to any Italian bishop. Nothing called for change in that highly desirable, sublime, historic, holy condition of affairs. Their attitude towards things as they were, was that of our old Tories, of our Castlereaghs and Wellingtons, of our *Morning Post,* towards our glorious constitution. They had inherited the constitution of the Roman Empire as refashioned in the third century by Diocletian; and its ideal of rigid unchanging stability, of forming the whole population into castes, so that one generation might step into the place of another, and nothing but the human material be changed. Their culture, the great Greek literature, of which Byzantium was the reliquary, they came to regard not as a stimulus and inspiration, but as a hieratic formula, an exercise of scholarship, a litany without meaning or interest. They mostly despised it as pagan and read lives of saints instead.

Under the paint and enamel of its outward civilisation Byzantium steadily grew more barbaric from age to age. With its stodgy conscientiousness and prim virtue went the cool and customary practice of atrocious cruelty. Palace revolutions were dramas of unmitigated horror—the Empress Theophano opening the door to the emperor's murderers; Zoë poisoning her husband; the

Empress Irene, who founded churches, monasteries and orphanages, and was canonized by the Greek Church, gouging out the eyes of her son after luring him from the throne by appeals to filial affection. To gouge out eyes, cut out tongues, emasculate, impale, crucify and flay alive, were the forms of punishment habitually inflicted. The Chalké gate of the Palace on the Augusteon, like those of the Seraglio of Turkish sultans, was usually decorated with blackening heads; the walls of Constantinople, after a victory over the Russians, were garlanded with festoons of severed hands; one of the few naval victories over the Saracens was celebrated by adorning the coast from Adramytos to Strobilos with the impaled bodies of the captives; and after surprising the Bulgars in the gorge of Kimbalongo, Basil II put out the eyes of fifteen thousand prisoners, sparing one eye to every hundredth man, that the groaning, bleeding multitude might grope their way back to their king. When provinces like Armenia revolted they were punished by wholesale massacres, rape, and devastation, and pyramids of severed heads were set up as a warning. The lapse of centuries did not bring about a trace of moral and humanitarian development; and the Turks, who took over much of the usages and traditions of the Byzantine court, have been blamed for the barbarity of the Byzantine peoples over whom it has been their misfortune to rule.

Thus did Byzantium proceed for ten centuries, unchanging, with its head turned backwards. But for the glassy coruscations of its hieratic mosaics, the gems and enamels of its ciboria, the gold of its scapularies, the lily pillars, and peacock panels, the marble tracery of its transennæ, the sepulchral splendour of its decorative craft which at once fascinates and chills us like the beauty of a dead woman; but for some insignificant details of bureaucratic administration—for the age of Justinian is to be accounted Roman rather than Byzantine—it has contributed nothing to human culture and civilisation, nothing to the resurrection of Europe. To those countries which developed under its influence, to Russia and to the Balkan people, it has bequeathed those elements which constitute not their civilisation, but their barbarism.

Such was the civilisation in which by unbroken continuity and in the fullest enjoyment of every conceivable advantage the Roman Empire and Christianity had resulted; such was the product of the fixed conservatism of the one and the theocratic dogmatism of the other. Historians labour to show that there was no break between the ancient and the modern world, they have sought to minimize the darkness of the Dark Ages, to exhibit Europe arising out of them by a continuous and uninterrupted process. The effect of such continuity is visible in the Byzantine Empire. Free cities arose in the West out of relics of Roman municipia, trade guilds out of the Roman associations; but anteriorly to the development of wealth and trade there were, and there could be, no free cities and no guilds. Mediæval culture grew on the soil of Greek and Roman literature, but under dogmatic domination and amid universal illiteracy those literatures were abolished, and before the operation and stimulus of other intellectual elements mediæval culture did not arise. The 'young and virile Teutonic nations,' those *christlich-germanischen Tugenden* of Giesebrecht and our Teutonic friends, which for all our historians, from Stubbs and Seeley and Green to the French Taine, are the source of the rebirth of the modern world, did not infuse life into it, but death and barbarism. The Christian-Germanic virtues did not result in progress, but in steady and growing barbarisation. It is not true that a new world began at once to sprout on the ruins of the old. On the contrary, for close on five hundred years Europe sank lower and lower; things went steadily and continuously from bad to worse. In the ninth century the conditions were more desolately dark and more utterly hopeless than they had been in the sixth or seventh. If we picture that dark continent of the ninth century isolated from the rest of the world and left to its own resources, there is no ground for surmising that it could ever, by virtue of any element of life existing within it, become civilised at all. Whatever possibilities might exist in that dark welter of degradation, whatever factor might under propitious conditions be turned to advantage, it contained no endogenous seeds of life and progress that had power to germinate by virtue of their intrinsic force. The fate of Europe might quite conceivably have been to become fossilised into a kind of barbaric Abyssinia.

The light from which civilisation was once more rekindled did not arise from any embers of Græco-Roman culture smouldering amid the ruins of Europe, nor from the living death on the Bosporus. It did not come from the Northern, but from the Southern invaders of the empire, from the Saracens.

IX

DÂR AL-HIKMET

(The Home of Science)

THE Semitic people who raised the banner of Islam were, like Europe, under the spell of a theological dogma, and it was in its name that they rose from their desert tents, and in a remarkably short space of time conquered an empire vaster than that of Rome, which stretched from Kashghar and the Panjab to the Atlantic and the South of France. But in addition to the vital contrast between the rich luxuriance of the Christian dogma, its stately and elaborate hierarchical organisation, and the bare, bald theism of Islam, with its negation of systematic theology, of myth, of tradition, almost destitute of ritual, and, above all, entirely without priesthood,—there were other and even more fundamental differences.

No conception could be remoter from the truth than that which commonly pictures the coming of Islam as a sort of Mâhdi rising, a *jihad* of wild darvishes fired to frenzy by religious fanaticism. The experiences from which such a picture is drawn, Muslim fanaticism, one might almost say Muslim faith, belong to a subsequent age, when Islam's civilisation had sunk to dust and its creed had become transformed by Ash'ârite theology. Its origin and its halcyon days were far different.

The Kûraish community in whose midst it first arose, though untouched in the patriarchal simplicity of its constitution, was by no means primitive in its mentality. It was a society of wealthy and travelled merchants, well in touch with the outer world, cultivating fine manners, delighting in social intercourse, in cultured female society, in poetry already grown artificial and frivolous, in tournaments of song; a society that had waxed too worldly and sceptical for serious convictions, having, like the more primitive Arab tribes around it, outgrown the conglomerate of traditional cults which it conventionally continued to profess. The simple-minded earnestness of one of their commercial travellers, Muhâmmad, made upon that society much the same sort of impression as a Unitarian missionary might expect to make in Mayfair. The prevalent feeling which he voiced was rather one of rationalistic dissatisfaction with the outworn palimpsest of cults than the enthusiasm of a religious revelation. And it was in fact as a very human destroyer of idols in the broadest sense, as a protester against all religious superstructure above the generalised idea of theism reduced to its simplest expression, that Muhâmmad, like a sort of Channing, without any thaumaturgic or supernatural pretensions, in the most undisguisedly commonplace, human way, presented his ideas of reform.

There was of course a nucleus of genuine fervour and enthusiasm in the closer associates of the prophet, around which were later formed the Shî'ite and Sunnite parties; there were leaders like the great 'Omar, the St. Paul of Islam, the moving spirit of its expansion and organisation, in a sense its true founder. But all those elements became almost immediately submerged and reduced to a subordinate position destitute of influence or importance. The whole subsequent development and marvellous expansion was not a religious, but a political movement, one whose sole aim, in fact, was conquest and plunder. The mass of Muslim tribes knew and cared nothing about Islam—amusement was caused on more than one occasion by their inability to recite a single prayer beyond the opening formula, *Bismillah er-rahman, er-rahim.* The dazzling rapidity of the conquest was chiefly due, not to Muslim prowess or to Byzantine inefficiency, but to the assistance and friendliness of the Christian populations of Syria and Egypt, sick to death of theocratic oppression and of theology.

After the first days of the 'orthodox' Khalìfs, when the Commander of the Faithful was pointed out to astonished pilgrims in the streets of Medina, clad in a tattered *jubba* eating sesame bread and onions, and when the great 'Omar journeyed on a camel to receive the homage of conquered Jerusalem, accompanied by a single attendant and with a bag of dates for luggage, the Khalìfate passed to the Kûraish Umayyads, the bitterest opponents of Islam, who made no secret of the purely political nature of their adhesion, and overtly flaunted their indifference. Never was a religion propagated with so little religious faith. We have in fact in Islam the rather extraordinary spectacle of a professedly religious movement which, while it gave rise later in its utter decadence to a wide-spread and earnest religious faith of great vitality, was in its origin and throughout its hey-day utterly indifferent to religion, a movement in which large populations were willingly converted by lukewarm and unbelieving apostles, and whose final triumph as a religion was effected by hordes of barbarian invaders who destroyed it as a civilisation. That peculiar evolution was the exact converse of that of Christianity.

The 'Abbâssid princes who became the founders of Islamic culture, owed their triumph over the Umayyads chiefly to the support of Persia, where they had been reared. The glorious and ancient empire of the Sassanids, which had always been the great trysting-place of Hellenistic and Oriental commerce and culture, had, when conquered to Islam by 'Othman, just reached under the two Chosroes the climax of a rich and large-minded culture. Gathering and inviting all the intellectual and industrial products of India and China, it also offered the only existing hospitable refuge to persecuted Christian sects; and the Nestorians, driven by fanaticism from their school at Edessa, had been encouraged to found an even more brilliant one at Jundi Shapûr. In that tolerant, latitudinarian atmosphere of Persia, which had seen so many 'new religions,' Islam was accepted in a philosophic spirit which soon further attenuated its already simplified theology into a mild theistic rationalism, known to Islamic pietists as the Mu'tazil heresy. Of Muslim faith no more than that slight nominal conformity was retained by the 'Abbâssid Khalìfs and those who built up the civilisation of Islam. "They are the elect of God," said Al-Mamûn, "his best and most useful servants, whose lives are devoted to the improvement of their rational faculties."

There were other propitious circumstances in the rise of Islamic culture. The Arabs had once, like the ancient Chaldæans, worshipped 'the heavenly bodies,' hence the interest of the desert-folk in astronomy. So likewise was the rude cultivation of the healing art and of botanical lore, in which Muhâmmad and Abû Bakr themselves had been proficient, a tradition of the race. And as the sons of Araby changed the tents of Shem for the luxury of Damascus and Baghdad, they had occasion to avail themselves of the services of the Nestorian physicians; and it was gratified admiration for their skill and learning which first prompted the Khalìfs to enquire into the sources whence they derived them. They thus became acquainted with the works of Hippokrates and Galen, and with those of the latter's admired master, Aristotle. Practically untouched in their desert home either by the old theocratic empires or by the conquests of Rome, they were still the nomad

Semites of primitive times. When they suddenly attained to wealth and power, and came into contact with the traditions of the great past civilisation, spectrally surviving in the Byzantine East, they were not, like the northern barbarians, held in awe by the great name of Rome, which had loomed for generations as the embodiment of god-like grandeur and power, and by the religion which was identified with it. While they coveted the material culture which lay sealed and idle in the hands of the Roman mummy, they despised the barbarian of Rūm.

There was indeed something of the old pagan, Hellenic joy of life in the spirit of that new splendour which arose like the fantastic creation of a jinni at the beck of the Khalîfs, and spread its glinting opulence and delicate wizardry over the civilisation of the *Thousand and One Nights*. A hedonism refined withal and tempered by the superb gravity of the Bedâwin, and a philosophic seriousness mindful while it quaffed the cup that it was but a small matter, and a frail tenure resting upon the caprice of Kismet. The incorruptible treasures and delights of intellectual culture were accounted by the princes of Baghdad, Shiraz and Cordova, the truest and proudest pomps of their courts. But it was not as a mere appanage of princely vanity that the wonderful growth of Islamic science and learning was fostered by their patronage. They pursued culture with the personal ardour of an overmastering craving. Never before and never since, on such a scale, has the spectacle been witnessed of the ruling classes throughout the length and breadth of a vast empire given over to a frenzied passion for the acquirement of knowledge. Learning seemed to have become with them the chief business of life. Khalîfs and Emirs hurried from their diwans to closet themselves in their libraries and observatories; they neglected their affairs of state—which they in general sorely mismanaged—to attend lectures and converse on mathematical problems with men of science; caravans laden with manuscripts and botanical specimens plied from Bokhara to the Tigris, from Egypt to Andalusia; embassies were sent to Constantinople and to India for the sole purpose of obtaining books and teachers; a collection of Greek authors or a distinguished mathematician was eagerly demanded as the ransom of an empire. To every mosque was attached a school; wazirs vied with their masters in establishing public libraries, endowing colleges, founding bursaries for impecunious students. Men of learning, irrespective of race or religion, took precedence over all others; honours and riches were showered upon them, they were appointed to the government of provinces; a retinue of professors and a camel train of books accompanied the Khalîfs in their journeys and expeditions.

It was under the influence of the Arabian and Moorish revival of culture, and not in the fifteenth century, that the real Renaissance took place. Spain, not Italy, was the cradle of the rebirth of Europe. After steadily sinking lower and lower into barbarism, Christian Europe had reached the darkest depths of ignorance and degradation when the cities of the Saracenic world, Baghdad, Cairo, Cordova, Toledo, were growing centres of civilisation and intellectual activity. It was there that the new life arose which was to grow into a new phase of human evolution. From the time when the influence of their culture made itself felt, began the stirring of a new life.

The fact has been set forth again and again. But it has been stubbornly ignored and persistently minimised. The debt of Europe to the 'heathen dog' could, of course, find no place in the scheme of Christian history, and the garbled falsification has imposed itself on all subsequent conceptions. Even Gibbon treated Islam depreciatingly, an instance of the power of conventional tradition upon its keenest opponents. Until the last century there did not even exist any accurate knowledge of Saracenic history and culture. "Those accounts of Mahomet and Islam which were published in Europe before the beginning of the nineteenth century are now to be regarded simply as literary curiosities." [1] At the present day, when wider and more exact knowledge is becoming accessible, scarcely any history of the Middle Ages gives Islamic culture more than an off-hand and patronising recognition. The history of the rebirth of Europe from barbarism is constantly being written without any reference whatsoever, except to mention "the triumphs of the Cross over the Crescent," and "the reclamation of Spain from the Moorish yoke," to the influence of Arab civilisation—the history of the Prince of Denmark without Hamlet. Dr. Osborn Taylor has even achieved the feat of writing two large volumes on the development of *The Mediæval Mind* without betraying by a hint the existence of Muhâmmadan culture.

That a brilliant and energetic civilisation full of creative energy should have existed side by side and in constant relation with populations sunk in barbarism, without exercising a profound and vital influence upon their development, would be a manifest anomaly. That no such suspension of natural law was involved in the relation between Islam and Europe, is abundantly attested in spite of the conspiring of every circumstance to suppress, deform, and obliterate the records of that relation. Its extent and importance have been beyond doubt far greater than it is today possible to demonstrate in detail. Like the geological record of extinct life, our knowledge in the matter is derived from the scattered and accidentally preserved fragments of evidence which have been spared by forces universally tending to blot them out. When those conditions, when the obliteration of evidence, its distor-

[1] Professor Bevan, *Camb. Med. Hist.*

tion, the persistent prejudice and misrepresentation which fastens upon every single fact, are borne in mind, there can be no doubt that our estimate of that influence must err on the side of under-, rather than of over-estimation. It is highly probable that but for the Arabs modern European civilisation would never have arisen; it is certain that but for them, it would not have assumed that character which has enabled it to transcend all previous phases of evolution. For although there is not a single aspect of European growth in which the decisive influence of Islamic culture is not traceable, nowhere is it so clear and momentous as in the genesis of that power which constitutes the paramount distinctive force of the modern world and the supreme source of its victory—natural science and the scientific spirit.

It must be admitted that, in recoil from the general conspiracy of silence of our histories, several writers who have sought to vindicate the claims of Arab culture have exaggerated the achievements of Arabian science. Against such loose panegyrics it has been objected, that Arab science produced no surpassing genius and no transcending discovery; that it was derived from extraneous sources. That is substantially true, but entirely irrelevant. Arab astronomy did not forestall Copernicus or Newton, though without it there would have been no Copernicus and no Newton. Although the complexity of the Ptolemaic system was repeatedly criticised by Moorish astronomers, although Al-Zarkyal declared the planetary orbits to be ellipses and not circles, although the orbit of Mercury is in Al-Farâni's tables actually represented as elliptical, although Muhâmmad Ibn Mûsa glimpsed in his works on *Astral Motion* and *The Force of Attraction* the law of universal gravitation, those adumbrations of the truth were not fruitful of any great reform. The only important facts brought to light by Arabian astronomy, the discovery of the movements of the sun's apogee by Al-Batâni, and of the secondary variations of the moon's motion by Abû 'l-Wafâ, exercised no perceptible influence upon the course of research, and had to be rediscovered by Tycho. Ibn Sina is said to have employed an air thermometer, and Ibn Yunis certainly did use the pendulum for the measurement of time; but neither of those devices, which were independently reintroduced by Galileo, can be counted as a contribution to the growth of science.

That, however, is entirely beside the point. The debt of our science to that of the Arabs does not consist in startling discoveries or revolutionary theories. Science owes a great deal more to Arab culture, it owes its existence. The ancient world was, as we saw, pre-scientific. The astronomy and mathematics of the Greeks were a foreign importation never thoroughly acclimatised in Greek culture. The Greeks systematised, generalised and theorised, but the patient ways of investigation, the accumulation of positive knowledge, the minute methods of science, detailed and prolonged observation, experimental inquiry, were altogether alien to the Greek temperament. Only in Hellenistic Alexandria was any approach to scientific work conducted in the ancient classical world. What we call science arose in Europe as a result of a new spirit of inquiry, of new methods of investigation, of the method of experiment, observation, measurement, of the development of mathematics in a form unknown to the Greeks. That spirit and those methods were introduced into the European world by the Arabs.

Greek manuscripts were collected and translated at the court of the 'Abbâssids with an ardour even more enthusiastic than that which inspired the Aurispas and Filelfos of fifteenth-century Italy. But the choice of the Arab collectors and the object of their interest were very different. Of the poets and historians of Greece, beyond satisfying their curiosity by a few samples, they took little account. Their object was information; and besides the writings of the philosophers from Thales to Apollonius of Tyana, and the textbooks of medical science, it was above all to the writings of the Alexandrian Academy, the astronomy and geography of Ptolemy, the mathematical works of Euklid, Archimedes, Diophantes, Theon, Apollonius of Perga, that they devoted their attention. For speculative theories and broad generalisations they showed little aptitude, valuing as they did information for its own sake and as a means to the extension of knowledge, rather than as the basis of generalising induction. They accepted the conclusions of the Greeks as working theories necessary to the pursuit of scientific enquiry, only venturing to criticise or modify them as the expansion of knowledge forced them to adapt them to new facts. They have been reproached with imposing a dogmatic spirit in science upon Europe. Christian Europe had little to learn in the way of dogmatism; and those theories, such as the Ptolemaic system, the geographical doctrine of 'climates,' the doctrine of alchemical transmutation, which it received from the Arabs, were not Arabic, but Greek. But the spirit in which the Arabs made use of existing materials was the exact opposite of that of the Greeks. It supplied precisely what had been the weak and defective aspect of Greek genius. For the Greeks it was in theory and generalisation that the interest lay, they were neglectful and careless of fact; the Arabian enquirers' zeal, on the contrary, was careless of theory, and directed to the accumulation of concrete facts, and to giving to their knowledge a precise and quantitative form. What makes all the difference between fruitful, enduring science and mere loose scientific curiosity, is the quantitative as against the qualitative statement, the anxiety for the utmost attainable accuracy in measurement. In that spirit of objective research and quantitative accuracy the whole of the vast scientific work of the Arabs was conducted. They accepted Ptolemy's cosmology, but not his catalogue of stars or his planetary table, or his measurements. They drew up numerous new star catalogues, correcting and greatly amplifying the Ptolemaic one; they compiled new sets of planetary tables, obtained more accurate values for the obliquity of the ecliptic and the precession of equinoxes, checked by two independent measurements of a meridian the estimates of the size of the earth. They devised for the carrying out of those observations elaborate instruments superior to those of the Greeks and exceeding in accuracy those manufactured in the fifteenth century at the famous Nuremberg factory. Each observer took up the work independently, sought to eliminate the personal equation, and the method of continuous observation was systematically carried out—some observations extending over twelve years—at the observatories of Damascus, Baghdad, and Cairo. So much importance did they attach to accuracy in their records that those of special interest were formally signed on oath in legal form.

The same objective and quantitative spirit is manifested in all their activities. When Al-Mamûn ordered his postmaster, Ibn Khûrdadbeh, to draw up an account of his dominions and of all the sea and land routes in use—the first of those numerous geographical works of the Arabs which opened a new view of the world and a new geography—he insisted that each place should be localised by accurately determined longitudes and latitudes. Al-Byrûny travelled forty years to collect mineralogical specimens; and his tables of specific weights obtained by differential weighing are found to be correct. Ibn Baitâr collected botanical specimens from the whole Muslim world and compared the floras of India and Persia with those of Greece and Spain; his work describing 1,400 plants is pronounced by Meyer[1] "a monument of industry." Contrast that spirit of scientific minuteness and perseverance in observation with the speculative methods of the ancients who scorned mere empiricism; with Aristotle who wrote on physics without performing a single experiment, and on natural history without taking the trouble to ascertain the most easily verifiable facts, who calmly states that men have more teeth than women, while Galen, the greatest classical authority on anatomy, informs us that the lower jaw consists of two bones, a statement which is accepted unchallenged till 'Abd al-Letif takes the trouble to examine human skulls.

The Arabs gathered their knowledge from whatever sources were at hand. The bulk of their astronomy and some of their mathematics came from Greek and Hellenistic sources. That ancient science of the Greeks had itself been originally derived from the Babylonians, migrants from Arabia to Mesopotamia, like the Arabs. Thus that ancient science which the latter restored to Europe was itself the achievement of their own ancient cousins from whom the Greeks had once borrowed it. But by a singular good fortune another source of scientific knowledge had become available. In the Gupta Renaissance of the fifth century in India a notable intellectual movement had taken place. Two writers in particular, Aryo-Bhatta and Brahmagupta, had produced important novelties in mathematics. In the hands of the Arabs those new methods became combined with the unwieldy and unpractical methods of the Greek mathematicians, and further elaborated. While the highest mathematical knowledge of the Christian West did not extend beyond a laboured use of the rule of three, and the simplest operations of arithmetic were performed by means of the abacus—the same device of wires and beads that is used in our kindergartens—the

[1] *Gesch. der Botanik*, ii. 233.

Arabs perfected the decimal system of notation by introducing the use of the cipher or zero (Ar. *zirr*); they created Algebra and carried it to the solution of equations of the fourth degree, and trigonometry, substituting sines and tangents for the chord of the Greeks, and thus multiplied a thousandfold the powers of human enquiry.

Not only did the Arabs create those mathematics which were to be the indispensable instrument of scientific analysis, they laid the foundation of those methods of experimental research which in conjunction with mathematical analysis gave birth to modern science. Chemistry, the rudiments of which arose in the processes employed by Egyptian metallurgists and jewellers—combining metals into various alloys and 'tinting' them to resemble gold—processes long preserved as a secret monopoly of the priestly colleges, and clad in the usual mystic formulas, developed in the hands of the Arabs into a widespread, organised passion for research which led them to the invention of distillation, sublimation, filtration, to the discovery of alcohol, of nitric and sulphuric acids (the only acid known to the ancients was vinegar), of the alkalis, of the salts of mercury, of antimony and bismuth, and laid the basis of all subsequent chemistry and physical research.

Like the Hellenistic materials of which it availed itself, Arabian science, and with it the science of the Middle Ages, was tainted with all the fantastic disorders with which it had always been associated in the Oriental and Hellenistic world. Its astronomy arose from Chaldæan astrology, its chemistry from hermetic alchemy. It was, in fact, largely from the same mystical atmosphere of the Hellenistic Orient whence the new religions, the theologies of the epoch of Christian origins, had sprung, that the materials of science were derived. But whereas in the case of theologies and religions those fancies constitute the very substance of the speculative fabric, in that of investigation into natural phenomena they are no more than the outward dress and terminology, the setting of scientific enquiry, which can up to a certain point proceed quite usefully and without being greatly vitiated in consequence. Astronomical observation has not been seriously impaired by being pursued as astrology. Tycho, Copernicus, Kepler were astrologers. The narrow spirit in which Ptolemy produced his compilation of astronomical knowledge, and the authority of his name, have, as a matter of fact, proved immeasurably more baneful to the progress of science than all the notions of astrology. And in experimental research the concepts of alchemy, far from being an obstacle to the progress of knowledge, were the fortunate occasion without which that difficult line of inquiry might never have been pursued. It was, rightly considered, a working hypothesis as good as could be devised in the absence of the knowledge to which it was itself to lead the human mind. All bodies and substances were conceived to consist of a uniform and universal 'materia prima' diversified by the admixture of the four Aristotelian elements, water, earth, air and fire. But from the presence and combination of those elements with primitive matter, could not be deduced the peculiar properties of substances; hence they were ascribed to 'occult virtues' connected in some way with the seven metals, which were imagined to bear some relation to the seven planets; and in order to discover those properties or virtues there was no other way but to study substances in themselves and in their various combinations, to endeavour to purge them from the masking elements and reduce them to their pure state, to discover the processes and reagents which could bring about in them the observed transformations. It should be noted that among Arabian and mediæval scientific inquirers the relative importance attached to mystic theory and ascertained facts varied widely in every degree, from that of vulgar charlatanism intent on exploiting popular superstition, to that of the intellectual enquirer concerned with results, and to whom speculative theory had only the interest of an hypothesis. Though to the mediæval popular mind all science was magic, and the Arab scientists were spoken of as necromancers, the most distinguished of them rose well above that atmosphere. Thus with all the great Arabian astronomers observation and analysis of results was the thing of importance, to the exclusion of the trade in horoscopes and astrological prediction, which they left to the vulgar practitioner. And in the case of alchemical ideas, that premature evolutionary theory was strongly contested by several leading Arabian chemists; and in the eleventh century the dispute between its defenders and opponents developed into a lively controversy. So great an authority as Ibn Sina himself said: "Those of the chemical craft know well that no change can be effected in the different species of substances, though they can produce the appearance of such change." Europe, where the Lateran Council of 1215 had proclaimed the dogma of transubstantiation, generally adopted the theory of transmutation of metals, which had fallen into discredit among the Arabs. "Theosophy and mysticism," says Sir Edward Thorpe,[1] "were first imported into Alchemy not by the Arabs, but by Christian workers."

Science is not a tradition, but the essence of progressive thought. The science of one generation is consequently looked down upon by succeeding ones from those very heights of knowledge to which it has helped to raise them. Our own physiological and biological theories will probably appear as quaint to our descendants as do the conceptions in which the infancy of science was swaddled. Not until a quite recent time has it cast them off. Kepler drew

[1] *Hist. of Chemistry*, p. 36.

horoscopes, Copernicus accounted for planetary motions by propelling angels, Newton himself applied his mathematical genius to the working out of the astrological prophecies in the Book of Daniel; the doctrine of alchemical transmutation was firmly held by Robert Boyle, by von Helmont, by Boerhaave, by Newton, by Leibnitz, and by Stahl; Priestley, obsessed with the theory of phlogiston, refused to recognise the significance of his own discovery of oxygen. It was not till the eve of the French Revolution that, thanks to Lavoisier, new conceptions of the various forms of matter supplanted the hypotheses under which, from the days of the Arabs, chemical analysis and the experimental investigation of nature had proceeded.

In the new methods which they introduced, in that star-gazing, in those alembics, in that new lore—uncouth and larded with gross fancies as much of it was—which differed entirely in temper from the old classic culture, and long preceded the revival of its study in Europe, lay the future of the world, the germ whence, after a maturation of several centuries, was to burst forth the titanic force of modern science.

Arabian knowledge began at an early date to percolate into Christian Europe. If there be any ground of fact in the legend of the alchemical pursuits of St. Dunstan, Arabian lore must have been much more widely diffused in the tenth century than can be shown by surviving records. Under absolute religious tolerance, Christians enjoyed complete freedom in the Spanish Khalìfate. They had their own bishop; several monasteries existed in the outskirts of the capital which served as hostels for travellers, and monks were commonly seen in the streets of Cordova. From all parts of Europe numerous students betook themselves to the great Arab seats of learning in search of the light which only there was to be found. Alvaro, a Cordovan bishop, writes in the ninth century:

"All the young Christians who distinguish themselves by their talent, know the language and literature of the Arabs, read and study passionately the Arab books, gather at great expense great libraries of these, and everywhere proclaim with a loud voice how admirable is that literature."[1] The famous Gerbert of Aurillac brought from Spain some rudiments of astronomy and mathematics, and taught his astonished pupils from terrestrial and celestial globes. Though his learning was not deep, and he is probably credited erroneously with introducing the decimal notation—he still used the Roman abacus—his keen taste for knowledge "stolen from the Saracen," in William of Malmesbury's phrase, made him, as Pope Sylvester II, the hero of fantastic Faust legends popular throughout the Middle Ages.

During the next two centuries the process of diffusion assumed an extensive scale. An African monk, Constantine, who had acted as secretary to Robert Guiscard, devoted himself with enthusiasm to the translation of Arab textbooks and to introducing the new learning into the mother house of the Benedictines at Monte Cassino, whence the path lay open for its transmission to the far-flung houses of the order. Another Benedictine, Adelhard of Bath, brought with him from Cordova a large collection of books and much doctrine, which he and his nephew actively spread abroad in France and England. From his copy of Euklid all subsequent editions down to 1533 have been published. Daniel de Morlay likewise proceeded to Cordova to learn mathematics and astronomy, published the fruits of his studies and lectured at Oxford. Plato of Tivoli translated Al-Batâni's astronomy and other mathematical works. At the end of the twelfth century a young Pisan merchant, Leonardo Fibonacci, while travelling in Algeria and Spain became enamoured of the new mathe-

[1] *Indiculus luminosus*, in Florez, *España Sagrada*, vol. xi, p. 274.

matical sciences of the Arabs, and after several journeys issued a translation of Al-Khwarismi's great work on algebra. He definitely popularised the perfected decimal notation, which became known, with the facilitated arithmetic resulting from it, as *algorism,* from the Arabian writer's name. Fibonacci, whose work had a wide influence, must be accounted the founder of modern mathematics in Christian Europe and the first of the long line of Italian mathematicians. Gerard of Cremona was the most industrious among the popularisers of Arab literature; he spent fifty years at Cordova and brought forth no less than sixty translations, among which the *Almagest,* and the *Astronomy* of Al-Haithâm. Michael Scot repeatedly visited Cordova for the purpose of obtaining manuscripts and making translations. The influx of students into Spain and the activity of translators went on till the last days of Muslim rule. Arnold of Villeneuve, and Raymond Lully, the friend of Bacon, studied in Spain and taught at Montpellier; Campanus of Novara studied mathematics at Cordova and taught in Vienna; and systematic schools for the translation of Arab textbooks were established in Toledo by Alfonso the Sage.

The Jews shared under the complete tolerance of Moorish rule in the cultural evolution of the Khalìfate; and as they scattered over Europe, especially after the Almohadean conquest, became the carriers of that culture to the remotest barbaric lands. They are found freely teaching and discussing with the inmates of secluded monasteries, whose curiosity for the strange learning prevailed over their religious prejudices.[1] French and German

[1] A passage of Joinville's, of interest in more than one respect, is worth citing in full in this connection. I slightly modernise the spelling: "Il [St. Louis] me conta que il eut une grande disputation de clercs at de Juifs au moustier (monastère) de Cluny. Là estait un chevalier à qui l'abbé avait donné le pain là pour Dieu, et requit à l'abbé que il li lessast dire la première parole, ce qu'il lui octroya à peine. Et lors il se

monks obtain from them the textbooks of the new sciences; and even literary nuns in Thuringian convents, such as the famous Hildegard and Hroswitha, did not disdain to avail themselves of their learning. They established numerous schools, such as that of the Kimhis and of Ben Esra at Narbonne, where Arabian science was popularised and Arabic books translated. Numerous Jews followed William of Normandy to England and enjoyed his protection, building there the first stone burgher houses which may still be seen at Lincoln and St. Edmundsbury, and establishing a school of science at Oxford. It was under their successors at that Oxford school that Roger Bacon learned Arabic and Arabic science. Neither Roger Bacon nor Francis Bacon has any title to be credited with having introduced the experimental method. Roger Bacon was but one of the apostles of Muslim science and methods to Christian Europe; and he never wearied of declaring that a knowledge of Arabic and Arabian science was for his contemporaries the only way to true knowledge. Discussions as to who was the originator of the

leva et s'appuya sur sa crosse, et dit que lui li faist venir le plus grave clerc et le plus grant mestre des Juifs, et si firent ils. Et lui fist une demande qui fut telle: Mestre, fist le chevalier, je vous demande si vous croyez que la Vierge Marie qui Dieu porta en ses flancs et en ses bras, enfantât vierge, et que elle soit mère de Dieu. Et le Juif répondit que de tout celà il ne croyait rien. Et le chevalier li répondit que moult avait fait que fol, quant il ne lo croyait, ni ne la lamoit, et estait, entré dans son moustier et en sa maison. Et vraiement, fist le chevalier, vous le payerez; et lors il hauça sa potence et féri le Juif près de l'orielle et le porta par terre. Et les Juifs tournèrent en fuite, et emportèrent leur mestre tout blécié; et ainsi demoura la disputation. Lors vint l'abbé au chevalier, et lui dist qu'il avait fait grande folie. Et le chevalier dit que encore avoit il fait plus grande folie, d'essembler telle disputation; car avant que la disputation feust menée à fin, avait il céans grand foisons de bons chrétiens, qui se furent parti tous mescréants, parce qu'ils n'eurent mie bien entendu les Juifs. Aussi, vous dis-je, fist le roy, que nul, s'il n'est très bon clerc, ne doit disputer avec eux; mais l'homme laïc, quant il oye médire de la loi chrétienne, ne doit pas déffendre la loi chrétienne, sinon de l'espée, de quoi il doit donner parmi le ventre dedans, tout comme elle y peut entrer." Intolerance and persecution of Jews was a feature of the later, rather than of the earlier Middle Ages.

experimental method, like the fathering of every Arab discovery or invention on the first European who happens to mention it, such as the invention of the compass on a fabulous Flavio Gioja of Amalfi, of alcohol on Arnold of Villeneuve, of lenses and gunpowder on Bacon or Schwartz, are part of the colossal misrepresentation of the origins of European civilisation. The experimental method of the Arabs was by Bacon's time widespread and eagerly cultivated throughout Europe; it had been proclaimed by Adelhard of Bath, by Alexander of Neckam, by Vincent of Beauvais, by Arnold of Villeneuve, by Bernard Silvestris, who entitles his manual *Experimentarius*, by Thomas of Cantimpré, by Albertus Magnus.

In the hands of Jewish doctors trained in Arab schools, where medical art had been carried far beyond that of the ancients, the practice and teaching of medicine remained throughout the Middle Ages. The pharmacopœia created by the Arabs is virtually that which, but for recent synthetic and organotherapic preparations, is in use at the present day; common drugs, such as nux vomica, rhubarb, aconite, gentian, myrrh, calomel, and the structure of our prescriptions, belong to Arabic medicine. The medical school of Montpellier was founded on the pattern of that of Cordova under Jew doctors. The example was imitated at Padua and later at Pisa, where together with the *Canons* of Avicenna (Ibn Sina) and the *Surgery* of Abû 'l-Kasim, which until the seventeenth century remained the textbooks of medical science throughout Europe, were taught the mathematics and astronomy of the Moors. Those were the nurseries which were one day to bring forth Fallopius, Vesalius, Cardan, Harvey, Galileo.

That power which has transformed the material and mental world is the product by direct filiation of the science of the astrologers, alchemists, and of the medical schools of the later Middle Ages; and those arose directly and solely as a result of Arabian civilisation. Down to the fifteenth century whatever scientific activity existed in Europe was engaged in assimilating Arab learning without greatly adding to it. Prince Henry of Portugal established under Arab and Jewish teachers his great nautical academy at Cape St. Vincent, which prepared the way for Vasco da Gama, and for the expansion of Europe to the uttermost ends of the earth. Columbus, writing from Haiti, says that the existence of America suggested itself to him from reading the works of Ibn Roschd (Averroes). The first mathematical treatise printed in Europe (1494) is but a paraphrase and in parts a transcription of Leonardo Fibonacci's translations by Lucia Pacioli, the friend of another Leonardo—Leonardo da Vinci. It was from Al-Batâni's tables that Regiomontanus constructed the Ephemerides which made the voyage of Columbus possible; Kepler carried out his work by means of the Hakemite tables of Ibn Yunis; Vesalius translated Al-Râzi. The spirit of science passed through the period of the Classical Renaissance without being influenced by it, and developed in seclusion, independently of classicising influences.

Science is the most momentous contribution of Arab civilisation to the modern world, but its fruits were slow in ripening. Not until long after Moorish culture had sunk back into darkness did the giant to which it had given birth rise in his might. It was not science which brought Europe back to life. Other and manifold influences from the civilisation of Islam communicated to it the first glow of a new vitality.

X

THE REBIRTH OF EUROPE

THE industrial and commercial activity of the East, of Moorish Spain and Sicily, created European commerce and manufactures. These gave rise to the wealth and power of the merchant classes and the commercial cities; the Burgher communities became strong enough to defy the feudal powers, and the new force of free republics and communes overthrew the tyranny and lawlessness of the barons. Thus, like culture, political liberty and organisation came to Europe with bales of goods from the Levant. Until trade and industry had developed, until burghers had waxed substantial through eastern traffic there were no communes, there were hardly cities. The coast towns of Catalonia and Provence were the first to rise to life and importance through trade with the Arabs. Free and autonomous republics were established at Marseille, Arles, Nice. Some notion of the source whence from earliest days that wealth had grown may be gathered from the account given by Theodulf, Bishop of Orleans, of a journey to the South of France as one of Charlemagne's *missi dominici*. On his arrival at Marseille, he says, "the people came to us in crowds, men, woman, children, old men, loaded with presents, persuaded that they had only to offer them to us in order to obtain their wishes. . . . One offered crystals and Orient pearls, . . . another brought a heap of gold pieces on which shone Arabic sentences and characters . . . another said, 'I have cloths which come from the Saracens and it is not possible to see aught more richly coloured or more delicately and better wrought' . . . another showed me hides of leather from Cordova, some white as snow, others red . . . another offered me carpets." [1]

The cities of Southern Italy next followed. Amalfi, Salerno, Naples and Gaeta rose gradually to wealth and freedom through commerce with their Muslim neighbours of Sicily, and extended their connections in conjunction with Arab traders to Africa and Syria. The Emperor Ludwig II accused Naples of being as Muhâmmadan as Palermo. Amalfi and the first Italian free cities of Southern Italy entered into alliance with the Muslims of Sicily (875) and actually assisted them when they advanced to the gates of Rome, defying the excommunications of Pope John VIII. When a crusade was moved against Islam, they refused to bear arms against the people who had helped them to wealth and greatness. Pisa, Genoa, and Venice used the opportunity to outreach Amalfi and Naples. Pisa, which the chronicle of Donizo describes in 1114 as "unclean with" swarming Saracens, "Turks, Libyans and Chaldæans," who possessed a whole quarter of the city, known as Kinsica,[2] rose, like Genoa, to importance by trade with Saracenic Sardinia. Such was the destitute condition of Europe prior to the development of that commerce, that, having neither native products nor money to exchange for the wares of the Arabs, the first Italian merchant-adventurers kidnapped the children of neighbouring villages, and paid for their goods with cargoes of human flesh. Genoa and Pisa joined forces to conquer Sardinia, which produced the finest wool, that of England excepted; the wool-trade passed thence to Lucca, where the art of weaving had

[1] *Mon. Germ. Hist., Poet. Lat.* I. 499.
[2] Muratori, *Ant. Med. Aev., diss.* 30.

been brought from Palermo, and whence, after the sack of the town by Uguccione della Faggiola, the master-weavers established themselves in Florence. Thus was laid the foundation of that Florentine wealth and greatness, which before long made the Tuscan merchant-princes the bankers of Europe.

The Arabs opened up the land-routes to India, to China, Malacca, and Timbuctoo, the emporium of Central African trade; and sent their caravans to the rich lands beyond the Sahara long before the Portuguese doubled Cape Verde. They held the monopoly of the sea-routes to India, and the Emosaïds founded along the eastern coast of Africa a line of trading colonies from the Sudan coast and Socotra to Mombaza, Mozambique, Zanzibar and Madagascar.

They improved the art of shipbuilding, taught Mediterranean seamen to construct lighter sailing-ships or caravels *(gâraf)*, to caulk their boats with tar—still known in Romance languages by the Arabic name of *gatrân* (Fr. *goudron*, It. *caltrame*)—to handle sails and cables (Ar. *hábl*). Moorish merchants established their *fûndaks* in the Christian ports, plied between the great seaports of Andalusia, Valencia, Almeria, and Malaga to those of Provence and the South of France, brought their wares to the markets of Montpellier and Narbonne. Arab *dinàrs* are to this day found as far north as the shores of the North Sea and the Baltic in greater abundance than Roman coins or Greek besants. The Moors introduced the system of bills of exchange, and the commerce of the Mediterranean was regulated by the institution of sea-consuls first adopted at Barcelona.

The fine linens, the cottons, the silks, the delicate and gorgeous fabrics of the Saracenic world, satins and sarcenets, Persian taffetas, damasks from Damascus, baudekin from Baghdad, muslin from Mosul, gauzes from

Gaza, grenadines from Granada, moirés, crêpes and chiffons (not 'rag,' but diaphanous *chiff* from Tripoli), chamlets, karsies, and radzimirs, created a demand for fine raiment among the coarsely clad populations of Europe. In the Nibelung lay Krimhild anachronicly adorns herself with

"Die arâbischen sîden wîz alsô der snê,
unde von Zazamanc der gruenen sô der klê . . .
von Marrock dem lande und ouch von Libîan
die aller besten sîden die ie mêr gewan."[1]

The looms of Syria and Spain—sixteen thousand were at work in Seville alone, and a hundred and thirty thousand silk-workers were employed at Cordova—wove the materials for the garments of nobles and the sacramental vestments of Christian prelates; and it was not an uncommon spectacle to see a bishop celebrating mass with an *'âyat* of the Kurân elegantly embroidered on his chasuble. The women of Europe learnt to wear an Arab *kamis* (chemise) and *jubba* (jupe, jupon). The warriors of Christendom were eager to wield blades forged in Damascus, Almeria, or Toledo, and to ride in Cordovan saddles. The sugar-cane was introduced and Europeans first tasted confectioneries, sweetmeats and sorbets. By and by the manufactures of the East were introduced and imitated in Christian Europe. Silk-looms were established in Norman Sicily. Venice copied with the aid of native craftsmen the glassware of Antioch; Lyons the damasks, Paris the 'tapis sarrasins,' and Rheims the linen of Syria. The rich dyes of the East were brought to Bruges, where they were used to prepare English wool for the market. The wares of Spain shipped from Majorca led to the establishment of Italian factories for the manufac-

[1] "The Arabian silks white as snow, and those from Zazaman green as the clover leaf . . . from the land of Morocco and also from Lebanon, the best silks that were ever won."

ture of 'majolica.' Sugar factories were transferred from Sicily to Italy, and from Spain to the South of France.

The Arabs introduced into Europe three inventions, each of which was to bring about a world-transforming revolution: the mariner's compass which was to expand Europe to the ends of the earth; gunpowder which was to bring to an end the supremacy of the armoured knight; and paper which prepared the way for the printing-press. The revolution effected by the introduction of paper was scarcely less important than that brought about by printing. The extreme scarcity of books was in a large measure due to the scarcity of parchment; the texts of ancient manuscripts were erased again and again to supply materials for writing missals and legends of saints, so that scarcely a manuscript older than the eleventh century survives today. The price of books was consequently prohibitive; a Countess of Anjou paid two hundred sheep and five measures each of wheat, rye, and millet for a book of homilies; and as late as the reign of Louis XI, when that king wished to borrow the medical works of Al-Râzi from the library of Paris University, he deposited in pledge a quantity of plate, and was moreover obliged to procure a nobleman to join with him as surety in a deed binding him to restore the book. The Arabs first adopted the manufacture of paper from silk as practised in China; and silk paper was manufactured at Samarkand and Bokhara. For silk they at first substituted cotton, (Damasc paper), and later linen. The linen-paper industry was long a monopoly of Xativa, near Valencia, whence it was introduced into Catalonia and Provence, and later to Treviso and Padua.[1]

The first parts of Europe to emerge from barbarism

[1] **We call paper by the name of Egyptian papyrus, but we measure it by reams (Ar. *razma* = a parcel).**

were those most directly under the influence of Moorish culture: the Spanish Marches of Catalonia, Provence, and Sicily.

It is an entirely erroneous conception which pictures the Moorish and Christian States of Spain as divided by intolerant hatred and incessant warfare. Spanish fanaticism is a later growth which owed its introduction mainly to foreigners. To those who lived in contact with the civilisation of Islam it was hardly possible to entertain the conceptions fostered among remoter populations by their priests, who represented the abhorred 'infidel' as savage fiends addicted to the worship of a hideous idol called Mahom. The gradual encroachment of the Spanish kingdoms over the Moorish dominions was as much the fruit of Muslim dissensions as of the ardour of the attack, and was brought about by crafty alliances with ambitious Moorish princes as much as by the sword. Friendly relations and intimate intercourse were the rule, not the exception. Since the days of Roncesvalles, when Moors and Christians had together defeated the marauding army of Charlemagne who, having crossed the Pyrenees at the invitation of Suleimân al-Arabî, a rebel against the first 'Abd-al-Rahman, was returning laden with Christian booty and without having fought a Moor, Christians and Moors had constantly fought side by side and lent each other support in their complex internecine quarrels. Spanish princes marched at the head of Moorish troops lent to them by a Muslim ally to recover their domains, Moorish Emirs led Christian troops against their rivals. Companies of soldiers of fortune both Christian and Muslim hired themselves out to masters of either religion. The most brilliant of Moorish generals, Al-Mansûr, won his victories, and sacked the shrine of Compostella, with Christian troops. The famous Rodrigo Diez de Bivar, transformed by legend into the doughty champion of the faith, was a *condottiere* who fought at least as often on the side of the Moors as on that of the Catholics, remained seven years in the service of the Emir of Saragossa, looted churches with as much gusto as mosques, usually dressed in Moorish costume, put his faith in a Moorish bodyguard, and is known to fame by the Arabic appellation of the Cid. It is no mere fiction, like the transmutation of the ignominious expedition of Charlemagne in Spain into an heroic epic, and its adornments with the magicians, knight-errants, dwarfs, dragons and enchanted palaces of Arabian romance, but an accurate tradition which in the tales and poems of chivalry represents Christian and Moorish knights as freely consorting on friendly terms, joining together in jousts and tournaments and entertaining each other as honoured guests. Spanish and Moorish princes and their retinues of men of science and minstrels constantly resided at each other's courts. Christian rulers entrusted the education of their sons to Arabian tutors; and when afflicted with some obstinate disorder betook themselves to Cordova to consult the most eminent physicians. Even between Christian ecclesiastics and Moorish princes there was friendly intercourse; the translation of the Arab Almanack by Bishop Harib, and a history of the Franks written in Arabic by Bishop Gobmar of Gerona, were dedicated to Khalîf Hakim. Intermarriage, common among the people, was not infrequent among the nobility, and even King Alfonso V of Leon gave his sister in marriage to Muhâmmad, King of Toledo, and Alfonso VI married Princess Zayda, the daughter of Ibn Abet, King of Seville. Al-Mansûr married Teresa the daughter of Bermudo II, who, with the consent of her family, adopted her husband's faith. Moorish princes who acknowledged the suzerainty of the King of Castile sat in the Spanish Cortes.

The lustre of Moorish elegance circulated unimpeded throughout the peninsula and the south of France. A shifting population of Mozarabians (Muslim Spaniards) and Jews passed continually from Andalusia to Catalonia and Languedoc. The papal legate charged the Counts of Provence with harbouring "Moors, Jews, and all manner of infidels." Provence, where the Moors had dwelt nearly two hundred years, became united to the Spanish March, where the same language was spoken, when Raymond Berenger, Count of Barcelona, married Douce, the daughter of Gilbert of Gévaudan, the last scion of the Counts of Provence. There and then it was that the first efflorescence of European culture and elegance, which was so tragically blotted out in blood in the ghastly Albigensian Crusade, blossomed forth under the stimulus of Moorish civilisation.

Rude, illiterate, unwashed robber-barons gave place to men who delighted in poetry and music, and foregathered in tournaments of song. Loose woollen gowns and leather jerkins were exchanged for close-fitting braided pourpoints, first known as *gipons* (Ar. *jubba*) and mantles of shimmering silk, the fashion for which gradually extended to Northern Europe. Women joined as equals, as in Moorish Spain, in the intellectual interests and artistic tastes of men. They discarded nun-like habits for fine apparel and jewels, developed a waist and rustled silken trains; instead of wearing their hair in long plaits they did it up elegantly, a change which came to be known in the North as 'cheveux à la Provençal'; they wore embroidered and jewelled Persian tiaras of *cendal* (Ar. *candal*), which in the fourteenth century were exchanged for the sugar-loaf and horned head-dresses known as 'bonnets à la Syrienne.' An Arab author, Ibn Jobaìr, thus describes the appearance of the women of the period: "They went forth clad in robes of silk the colour of gold, wrapped in elegant mantles, covered with many-coloured veils, shod with gilt shoes, laden with collars, adorned with kohl and perfumed with attar, exactly in the costume of our Muslim ladies." Such dalliance did not fail to call forth the shrill denunciations of monks who, elsewhere supreme arbiters of life, slunk away in impotence before the indifference of the people and the *sirventes* of the poets. Song and music, which filled the rose-gardens of Andalusia, where every court rang with the sound of romances and quatrains, where poets and musicians formed part of the retinue of every Moorish prince and every Emir, where skill in versification was counted an indispensable accomplishment of every knight and every lady, spread to the adjacent lands of Castile, Catalonia and Provence. Stringed musical instruments, which are throughout the Middle Ages spoken of as 'mauresques,' were first introduced into Europe, the lute or laud (Ar. *al 'ud*), the viol or violin, known at first as rubeb (Ar. *rabab*), the psaltery (Ar. *santyr*), ancestor of the piano, the zither, the tabor, and the guitar (Ar. *kuitra*).

To what degree the Catalonian and Provençal poetry which was sung to the accompaniment of that Moorish music was moulded by that of Arab Spain, is the subject of controversy among specialist scholars. What measure of prejudice may enter into the conclusions of those who pronounce the literature of Provence to have been "an extraordinary instance of spontaneous growth," may pardonably be suspected when the manner in which every other contribution of Arab culture has been treated by European scholarship is borne in mind. There was a popular vernacular poetry in Provence as everywhere else, but only there did a courtly fashion for verse appear, distinct from popular song, and court-singers identical in function with the *ruwâh* of Moorish courts. Rhyme of a rude kind had previously been used in monkish doggerel, but its elaborate pattern in Troubadour song, the assonant repetition of the same word in alternate lines, the research of 'difficult rhymes,' the *tornada* or *envoi* (invariably used in the *ghazal*), are traits of Arabic poetry, and of the Spanish school in particular, which invented the *muwashâh* and *zajâl* stanzas, and was as partial to *hûshi,* or learned obscurity, as Guirant de Bornelh and so many Troubadours to the *trobar clus.* More even than its technical features, the new song reflected the somewhat euphuistic sentiment, the conventionalised erotics of Arabo-Persian poetry; and Bernard de Ventadour and his fellow-poets who lament "*De la donha me dezesper,*" were, like their Andalusian brethren, *'sarî al-ghawâni,'* 'victims of the fair.'

Spanish and Provençal poetry is the birth-song of European literatures, awakening poetic echoes throughout Europe, from the Minnesingers of Germany to pre-Dantesque Italy, calling the 'vulgar tongues' of the new Europe to literary life. The earlier Italian singers, Malaspina, Zorgi, Sordello, Lanfranc Cigala, used the language as well as the prosody and style of the Provençal Troubadours. It was in Sicily at the Saracenised court of Frederick II, that the first Italian lyrics were produced in the native tongue—*il dolce stil nuovo* of Guido delle Colonne, Jacopo Lentini and Pier delle Vigne. Dante hesitated long whether he should write his great poem in Latin; his decision was determined by his admiration for the achievements of Provençal song, and from them his language, form and treatment were derived. Without the Spanish Moors no Troubadours, without the Troubadours no Dante.

It was the conquest of Muslim Sicily and of Southern Italy by Norman mercenaries which moved William the Bastard to that of England. When after a struggle of thirty years the Muslim kingdom and its capital of Palermo, which rivalled Cordova itself in splendour and culture, at length submitted to the Hauteville adventurers, it was only on condition of being granted full and equal rights and liberties; and so willingly were the terms carried out in letter and spirit, that Roger, the first King of the Two Sicilies, and his successors were, not without good ground, accused of being more Muslim than Christian. Sicily down to the last Hohenstaufen rulers remained a centre of Muslim culture and became the focus of awakening civilisation. It was—strange irony of fate! —by Muslim troops that Pope Hildebrand was rescued from Castle S. Angelo when Henry IV sought to wipe out the shame of Canossa. Not only were the troops, the religion, and to a large extent, the administration of the Muslim retained under the Normans and Suabians, but the posts of honour and command remained in Moorish hands. Their *amyr al-bahr* became in latinised form *ammirati,* or *admirals;* their *diwâns,* or government offices, became *dohanas* or *douanes*. Sicilian administration served as a model to Europe. The English fiscal system, like the name which it bears today, the Exchequer, was derived from Muslim Sicily, whence Thomas Brun, who served as *Khaid* under Roger II, introduced it when he transferred his services to our Henry II. Between Norman England and Norman Sicily there was continuous intercourse through which many elements of Muslim culture came directly to distant Britain. Its far-reaching civilising influence over barbaric Europe reached its height when the kingdom passed into the hands of the great Italian-born Emperor Frederick II, whose radiant figure filled the Middle Ages with wonder. If the name of any European sovereign deserves to be specially associated with the redemption of Christendom from barbarism and ignorance, it is not that of Charlemagne, the travesty of whom in the character of a civiliser is a fulsome patriotic and ecclesiastical fiction, but that of the enlightened and enthusiastic ruler who adopted Saracenic civilisation and did more than any other sovereign to stimulate its diffusion.

His brilliant court where, under the stalactite roofs of Moorish halls, and amid Oriental gardens adorned with murmuring fountains, and aviaries filled with rare birds, and menageries of strange animals, the gifts of friendly Sultans, the professors of Arabian science foregathered as honoured guests, and discussed mathematical problems and questions of natural history; where troubadours from Provence and Moorish minstrels sang to the music of lutes and tabors, and inspired the first-fruits of Italian poetry; that wonder court, the seat of learning, refinement and beauty, so utterly contrasting with the gloomy, rush-littered halls of other European potentates, which swarmed with monks and vermin, ignorance and superstition, was an object of astonishment and malicious rage. Among the accusations and denunciations that were hurled against Frederick, it was alleged with horror that he indulged in a daily bath—even on Sundays. He established universities in Naples, Messina, Padua, renovated the old Byzantine medical school of Salerno in accordance with the advances of Arab medicine; encouraged by his patronage Plato of Tivoli and Leonardo Fibonacci, the founders of European mathematics; gathered Jewish and Arab scholars to undertake translations of every procurable Arabic book; sent his friend Michael Scot to Cordova to obtain the latest work of Averroes, and distributed copies to every existing school.

The course, not only of political history, but of European development and culture would doubtless have been very different had he, as was his dream, united Europe under a new empire with its capital in Italy. But the opposing forces of ecclesiastical power were as yet too strong. The popes moved heaven and earth against the Hohenstaufen Emperor. Gregory IX stirred the Lombard cities to revolt, and secured their loyalty by setting up the Inquisition in their midst, burning a few hundred of their citizens—*pour encourager les autres.* Mendicant monks penetrated into the very palace of the Emperor, threatened and bribed his closest friends, and thrust daggers and poison into their hands.

The Church dreaded, no less than a united Italy and the loss of its temporal dominions, the new intellectual light which was being flashed across the darkness of Europe. Gregory declared Frederick to be the Antichrist. "That pestilent king," wrote the Pope, "affirms that the world has been deceived by three impostors, Moses, Jesus and Mahomet. He further dares to utter lies to the extent of saying that none but fools can believe that the all-powerful Creator of the world was born of a virgin. He maintains the heresy that no man can be born without the concourse of a man and a woman. And he adds to those blasphemies that what is proved by the laws of things, and natural reason, is alone worthy of belief." The supporters of the Emperor throughout Italy were regarded as infidels, the name of Ghibelline was synonymous with 'epicurean,' the current designation of the time for philosophic unbelievers; and when Guido Cavalcanti walked through the streets of Florence, absorbed in thought, the populace, Boccaccio tells us, whispered that "he was thinking out arguments to prove that there is no God." The interdicts, the anathemas, the repeated excommunications of the Church, proved a more formidable weapon than even the swords of the Guelphs. Vanquished, baffled, betrayed, harassed, disheartened, embittered by long years of strife and daily peril, the Emperor craved for terms from his implacable foe. He agreed to depart from Italy on a crusade to Palestine; and betaking himself to Jerusalem, that strangest of crusaders was there received as an honoured friend by the Sultan Melik al-Kamîl. As he walked arm in arm with the noble and learned Melik on the terrace of the mosque of 'Omar, discoursing of the latest advances in his beloved mathematical sciences, and of the folly of men who like darkness rather than light, he cast a scornful glance on the fanatical crowds that crawled on their knees before the gates of the Holy Sepulchre, and exclaimed, like Philip Augustus, "Happy Sultan who knows no pope!" As a token of his regard, Melik presented him with a marvellous clock, in the form of a large domed tent, in which the sun and moon were moved by mechanism, and made to rise and set, showing the hours.

Christian and Saracen mingled their tears when the great Hohenstaufen *'che fu d'amor si degno'* was laid in the crypt of Monreale, leaving behind him the foundations of a power greater and more mighty than any empire he had dreamed of, a power that was one day to avenge him, and break the tyranny of pope and priest like a reed.

A cause more immediate in its effects than physical science and deeper than romantic and poetical literature aroused the European mind from its lethargy. It has not in general been sufficiently emphasised that one of the chief agencies by which the dead hand of theological dogma was shaken off, was theology itself. "The naïve mysticism and emotional inconsistency of a religious creed," as Al-Ghazali remarked, "cannot be brought to an intellectual focus without being dispelled." Already in the ninth and tenth centuries there were sporadic signs of insubordination in Christendom. In England and Ireland, partly owing to the tradition established by Theodore, an Eastern monk with an ardent taste for literature, who, under Pope Valerian, had been appointed to the see of Canterbury, partly in consequence of the protection from the Gregorian obscurantism of the central Church government, afforded by isolation and remoteness, the status of culture among the monks of the Benedictine order and of St. Columba was distinctly higher than on the Continent. Egbert, Bede, Alcuin are examples of that pre-eminence. Not that it amounted to much; but by comparison with the almost complete illiteracy of other countries, the taste of the English, and, above all, of the Irish monks for Latin authors, and even an occasional, though rare, acquaintance with Greek, placed them upon a higher level. The consequences were not long in showing themselves in reading Scripture and the Fathers, they dared to exercise their mind. The Irish monks are spoken of as "*sophia clari,*" and a chronicler describes the disturbing inroads of those herds of philosophers—"*philosophorum greges*"—across the stormy sea. St. Boniface, while engaged in Christianising Germany, encountered nothing but trouble with his Irish assistants. One Brother Vergil had the assurance to speak of 'antipodes'; Father Clement flatly scorned the authority of Jerome, Augustine, and Gregory, and even that of the Canon, and aired views about marriage with a deceased wife's sister, and the marriage of bishops, which made one's hair stand on end. Father Macarius was no better than a pantheist, and he set the devil loose in the monastery of Corbie, whence presently Father Ratramn came forth denying the miracle of the Eucharist. But the boldest and greatest of those Irish disturbers of the Faith was John Erigena, a superior man, who had travelled in the East and knew Greek, and who with great power and learning endorsed Ratramn's view of the mass, accounting it a mere symbol, and expressed purely pantheistic views. There was no one in that day capable of even appreciating the magnitude of his heresies, much less of making any show of argumentative fight against the terrible Irishman. Theology merely consisted in the submissive reading of the Scriptures and the Latin Fathers, and had no weapon but their authority. The eucharistic heresy smouldered for over a century in the Benedictine monasteries until it was—it was hoped—adequately laid at rest by Archbishop Anselm of Canterbury. But that hope was cruelly shattered by Roscellin, who hanselled the new weapon of Aristotelian logic lately come from Spain in his fierce onslaught upon Anselm. One of the disciples of Roscellin was the great Peter Abélard, who with impassioned eloquence proclaimed not only that reason had a right to examine all authority, but that it was the supreme and sole authority.

In what measure the earlier disputes of 'pre-scholastic scholasticism' were influenced by Muslim thought, we have little means of knowing with accuracy. The first systematic body of heretical doctrine within the Roman Church which resulted in widespread theological controversy, arose in Muslim Spain, and originated in the ninth century with Bishop Elipandus of Toledo, who infected with the Adoptionist heresy the clergy of the South of France. Muhâmmadan philosophy and theology had, we know, been carried to the Benedictine monasteries through the Jews, and the metropolitan house of Monte Cassino; and Alvaro of Cordova tells us that many Christions in the ninth century "studied the Muhâmmadan theologians and philosophers," not always, he adds significantly, "with a view to refuting them." Peter the Venerable, the Abbot of Cluny, with whom Abélard took refuge after his condemnation by the Council of Sens, lamented that, during his stay in Spain, he had seen troops of students from France, Germany, England, flocking to the Moorish seats of learning. In order to do something to stem the tide, he had the Kurân translated into Latin, naïvely remarking that the text of such 'inspired' books constitutes their most effectual refutation. The exact parallelism between Muslim and Christian theological controversy is too close to be accounted for by similarity of situations, and the coincidences are too fundamental and numerous to be accepted as no more than coincidences. A single metaphysical quibble raised in the *Isagogue* of Porphyry concerning 'universals' supplied the cardinal formula about which the whole edifice of controversial thought both in Islam and Christendom was raised. The same questions, the same issues which occupied the theological schools of Damascus, were after an interval of a century repeated in identical terms in those of Paris.

The culture of the courts of Damascus and Baghdad had been eyed askance by the zealots of Islam; and when Al-Mamûn established his famous school of translators, the Dâr al-Hikmet or 'Home of Science,' he had to placate the pietist conscience by assurances that it was merely a college of physicians. To the Muslim faithful and their 'Ulama, the whole cultural movement remained from first to last a thing accursed; Harûn and Al-Mamûn had sold their souls; and in Moorish Spain there were constant outbursts of fanatic zeal in which the books of science were consigned to the flames. The attitude of religious ardour towards intellectual culture was the same in the Muslim as in the Christian world. Only there was this difference, that in the former it was the intellectuals and heretics who for a time held the whip-hand of power; the pious had perforce to rest content with sour looks and suppressed growls, and to wait patiently until the Turk, the Berber, and the Spaniard came to their assistance, and plunged Islam back into the purity of faith and the darkness and ignorance of barbarism. If, while in the tenth century European aspirants to knowledge sought the schools of the learned Moors, in the twentieth century anthropologists journey to Morocco to study the ways of primitive barbarism, it is because in the two worlds the contest between light and darkness had opposite issues. In the one dogma was defeated by rational thought, in the other it prevailed over it.

Although the intellectual energy of the Arabs employed itself by preference with objective mathematical and scientific pursuits, it was inevitable that it should be applied to the interpretation of religion. From their Nestorian teachers and from Galen they derived a profound veneration for Aristotle, whose orderly and encyclopedic cast of mind chimed with their disposition. He was *'al-elahi,'* the 'divine' Aristotle, *the* philosopher, and pilgrimages were made to his supposed tomb in Palermo as to the shrine of a saint. The Arabs applied his terminology, metaphysical ideas and classification, and logical method to the endeavour to make more definite and precise, and reduce to a rational order, the dogmas of their religion. A maze-like structure arose out of the subtle disputations of theology, *al-katan,* the 'science of the Word.' And intellectual thought set about the endless task of 'reconciling' religious dogma and rational thought. Al-Farabi paraphrased Aristotle, enumerated the principles of 'being,' elaborated the doctrine of the double aspects of the intellect and the question of universals. Ibn Sina sought, upon the basis of Farabi's work, to spiritualise the naturalism of Aristotle by a free admixture of mystic Neo-Platonism derived from Jewish and Alexandrian sources. Others rationalised the mysteries of the faith into pantheism; and Ibn Roschd (Averroes), the last of the Arabic philosophers, proclaimed the unity of the intellect, and put forth the fatal solution of 'double truth,' that a thing may be true in theology and false in science—or, as Professor Bury has aptly expressed it, that a thing may be true in the kitchen but false in the drawing-room.

The whole logomachy passed bodily into Christendom.

The catchwords, disputes, vexed questions, methods, systems, conceptions, heresies, apologetics and irenics, were transferred from the mosques to the Sorbonne. The deification of Aristotle, introduced by the Arabs, together with his works, which had previously only been known in meagre fragments in Cassiodorus, Capella, and Boethius, stood at first for the assertion of the rights of reason. The reading of his works, and of the Arabian commentaries, was in Paris forbidden.

It soon, however, became apparent to the defenders of orthodoxy that their original principle—that the methods of rational thought must not be applied to religious dogma—condemned them to an unequal fight. They accordingly abandoned it, and reversed their policy. It was determined to fight intellectual insubordination with its own weapons, to enlist Aristotle in the cause of faith. The canonisation of Aristotle was the first of the long series of surrenders of theology to rational thought. The Dominicans devoted themselves to the task of harmonising 'the philosopher' with religion. It had already been performed for them. Albertus Magnus, and Thomas Àquinas, both proficient in Arabic literature—the former was no less famous as an alchemist than as a theologian, and the latter had been a pupil in Frederick II's university of Naples—reproduced the arguments, formulas, and methods of Ibn Sina and his predecessors in the 'reconciliation of reason and religion,' Al-Farabi and Al-Kindi.[1] They were met by their antagonists with the bolder logic of "the impious and thrice-accursed Averroes," (Erasmus).

The banners under which the battles of intellectual progress have been fought have been subject to strange mutations. The same Muslim infidel, Ibn Sina, furnished

[1] "Albertus Magnus owes everything to Avicenna; St. Thomas, as philosopher, owes a great deal to Averroes." Renan.

both the weft of the Tomistic, or official philosophy of the Catholic Church, and the text-book of the medical schools; nurtured the Vatican and the Holy Office with one hand, and Galileo with the other. We are accustomed to think of Aristotelian authority and of 'the schools' as the foes against which the European intellect had to win its victory. When science and modern thought at last unfolded their wings with Galileo and Descartes, it was by the overthrow of Aristotle and his authority that that first liberation was marked. But at an earlier stage it was those same authorities which the Arabs had transmitted to Europe, it was that very Aristotle, which had stood for intellectual freedom, for reason against obscurantism and mysticism. Aristotle was the shield under which in the universities and the medical schools, thought and science were brooding and maturing. When the humanists of the Renaissance, when Petrarch, when Erasmus inveighed against Aristotle and Averroes, it was not dogmatism or authority which roused their ire, but science, 'impiety,' 'materialism.' They were occupying the same position as the opponents of Copernicus, of Darwin, of that science whose chrysalis was wrapped in the 'authorities' of the Arabs.

Scholasticism, like Greek Sophism, is one of those vanquished things whose names have been branded by the triumph of their opponents. Nevertheless those argumentative contests which seem to us absurd and unintelligible, were the first stirrings of the mind in Europe after the death-like trance and Cimmerian darkness that went before. In the hair-splitting subtleties and grotesque disputes of the schools, the weapons were tempered that were to arm the human mind for the battles of its liberation and triumph. "To the Schoolmen," J. S. Mill rightly observes, "we owe whatever accuracy of thought, and lucidity of logic, we can boast." We may laugh at some of the problems on which the scholastic disputants exercised their wit—"whether divine essence engendered the Father, or was engendered by the Father; whether attributes or substance determine persons" (Peter Lombard), or "whether the Holy Ghost appeared as a real dove; whether Adam and Eve had navels; whether Christ took any clothes with him to heaven" (Thomas Aquinas);[1] but the laugh would not be altogether on our side if some of the paralogisms which sometimes pass today as arguments with untrained and slovenly thinkers, could be submitted to the mediæval worshippers of Aristotle. 'Formal logic' is pedantic, and the syllogism is not the sum of rational method; but they have supplied a very beneficent and useful training. And it is by passing through the mill of scholasticism that the European mind has acquired that appreciation of accuracy, that habit of precision, that care in the use and definition of words, that protective immunity against plausible fallacies, that indisposition to being put off with irrelevant and lofty phrases, which have been its strength, and to which it owes its growth and achievements.

And it was that unflinching application of logic which in the days of Roscellin and Abélard had struck terror in the champions of dogma and tradition, which ultimately shook off their intellectual tyranny, in spite of their attempt to press the two-edged weapon into their own defence; and which produced Roger Bacon and William of Occam, who dealt the death-blow to the phantasms of dogmatic abstraction, and pointed to the methods of accurate observation, enquiry, experiment, and mathematical analysis, introduced into the world by Arabian science, as the basis of rational judgment and knowledge.

By the end of the thirteenth century, among the propositions which the Paris Sorbonne was called upon to

[1] It is, of course, on the orthodox or "realist" side of scholasticism that such speculative gems are to be met.

censure, we find the following: "The discourses of theologians are founded on fables"; "True knowledge is made impossible by theology"; "The Christian religion is an obstacle to education."

The spell which has held the human mind captive during the Dark Ages was broken forever.

XI

THE SOI-DISANT RENAISSANCE

It was in the first three centuries of the present millennium that the rebirth of Europe took place. The term 'Renaissance' applied to the Italian and Italianate culture of the fifteenth and sixteenth centuries is a misnomer stamped upon current notions by the traditions of that culture itself. The greater splendour of European culture at that epoch was the outspreading of overblown blossoms which the previous centuries had called to life and unfolded. Its freer and more fertile vitality was not the outcome of humanistic culture, but of a momentous new agency: the printing-press.

Human evolution as a whole has three times been raised to new planes of power by the development of new agencies for the dissemination and perpetuation of thought: by the development of speech, the invention of writing, and that of printing. Speech raised humanity above the brute world; writing made civilised culture possible, and separates history from pre-history as speech separates humanity from animality; printing brought into existence the modern age. Each step was an extension of the nervous system of humanity, a stage in the transference of evolutionary development from the individual to the race. Printing afforded for the first time a medium for the dissemination of thought which could not be altogether silenced and suppressed. Speech can be effectively silenced; the written manuscript, limited in its circulation to a narrow coterie uniform in tradition, could never serve the purpose of unfettered criticism. No radical challenge of established opinion has ever been set down in the manuscript age. But no censorship can effectively suppress the printed book. The press gave to independent thought a freedom which it had never before enjoyed. To that new power, not to the revival of ancient literature or to any specific form of culture, the enhanced activity of the period of print was due.

The antecedent impulse which had aroused Europe in the twelfth and thirteenth centuries, and had broken the spell of authority and the power of absolutism, supplied the momentum of renewed growth. The paramount part of Arab culture in bringing about that awakening, on which I have dwelt at some length—proportionate to the grossness and insistence of traditional misrepresentation—it would be difficult to overestimate. The fruits which that influence bore in Europe were, however, of a quality which could never have been attained by the Oriental mind. Had the culture of the Islamic world not succumbed to fanaticism, it is doubtful whether it would have pursued a career of prolonged growth. Europe, making use of what it had acquired from Islam, outstripped it, as Greece had surpassed the Oriental cultures whence hers derived. Arabised knowledge, in passing into Europe, acquired a new virtue which vitalised and fertilised it. There was in the European mind, however barbaric, a quality which no Oriental culture can possess. That quality is not an intangible and undefinable racial mystery; it is a quite definite fact. The European mind owes it to its geniture and parentage from the clear discursive spirit of Greece. It differs from the East because it has Greece and Rome at its back. Nothing could obliterate that difference. The mediæval Church, despite its obscurantism and tyranny, and its Oriental religion, could not obliterate it; it, too, derived from Greece and Rome. Europe has grown and remained vital because it issued out of that 'antiquity,' which was the civilisation of the Greek mind; and even in the darkness of degradation and the depth of ruin, the dust of that civilisation preserved, however faintly, some element of its intrinsic Hellenic quality.

'Renaissance' humanism was in its form representative of that paramount fact. I say 'representative,' no more; for it neither initiated, nor determined, nor in any essential degree established its action. Roman, and subsequently Greek literature, were sought and cherished before the rise of Italian humanism and the advent of Greek refugees. The patriotic enthusiasm which looked back upon the only national literature, the only great European literature, then existing, and saw in its 'revival' and cultivation the only issue out of the dark sterility of the times, existed in Italy before Petrarch. Vilgardus of Ravenna early in the twelfth century paid to the Latin poets the same extravagant and superstitious worship as the humanist idolaters of the Renaissance. Those studies extended in the same measure as all other intellectual activities. But that quality and influence of which I have just spoken, is in truth something deeper and more subtle than any effect of book study. It lies in the very genesis and constitution of Europe, in its language, its forms of thought, its memory, its whole mentality. Study of ancient literature is but a small and accessory part of it.

The humanism of the Renaissance gave a new impetus to the perusal of the only secular literature then existing, and thus helped to establish the dominion of secular thought in the modern world. The republished works of Greece and Rome did not bring life and power by virtue of their specific contents, by virtue of any particular contribution to knowledge or ideas, of any concrete 'wisdom,' or any forgotten and regenerating inspiration which they transmitted, but by helping, in virtue of their secular character, to sever the bonds which had held the human mind fettered in the *bolgia* of ecclesiastical thought.

But everything that can ungrudgingly be set to the credit of 'Renaissance' humanism is more than counter-weighed by influences the most baneful and pernicious, which it exercised on the development of Europe.

"It may be doubted," justly remarks an historian,[1] "whether the human mind has gained by ceasing to develop along the path upon which it has been set during the Middle Ages, and by suffering that revolution which is called the 'Renaissance.'" While it crowned the antecedent growth of the twelfth and thirteenth centuries, the Italian Renaissance was in reality a phase and manifestation of essential decay. It was in intrinsic respects as much a set-back and a falling off, as the rule of the petty usurpers whose aulic influence fostered the literary vendors of flattery and 'immortality' was a falling off from the vitality and spirit of the communes and republics they smothered. Availing itself of the powers which a healthier and more creative age had developed, it wasted and prostituted them and remained essentially sterile.

The literature and thought of Greece and Rome are among the greatest, most glorious achievements of humanity. But Renaissance humanism and its far-reaching effects afford a conspicuous illustration of the truth that no matter how excellent a thing may be in itself, its influence is rendered wholly pernicious from the moment that it becomes an object of idolatry, and is invested with a superstitious authority. Instead of being vitalising and inspiring it becomes deadly and paralysing. The 'ancients' and what was conceived by the humanists to be ancient taste were by them set up as idols. Lamps were kept alight before the bust of Plato; Alfonso of Naples sent Beccadelli to Padua to beg for an arm-bone of Livy. The cult

[1] Wahl, in Lavisse et Rambaud, *Hist. Générale.*

of the 'antique' became a delirious and paralysing superstition. A spirit of intellectual parasitism more abject than that of the schoolmen for the *ipsissima verba* of Aristotle, extended a canonical authority to all the newly consecrated 'classics.' Plato, or rather a mystic farrago of Neo-Platonism, supplanted Aristotelian authority. So completely was intellect dulled by slavish deference that it was scarcely capable of discerning the incompatibilities between the authorities it worshipped. Intellectual views, theories, ideas, thoughts, information, were indeed of little or no concern to the pedants of Italian humanism. They cared for none of those things; the only things that mattered, the things which became the supreme objects of intellectual interest, were words, syntax, style. It was not as thinkers, as creators, as cogitating beings that the 'classics' were canonised and worshipped, but as dealers in words and periods. The Greeks had been concerned with ideas, the Arabs and Arabists with facts, the pedants of the Renaissance were concerned with words.

It had been the plausible ideal of those who in ages of semi-darkness turned, like Petrarch, to the literature of Rome, to revive the culture which had existed in the past and existed no longer, while the embryo of a new culture was only then struggling into feeble, though healthy life. They were inspired by the wish to bring back the glories of Rome; what they brought back was the palsy of its dotage. The 'revival of learning' was the revival of pedantry. The spirit of the culture that was set up by the humanists was that of their teachers, the Byzantines round whom they crowded to learn Greek. It contained as much of the spirit of progress and life as that culture which had for ten centuries rotted in its mummy cloths on the shores of the Bosporus. It very nearly succeeded in smothering the young life of the European intellect which was moving in the new world.

'Scholarship,' which is the tradition of humanism, is in itself a precious and delightful thing. But when, from being a means and a medium, it becomes an end, scholarship becomes pedantry. Pedantry, in the fatuous complacence of chartered self-esteem, accounting itself the measure of intellectual worth, repudiates the fact that it is compatible with the crassest ignorance and imbecility. The pedant claims for scholarly irrationalism precedence over living thought, and is ready to damn truth on account of a false accent or faulty latinity. Renaissance humanism was fiercely opposed to science, and academic humanism has consistently remained the bulwark of authority and reaction.

Never, except in the last phases of Rome and in the Byzantine Empire, have the contents of the human mind been so completely displaced and supplanted by borrowed verbal vacuities as in the period of the so-called revival of learning. Of rational thought, of even a tendency towards a critical and independent attitude, there is among the pundits of Italian learning in the fifteenth and sixteenth centuries little trace. Whatever serious intellectual activity existed in Italy during that period, in men like Telesio, Giordano Bruno, Campanella, Pomponazzi, stood apart from the humanistic movement, and except as regards the last, exercised no influence. Alone among the Italian humanists, Lorenzo Valla, who was thought cold and aloof, regarded Latin and Greek scholarship as a means to more vital ends, and he may be said to have initiated historical criticism by his exposure to the frauds and forgeries—the alleged decretals from the pseudo-Dionysius, the deeds of donation of Constantine—which constituted the credentials of papal power. The greatest mind of all brooded in complete silence and solitude; "I am no humanist," declared Leonardo da Vinci.

But one may look in vain among the lights of the time,

in Poliziano, Ficino, Poggio Bracciolini, Filelfo, for a spark of spontaneous thought. Nothing can match the intellectual impotence, the sterility, of the authors of that strange 'revival of learning,' who prided themselves upon their Latin style and Greek hexameters, and made the discovery that what they have dubbed 'scholarship' is the one goal of the human intellect. They were arid pedants, grammarians, translators, imitators in whom all faculty for thought had become atrophied. Imitation, more imitation, and still closer imitation was their highest ideal. Truth of thought or justice of feeling had no place in their scheme of mind, and the only quality which they could conceive as worthy of endeavour and of appreciation was an aping faculty for Ciceronian periods and Platonic sentiments. The works of Marsilio Ficino, the leader of the Florentine Academy, are a hotch-potch of mystic rubbish beside which the writings of Madame Blavatsky are products of intelligence. Covered with amulets and charms, "the greatest philosopher of the age" went abroad in fear of the evil eye and of goblins. That intellectual level was representative of that of his contemporaries. The controversies conducted with ponderous classical elegancies and scurrilous personal vituperation between Poggio and Filelfo, are more grotesque than the most puerile scholastic disputations. The 'divine' Poliziano reached at a jump the most fulsome heights of that charming literary style which the 'Renaissance' has bequeathed as a curse to succeeding ages. He cannot speak of Florence, but must say, 'the city of Sylla'; he cannot mention that some one is ill, but must needs describe the 'Goddess of Fever' sitting at his bedside. Pico della Mirandola wrote a tract against astrology, and one might imagine that he was moved by some rationalistic impulse; but the absorbing interest of that champion of common sense lay in the Cabala, and his influence on Erasmus, Reuchlin,

Colet, and More, was that of the morbid fascination which vapid mysticism exercises.

Renaissance humanism was the bitter opponent of the new knowledge which was growing to momentous importance in the universities founded on Arabian science. Padua and Pisa, which owed their prosperity to commerce with the Arabs, were likewise the centres of that rationalism, realism, and scientific research which were to develop into modern science. Against those nests of heresy, of 'materialism,' of 'Averroism,' the champions of 'scholarship' never ceased to hurl their fanatical denunciations. It was the proud boast of the Venetians that humanism never gained a footing in the Republic. The cult of classicism had not a single representative there in the fourteenth century, and in the fifteenth the names of Ermolao Barbaro and of Aldo Manucci are the only two which were associated with the humanist movement. Barbo, who became Pope Paul II, ascribed to its aloofness from humanism the prosperity and intellectual vitality of the Venetian Republic. Instead of writers of Ciceronian Latin, it brought forth thinkers like Pomponazzi, Vanini, Bruno, it nursed Aquapendente, Galileo, Harvey. Humanism fought tooth and nail against science and progressive thought, and from the first waged a fierce war for the possession of the universities, where it eventually succeeded in substituting classical 'scholarship' for science, and in ousting those studies upon which, down to the present day, the academic tradition of humanism has showered contempt and which it has sought to exclude from education.

The religious scepticism of the later Italian Renaissance was not the outcome of any critical process of thought, but of entire lack of mental earnestness. The contempt of religion began with the clergy. In secure and undisputed possession of their claims and powers, they had come to treat their business overtly as one of undisguised exploitation. What men thought was of no account so long as the powers and revenues of the Church remained secure. Of dogmatic zeal and persecuting spirit there was little in the higher Italian clergy. They smiled on a declared atheist as long as he paid his Church dues and was not an earnest propagandist. Nicholas V appointed Valla to a post at his court; Leo X invited Pomponazzi to discourse before him on the mortality of the soul; and he and his advisers allowed Luther to gain time and ground through their avowed indifference to the theological issue. Only when political power was at stake did heresy call forth severity. And the courtly scepticism of the Renaissance, while it laughed at dogmas and ridiculed monks, was perfectly loyal to the Church as a social and political institution. Men like Machiavelli who treated religious dogma with scepticism and ridicule, did not do so because of any shock to their intellectual conscience. They were utterly devoid of such a sense. To the relation between dogma and truth they were indifferent. The passion for truth, the mark of all real intellectual activity, even the most languid interest in abstract truth, are things conspicuous by their absence in the Italian mind of the Renaissance. It believed as little in reason as it did in inspiration, and in general assumed religion to be an expedient, and, on the whole, beneficent institution; at the worst a necessary evil. That there is any connection between truth and what is practically desirable and expedient, was not suspected. That good can come out of a lie was never doubted. The practical concern of the Italian intellect was not to distinguish between truth and falsehood, but between the respective expediency and desirability of various lies.

Thus the pseudo-scepticism of the Italian Renaissance never approached to anything like consistency. It was quite usual for the commonplaces of sceptical ridicule to be combined with a practical belief in the essential doctrine on which the power of the Church was founded—fear of hell. Lorenzo de'Medici scoffed as freely as any one, yet cringed in terror on his death-bed, and sought absolution from Savonarola, "the only priest he knew who was not a hypocrite." Even the grossest popular superstition was by no means incompatible with that superficial scepticism. Machiavelli himself believed in ghosts. There is no length of incongruity to which that worthless and irrational scepticism could not proceed. Aretino, *"che disse mal d'ognun fuorchè di Dio, scusandosi col dir 'Non lo conosco,'"* composed manuals of devotion. Blasphemy, like murder and treachery, was the outcome of moral unscrupulousness, and absolution was sought for the one as for the other. The writers of the Cinquecento pass by a quite natural transition from religious satire to prayer. Pulci, in whose poem gastronomical parodies of the *Credo* alternate with hymns to the Madonna, may by his tone seem a distant progenitor of Voltaire; but the resemblance is only superficial. Mocking, scoffing Voltaire was in grim and deadly earnest; the sceptics of the Italian Renaissance never were.

In France, in Germany, in England the same tedious foolery went on as in Italy. Latin verses and Sapphic odes, epistles spun of platitudes and commonplaces were profusely exchanged; dedications, prefaces, testimonies of learning in Latin verse and prose, were composed for each other by the members of a mutual admiration society in which every scribbler of sham Latin verses was a 'modern Horace,' and every compiler of a compendium combined 'the elegance of Sallust with the felicity of Livy,' exercises diversified by prolonged controversies conducted for the entertainment of the 'republic of letters' and adorned with the amenities and ponderous *facetiæ* of classical billingsgate, in which each *vir doctissimus* became *asinus ignarus*.

But in the northern lands humanism did assume a more serious complexion than in Italy, tending in general to theology. It thus became mostly associated with the Reformation initiated by Friar Luther, who denounced in the same elegant terms both Rome and reason—"*Die verfluchte Huhre Vernunft.*" In the European world, flooded for the first time with books, thought circulated and fermented, and the revival of thought which rapidly superseded the outlook of the ancient world proceeded in spite of the 'revival of learning' and the 'reformation of religion.'

But in the land where it swayed unmodified the products of the humanistic movement were intellectual death and corruption. The blight of mere artificial imitativeness fastened on men's minds, and the Italian intellect never fully recovered from the hollow and false spirit of the Renaissance. "This was it which damped the glory of Italian wits, that nothing had been written there now these many years but flattery and fustian." (Milton.)

Torrents of nonsense have been, and are still daily, gushed forth about the Italian Renaissance. The charm of the period in a land which lay closer to the old springs of culture, that efflorescing brilliancy and pagan opulence of artistic production which still affectionately holds us, were not the fruit of humanism, but of the time when the Italian mind was stimulated by the culture of the Moors and of Provence, when the Italian spirit was stirred to vigorous life in the struggle for freedom against pope, Emperor and feudal lords. That was the age which produced Dante and Giotto and brought to life Italian art and literature. Their resources were used as a means of power and pleasure by the ambition of the princes who crushed liberty, and their course, which had begun in freedom and vital energy, though borne onward for a short time by the initial impulse after they had become the creatures of aulic patronage, was one of rapid parabolic decline. Italy has produced no second Dante. No Italian poet after him can be named in the same breath. Instead of the *Divine Comedy* the Renaissance produced Sannazaro's *Arcadia*. Not only did the Italian Renaissance produce no Dante, it was incapable of appreciating him; it set him aside and disparaged him, "banished him," in the words of one of the humanists of the time, "from the assemblies of the learned and made him over to wool-carders and bakers." Latin was restored to the position of literary language and the growth of Italian literature stamped down. This had already been the ideal of Petrarch, the father of humanism, who chiefly prided himself on his Latin epic, the *Africa;* and Boccaccio, though superior to all his successors, already shows in his weakness for Ciceronian 'elegance' in his Italian writing the poisonous imitative spirit which was to kill off so much of native genius; and he apologizes for having written "things in the vulgar tongue fit for the ears of the populace." From that time on, while humanism reigned supreme, Italian literature sinks into mellifluous euphuisms, elegant conceits, and sugary ornateness, till in the seventeenth century it becomes a by-word for hollow bombast and turgid absurdity—"flattery and fustian." Before its final sinking into utter degradation we have, it is true, a Tasso and an Ariosto who charm by the sonorous suavity of the verbal music in which their sensuous fancy is clothed. But you may search their pages in vain for a character or a thought. And the manner in which their felicitous talent was appreciated by their princely patrons of culture is sufficiently well known. Tasso was cast in prison, and Ariosto's florid adulation was by Cardinal d'Este received with the words, *"Dove diavolo, Messer Lodovico, avete trovate tutte queste corbellerie?"*

Italian painting, which quickly grew in technique

through the Lippis and Masaccio, was at its technical height under Raphael already stricken with the canker of mawkish grace and artificial ornateness, and sank with him into rapid degradation and hollow formalism. Only in such men as were least tainted with the spirit of the times, in whom something of the proud independence and enthusiasm of an earlier age survived, in Leonardo, Michelangelo, and the Venetians, whose minds dwelt outside the current of courtly elegance and modish classicism, was true creative power manifested. And their faults were proportionate to the pestilent influence upon them of prevalent taste, from which not even Leonardo or Michelangelo could altogether escape.

It was indeed a precious revival of 'taste' and of 'appreciation for antiquity' which inspired its patrons and arbiters, the papal princes, to tear down the venerable historic basilica of St. Peter's, and set Michelangelo and Raphael quarrying the sacred remains of the Roman Forum in order to erect them into that pile of overgrown hideousness on the Vatican hill!

Immediately its transmitted impulse was spent the culture of classical humanism resolved itself into its elements, and issued in the basest degradation of literature and art which the world has looked upon—baroque classicism and rococo taste. If it has contributed any spark to the fire which lit the new life of Europe, almost everything that is base and false in the ideals and tastes which for nigh three centuries have oppressed it and warped its growth, is likewise to be traced to Renaissance humanism. That pestilent pseudo-classic 'elegance' which infested Europe during the seventeenth and eighteenth centuries, that cold blight which poisoned the literature of France in the critical period of its growth and its influence, so that its men of talent lay palsied for two centuries gibbering about 'Cupid's darts,' 'the Graces,' 'the Muses,' and 'divine Chloë'; that corruption which degraded the tongue of Villon and Rabelais into that of Vauvenargues and the Hôtel Rambouillet, Elizabethan English into that of Addison and Pope; that deformity of literary ideals which praised Racine and scorned Shakespeare; that baseness and blindness which covered Europe with *perruques allongées,* Wren architecture, 'artificial ruins,' and 'classic' colonnades, with furbelowed Romans striking Raphaelesque attitudes with outpsread fingers, and goddesses sprawling on clouds, and of which all that is artistically mean and hideous in the modern world is the outcome; the unspeakable absurdity in notions of polite education which weighs to this day upon the most vital functions of our culture and life—all those things are the legacy of Italian humanism. We owe, if nothing else, to Ruskin that he first boldly exposed the contemptible worthlessness of that Renaissance taste whose tyrannous influence so blinded our grandfathers that even a Goethe could go into ecstasies over the sugary counterfeits of Palladio and pass by the genuine glories of Italian Gothic, snatch at the tinsel and cast aside the gold. That baseness is but the reflection in art of the imitative artificiality and unreality in which the pedantry of humanism moved, and which extinguished in it every impulse of rational and critical thought.

XII

THE BIRTH OF NATIONS

EUROPE is singular in the multiplicity of powers which, during the whole course of its development, have contended for rule over it. In the ancient civilisations of the East the sole ruling power was that of the priest. In Rome it was that of the owners of land and slaves. The Greek city-states had sought to maintain the democratic character of the pre-civilised tribe, but they could do so only by means of slaves and commercial wealth. The Hellenistic kingdoms and the empire of Rome were maintained by the power of the sword. In Europe every form previously assumed by ruling power was represented in its full vigour. A theocratic absolutism more strongly organised than any the Orient had known, and more uncompromisingly jealous of its claims to control the lives and the resources of men, towered at first over all, and aimed at the absolute theocracy which the Church of Hildebrand and of Benedict VIII regarded as the logical right of its divine authority. The Church, after setting up local kings, sought to create a successor to the Roman emperors of the West, who should, as her mandatory and secular arm, wield temporal suzerainty over Christendom. But no strong centralised power was possible in barbaric Europe. Even the power of the kings could not, during the barbaric ages, become fully established. The actual temporal rulers were the feudal chiefs, dukes, counts, barons, marquises or margraves, or whatever they might call themselves, among whom Europe was parcelled out into domains varying in size from the few acres round their castles to provinces as large as kingdoms, and who, besides being actual possessors of the soil, exercised unrestrained arbitrary power over its inhabitants as their serfs and villeins.

Commerce with the civilisation of Islam early gave rise to a fourth form of power, that of the traders, the power of money. They were enabled to defy other powers, to wring charters from them, to set up communes. Their example was followed everywhere in Europe; towns purchased home-rule for cash from barons rendered penurious by their own devastations, by the crusades, from kings, from emperors. A lively trade was driven in charters, to the intense disgust and indignation of the more powerful nobles and bishops, who cried that the foundations of society were being sapped by those "execrable inventions by which," in the words of Abbot Guibert of Nogent, "contrary to law and justice, slaves withdrew from the obedience which they owed to their masters."

The immediate result of that multiplicity of rival powers was a series of long and desperate conflicts among them all. Popes and emperors, kings and priests, feudal lords and kings, communes, barons, all flew at one another's throats, covered Europe with pikes and battlements, and filled its annals with battles and blood. Europe, though it bled, profited by the quarrels of its masters. All of them got weakened. It was the obvious policy of each to play off its less powerful against its stronger rivals. Thus the Church instigated the kings, and set up the Lombard communes, against the emperors; the emperors and kings set up bishoprics and abbots, and communes against the barons; the English barons played off the commons against the kings, and the kings in turn played them off against the barons. The moneyed burghers in general profited.

At first the centralised power of the kings was like those

of all barbaric war-lords, extremely small. Dukes, counts, who in theory held their lands of the king in fief, ruled over far larger domains, flouted his authority, and carried on predatory wars on their own account against their neighbours. But the weaker lords naturally appealed to the king for protection against the stronger, and thus more power gathered round him. It was ultimately found that, instead of fighting private wars on one's own account, it was equally advantageous to lend one's serfs and vassals to fight in the king's wars, and to share the spoils in the form of royal favours and gifts. Hence the phrase 'to fight for king and country.' Henry VIII consolidated Tudor despotism by giving his nobles the Church-lands to loot. In France, in Spain, the central power was gradually extended by alliances, marriages, conquests, purchases; in England it had been unified by the Norman Conquest. Italy was kept fragmented by the Balance of Power maintained by the Pope, and Germany by the power of the elector princes and bishops. The Church, having utterly weakened the emperors whom it had so thoughtlessly helped to set up, found it to be to its interest to make common cause with the kings. The advantage was mutual. The kings received their crowns from priests and became the anointed of God, the representatives of Divine power, sacred persons that could do no wrong, answerable to God only, and the people were taught the duty of submission to the Divine Right of kingly power.

No sooner had the centralised power of kings become sufficiently consolidated in their own domains than they sought to overpower their neighbours and seize theirs. To the class wars between orders of power, succeeded the strife amongst the centralised powers themselves. England, being, thanks to geography and the Norman Conquest, the first to get consolidated, was accordingly the first to attack its neighbours. The inhabitants of France failed at first to perceive any distinction between the aggression of one royal power-system against another and the local wars of duke against duke, and king against duke to which they were accustomed; and they remained as indifferent in the one case as in the other. It took nearly a hundred years of English pillage and devastation to rouse them against the nuisance, and for that sentiment to assume the form of patriotism and loyalty to their king. No sooner had the English been swept out of France than the French king, confirmed in turn in his power, hastened to follow the example they had set, and to start predatory wars on his own account, attacking Naples and Milan on the pretext of precisely such a title as that of the English king to the crown of France. The Pope next bethought himself that he, too, would like to capture a couple of towns and villages to which he also had a 'title,' albeit a forged one, and set France, the Emperor, Aragon, and the Italian princes route-marching against Venice; and, having secured his loot, suggested that the allies should now turn, for want of better to do, upon France. And so the dance went on that never since has ceased. The personal duel to which Francis I challenged the Emperor Charles unfortunately never took place; but they instead fought six wars, devastated Italy, Artois, Navarre, and successfully ruined Spain and the Germanic Empire. For a share of the disintegrating corpse of that empire, German and Austrian princes, Dukes of Savoy, Sweden, Denmark, France, scrambled for thirty years, killing two-thirds of its population. The King of France, the chief profiter, continued the plunder by seizing Alsace and Flanders, and laying out picturesque ruins in the Palatinate. The settling of his family in Madrid gave rise to a European war which went on until every one was weary and forgot what it was about, except Marlborough, who protracted it in view of commissions from the army-contractors. It left the map unchanged, and the chief profit to England of her most glorious victories was the monopoly of the slave-trade, which was secured to her by the Asiento Contract. Frenchmen first became acquainted with Russian *moujiks* on the Vistula, because Stanislas Lecszinski was not *persona grata* with the Russian Tzar and the Austrian Emperor. In order to find an income for her children Elizabeth of Parma, with the help of the gardener's son, Alberoni, kept Europe on tenter-hooks for twelve years. Another little family arrangement of the Austrian Emperor Charles VI—for the sake of which he sold the trade of Belgium to England who, in turn, bestowed Serbia on Austria and Greece on Turkey at Passarowitz—started a European war which lasted seven years. But the worst evil which the blundering Charles VI inflicted upon Europe was to save the life of Frederick Hohenzollern, who was about to be shot by his father, and whose first act was to attack and rob the daughter of his preserver. Maria Theresa refused Sir Thomas Robinson's pressing offer to join England and Prussia against France, and dried her Silesian tears with a share of the loot of Poland. The robber of Potsdam, assisted by English subsidies of money and men, ran amuck, and kept Europe well occupied while he created the German Empire, thus enabling his English partner to create the British Empire.

Europe has been turned into a cockpit during five centuries and more by reason of issues that concerned none of its peoples and which none even comprehended. By the side of dynastic wars, wars of religion are a relief from the baseness of naked greed. But religion was but a euphemistic pretext for political motives and the scramble of rulers for possession and power. The Protestant Hollanders called the Catholic French under the Duke of Anjou to their aid against Alexander Farnese. In the Thirty Years' War "there is no trace," Gardiner sums up, "of mutual hostility between the populations of the Catholic and Protestant districts apart from their rulers." French soldiers whose fathers had massacred the Huguenots and whose brothers were engaged in putting them down were sent by a Cardinal to support the Lutherans against the Catholic emperor.

European wars have been fought by populations heterogeneous in race, language, and religion, in the interests of systems of centralised power carved out by violence and greed of barbaric chieftains. Those wars have been largely conducted by means of hired mercenaries and troops lent by allied powers. Charles VIII and Francis I fought with Swiss and even with Turkish troops; the Burgundian Charles V sacked Rome with Spanish and German troops led by a Frenchman; the armies of Tilly, Wallenstein, Maximilian, Mansfeld, Christian of Brunswick, Gustavus Adolphus, which well-nigh blotted out civilisation from Central Europe, were composed of adventurers from every country, "raised out of the scum of the people by princes who have no dominion over them," as Lord Chichester wrote, who passed as occasion offered from one side to the other, were paid and fed by plunder, and were more dreaded by their 'friends' than by their 'foes.' The Prussian army was founded by Frederick William with likely-looking fellows kidnapped by his recruiting officers from Scandinavia to Transylvania, from the Liffey to the Niemen; and of Frederick's armies in the Seven Years' War and at Rossbach, where they defeated a thoroughly German army, not one half were Prussians. The Queen of Hungary defended herself with Italian troops; and England garrisoned Gibraltar, Minorca, and India with Germans.

The conflict of cupidities in the barbarian-born world of Europe has been rendered more vile by the travesty of every purpose and motive. Reared under the dominance of theocratic power which, however sincere, must needs clothe every aim in the terms of its ethical and spiritual conventions, European society has from the first been trained to give to all its acts and purposes the garb of moral self-righteousness. Priests, often mere barbarians raised to ecclesiastical offices by kings and dukes, were the first ministers and diplomatists of European states. To them fell the task of translating into unctuous language the unscrupulous lusts and shameless treacheries of barbarian chieftains. Dissimulation and perjury were the ordinary adjuvants of force. The traditions of European statecraft grew up in an atmosphere of perfidy and sanctimony. Of those arts of statecraft and diplomacy, the Roman court came to be the recognised mistress and model. The task of keeping the petty Italian principalities divided among themselves, of warding off powerful influences from the peninsula, of maintaining 'the Balance of Power,' in order to safeguard the couple of provinces which the popes claimed as their temporal domain, developed craft, intrigue and deceit into a fine art which became the atmosphere of Italian political thought and its absorbing interest in the sixteenth and seventeenth centuries. The name of Machiavelli has come to be linked with that political rascality and unscrupulous fraudulence, and he is, rather unjustly, branded as the originator of pernicious doctrines of systematic depravity. But the *Prince* is no more than an exposition of the accepted principles of political action in the Italy of his day. The industrious Florentine secretary would have been greatly astonished at being regarded as the theorist of political perversity on the score of the journalistic task he had undertaken of setting down the currently approved maxims of government. All European powers have, like Frederick of Prussia, loudly disowned and denounced Machiavellian principles as their scapegoat and sedulously practised them.

Italian statecraft became the admired model of governments. The heart of Louis XI so melted with tender admiration for Francesco Sforza, the perfection of political rascality, that he refrained from robbing him. Thomas Cromwell, while carrying out the policies of Wolsey and Henry VIII, prided himself on his Italian training, and carried the *Prince* in his wallet. Women became the competitors of princes and prelates in the arts of mendacity; Louise of Savoy and Margaret of Austria showed themselves at Cambrai equal to any envoy in the arts of haggling and overreaching. Catherine de Medici, to whose grandfather Machiavelli had dedicated his manual, Mary Stuart, the pupil of the Guises, were only surpassed by Elizabeth in the tortuosities of deceit on which the latter plumed herself. The intricacies of crooked schemes, plots, intrigues, and machinations were to such a degree the habitual means of political action that rulers became blind whenever an obvious and straight path to their ends presented itself. When, by the death of Charles the Bold, the chief prize which the king of France had for years schemed to obtain was ready to drop into his mouth, he lost Burgundy because the means of obtaining it were so obvious that he devised instead circuitous machinations. The most assured and insidious means of dissimulation, as Bismarck declared, was to speak the truth. Historians have long conceived it to be their chief function to penetrate through the manifold palimpsest of ostensible pretexts and intricate mendacities to the actual purpose which the chief actors on the stage of history had in view.

Thus have the traditions of European diplomacy and politics been formed, that *haute diplomatie,* those sapient webs of combinations and intrigues, that polished and punctilious fraudulence, those cat's-paw schemes and overreaching mystifications, the felicitous phrasing of 'formulas' that enable unavowable vileness to utter itself in words, and convenient crime and cool atrocity to be glossed over with simulated rectitude, that decorous rascality that stinks in the grand manner, those oblique and secret transactions of pilfering designers in which the destinies of mankind are played away with loaded dice—thus hitherto has the government of the human race been constituted. In the year 1648 the power-states of anarchic Europe, exhausted, depopulated, ruined, fatigued and unnerved by thirty years of the most devastating of wars, sent their delegates to the first European Peace Conference at Münster and Osnabruck, that some 'settlement' might be effected. But even in the extremity of universal need and suffering the dominant anxiety of great and small was not at all to 'settle' anything, but to scramble for loot, for Naboth's vineyards, for 'satisfactions,' 'compensations,' 'indemnities,' and to seek increase and profit out of the misery of humanity.

At the outset, thanks to the ecumenical tradition of the Roman Empire and the Church, Europe, Christendom, was thought of as a single community. No portion of it was shut off from the rest, or grew in isolation. Considering the conditions of the early Middle Ages the closeness and extent of intercourse was remarkable; it was relatively closer and more extensive than in our own times. Monks from Ireland and England travelled and settled in Germany, France and Italy; Italian priests became archbishops of Canterbury and chancellors of England, and an Englishman became chancellor of Sicily; an Irishman was the friend of the Emperor and studied in Spain; every Englishman who cared about such education as was obtainable went at least as far as the Paris schools; the early universities in Paris, Bologna, Padua, Naples, Montpellier, Vienna, Oxford were divided into 'Nations' of students gathered from every part of Europe; Frenchmen swarmed in England, Spaniards travelled in Germany, Germans in Spain. There was the closest constant intercourse between the Norman courts of Winchester, Rouen and Palermo; between the courts of Barcelona and Toulouse, of Carolingian France and Germany, of Naples and Vienna; and between every country and the papal court of Rome or Avignon. Merchants spent their lives trudging backwards and forwards from Italy over the Brenner Pass, through Switzerland and along the Rhine to the Hansas and Flanders, and vice versa; postal correspondence was unsatisfactory, so people went themselves. Priests, poets, students, and Jews wandered everywhere; pilgrims from Normandy or Ireland went to Rome, to the Holy Land, to the shrines of Southern Italy. The population of the eleventh, twelfth, and thirteenth centuries were far greater travellers, considering the different conditions, than those of the age of railways.

Western civilisation has always been international, that is to say, European. The political constitution of Europe is no more the outcome of race, or religion, or language, or of any cultural aspect, than European wars are the outcome of issues affecting the interests of the people of Europe. Political unity was impossible in the Dark Ages because the barbaric anarchy of Europe was such that no centralised government could govern. Thereafter it has remained impossible because that anarchy of the Dark Ages has been perpetuated by the consolidation of barbaric kingdoms. The domains carved out of the ruins of the Roman Empire by barbaric chieftains and shaped by their predatory conflicts are war-made systems whose external relations with other political systems depend, in war or in peace, upon their strategic power. By no act can such strategic systems abolish the state of war. No person, acting as representative to those strategic systems, can in any parley or pact curtail by one hair's breath the strategic power of the system he represents without being a traitor, and no European state which enjoys any strategic advantage over others can, except by an act of suicide, surrender that advantage. Born of barbaric anarchy, the sovereign states of Europe are thus bound in the twentieth century within the vicious circle of the anarchy which gave rise to them in the tenth.

While they remain thus unaltered and unalterable in their external configuration as instruments of war, the states of Europe have undergone a progressive change in their internal constitution, although that change has not been so fundamental as it is conventionally represented to have been.

The heterogeneous powers which ruled them, the power of feudal landowners, of kings, of priests, of moneyed burghers, which had at first struggled for mastery, torn one another to pieces, and turned Europe into a shambles by their desperate conflicts, have by a natural process tended to become fused by a mutual adjustment of their interests, and to make common cause. The interests of kings and feudal aristocracies, of Church and State have become united by reciprocal adjustments. Even the burghers, after many fierce and desperate struggles, which constitute the revolutions that have led from absolutism to Democracy, found it advantageous to make common cause with king, nobles, and Church.

In England, "this fortress built by Nature for herself Against infection and the hand of war; This precious stone, set in the silver sea, Which serves it in the office of a wall Against the envy of less happier lands," large armies were unnecessary for defensive purposes, and therefore expensive. For the purposes of the king's offensive wars money had constantly to be obtained, and the burghers who held the purse had therefore to be treated with consideration. The parliament of embarrassed and open-mouthed burghers which Simon de Montfort, the son of the leader of the Albigensian crusade, had set up against the king, acquired extraordinary importance. England's chief means of aggression, as well as of defence, lay, moreover, in a navy rather than in an army; and ships were chiefly the property of the trading class who, now that Vasco da Gama and Columbus had changed the channels of the world's commerce, served all other interests as well as their own by supplying the Spaniards with slaves and relieving them of gold galleons, and by building empires overseas. The trading moneyed classes thus rose in England to great power, and the institutions of the 'nation of shopkeepers' became an exemplar to 'less happier lands.'

In the continental states whose existence depended upon strong permanent armies, the absolutism of the kings who disposed of that force, maintained itself much longer. But the growing power of money eventually compelled every other form of power to compound with it.

In no part of Europe has the conflict between the various powers been more desperate and more prolonged than in Germany. The power of the elective emperors was jealously resisted and kept down by the popes; that of the territorial lords and bishops in whom the elective rights were vested inevitably came to overshadow completely that of the nominal ruler. The emperor was destitute of revenues; Charles V's predecessor was known as 'Maximilian the moneyless,' and the great Charles himself was ever at a loss to cope with his penury. Every rood of land of the imperial domains eventually passed away in bribes to the Electors. The trading cities of Hansa threw off all allegiance to emperor or territorial lords. Germany became ultimately fragmented by the incurable separatist tendencies of its conditions, and ruined and devastated by the fierceness of its conflicts. It was rent asunder by three different religions. Every form of power, that of emperor, priests, barons, and burghers became crippled and exhausted by the perpetual conflicts between them all. Yet on the eve of Germany's fatal bid for *'Weltmacht oder Niedergang,'* all those powers which for centuries had been engaged in a death-struggle against one another are found firmly united in the bonds of common ambitions and interests. The Kaiser, representative of the mediæval ideals of Divine Right and empire, is at one with the Junkers, successors of the Teutonic Knights and robber-barons; the financial interests, the Frankfort bankers, the Hamburg shipowners, the industrialists, the Essen steel magnates, representatives of the trading burghers, assisted and promoted by Kaiser and militarists, make the aims and schemes of the latter as much their own as court and camp; even the Vatican is not altogether unsuspected of having a finger in the plot.

Thus ultimately have throne, altar, the sword, the pen, and the guinea come to stand side by side in a Holy Alliance. That alliance constitutes the modern state, the Nation. The kings who with the aid of the Church have carved out domains by the sword out of Roman Europe had called themselves 'England,' 'France,' 'Spain,' as bishops called themselves 'Canterbury,' 'York,' 'Winchester.' From being originally the names of kings, those denominations have come to be understood as denoting nations, imagined as varieties of the human species. The latter fiction is as fantastic as the former. No less fictitious is the convention that the nation is the people, and consists of their collective interests. It consists of the interests of holders of power. That power has undergone transformations. It is no longer exclusively the power of a priest, of a king, of war-chief, of landowner. The merchant and industrial burgher who from earliest times was able to defy kings, nobles, and priests, has in the modern European state absorbed most of their authority. In his conflicts with them he called himself 'the people.' But under the illusion of Democracy, of franchise, and self-government, the civilised State remains the essential relation which constitutes it what it was when it first arose at the dawn of history, the organised power of rulers wielded over men. Industrial and commercial interests, not those of a theocratic priest, of a war-leader, or of a feudal lord, are paramount in the modern state. But the interests of the industrialist and of the merchant are, as a consequence of the historical evolution of the State, bound up with every tradition which in the course of that evolution has served to support authority and constituted power. Thus it is that the industrial magnate, the Jew financier, the newspaper lord, are, in the modern nation, vehemently interested in the conservation of that tradition. The prestige of the feudal aristocracy, the consecrated authority of religion, are no less vital interests of the English manufacturer or stockbroker than the acquisition of new markets or sources of raw material for the empire. Every force which menaces the tradition of authority upon which rests that of the State jeopardises his own power to turn the control of men into wealth.

To the variety of conflicting powers out of whose mutual struggles the interests that rule European civilisation have arisen, leaving no form of power unchallenged and uncriticised, Europe owes in part its distinctive faculty for development and change. It cannot stagnate like an antique Oriental empire. For the same reasons that have caused the conflicts which have rended it in the past, it cannot endure while the foundations of its structure are open to challenge and criticism. The weapons by which has been waged the strife of interests that have moulded its present form have been, as are all that establish power over men's lives, weapons of the mind. To the attack of the same weapons, to the attack of human reason, the powers which rule it today stand exposed.

XIII

REASON'S BATTLE FOR JUSTICE

In the essential principles of its structure, modern Western civilisation is substantially identical with all other civilisations that have flourished since the breaking up of tribal humanity. Like the first theocracies of the ancient Orient which arose by the subjection of the bulk of the people to the power of a small class of priests, European civilisation is founded on the power wielded by the few over the many. That in modern Europe that power, instead of resting, as in ancient Babylon, on the claim to control supernatural agencies, rests upon the claim to control wealth and labour, does not affect the essential relation.

Some vague notion exists that while early theocracies, autocracies, and despotisms were tyrannical usurpations imposing upon the bulk of the population the outrageous domination of those who, for their own benefit, maintained that tyranny, modern democratic society is, on the contrary, an organisation planned for the general benefit of humanity. That notion is, of course, conducive to appreciation of the sanctions on which the existing order stands, in the same manner as belief in Divine Right was conducive to appreciation of the sanctions upon which autocratic despotism was founded. It would be interesting to know when civilisation, founded as a means of exploiting the many for the advantage of the few, changed its character, and became instead a benevolent scheme inspired by anxious concern for the welfare of all. Civilised society has, it is true, gradually tended to become farther and farther removed in its principles from those which originally gave rise to it, and to approximate more closely to the object and purpose ascribed to it. But that change has been an evolution which has gradually modified its constitution, without, however, reconstructing it, and it has left the fundamental relation untouched.

The chief difference between the structure of civilisation in ancient Babylon and in modern Britain, in ancient Egypt and in modern Europe, lies in the distribution of established power. The conflicts between the multiple forms of power struggling for mastery in the European world have, as an inevitable result, abridged privileges and extended rights.

Speaking absolutely an individual has no rights. A right presumes a contract; and there is no contract, formal or tacit, establishing any claim advanced in relation to life, liberty of conduct, of thought, of speech, or to any other demand made upon organised society by individuals or by classes in the name of right and justice. Right exists only as the correlative of wrong. The notion of individual right derives its meaning from the circumstance that there are wrongdoers, that man is liable to be oppressed by the power of other men. Because there have been men who have wielded power over others, and used that power to oppress them, because there have been murderers and despoilers, because the holders of power have compelled their fellow-men into slavery, appropriated their labour, and crushed their lives, the notion of 'the rights of man' has arisen, the rights, namely, not to be murdered, despoiled, enslaved and crushed. Right is but the right not to be wronged. Hence it is that all ethical law, in its primitive form at least, is negative in form, 'Thou shalt not . . .' The affirmation of human right is the denial of the claim to inflict wrong. Morality, as Nietzsche declared, originates with the weak, with the oppressed. It is protective, protesting. 'Thou shalt not . . .' means '*Thou* shalt not injure me.' It could not, manifestly, have originated with the wrongdoer and the oppressor, as 'I shall not . . .' It is the expression of wrongs suffered by the weak at the hands of the strong, the protest of the oppressed against the powerful. When the weak and the oppressed protest against power, they are protesting against moral wrong; when they defend their interests, their rights, they are defending moral Right, righteousness. The oppressed are always morally in the right.

And holders of power are always morally in the wrong. All power wielded by man over man is an aggression. It seeks the profit of the strong at the expense of the weak. Power and wrong are, in their primary relation, coextensive. Even when expedient or necessary as an organising function, when beneficial as protection, as the guidance of wisdom, the strength of leadership, power is, of its intrinsic nature, an injustice.

It has long been discovered that absolute power is intrinsically bad, no matter by whom exercised. History shows that to invest a saint with absolute power is to throw open the gates of hell. Louis IX of France, canonished by universal opinion no less than by the Church as the crowned saint whose sole end is righteousness and his people's good, was in fact a persecutor who accounted the sword the only argument against heresy, and crushed the last liberties of the French communes. It would be difficult to point to a figure, in the Renaissance period, more admirable in its quiet wisdom and gentle idealism than that of Sir Thomas More; yet his brief spell of power as Chancellor of England is marked by bloody persecution and heinous injustice. Absolute power has been abolished not because rulers are bad men, but because absolute power is necessarily bad. "Power tends to corrupt," Lord Acton observes, "and absolute power corrupts absolutely. Great men (meaning powerful men) are almost always bad men, even when they exercise influence and not authority." There is scarcely a sovereign in English history from William I to George I who, tried on the count of murder alone by the same standards as common delinquents, would have escaped the gallows.

What is true of absolute power is correspondingly true of power in every form and degree, whether it be that of privilege, or of the strong hand, of money, or of intellectual authority, of a ruler or of a Jack-in-office. The power of an autocrat is indeed by no means the worst. Far more pernicious is that of a class, and most pernicious of all that of a majority. Paddy's proverbial attitude of being 'agin the government' is in accord with the universal law that all power, no matter by whom exercised, tends to abuse and injustice. All chances are, therefore, that in order to be on the side of right one must be 'agin the government.'

Power results in injustice not because men are wicked, but because power corrupts judgment. The highest ideals and the noblest sense of the obligations of his function cannot save the holder of power from viewing the entire world in that perspective which is best suited to sanction and justify the power he wields.

That power, it is commonly supposed, rests upon physical force, or upon economic pressure, or some other form of coercion. Those means of power can only be of incidental and secondary use. Physical force requires the loyalty of those by whose agency it is applied. By economic facts is meant the power to coerce by economic pressure or by the control of physical force which wealth affords; they are the facts of existing economic power. But that power only exists so long as it can succeed in being tolerated. Its security rests, like that of all other forms of power, upon the ideal sanctions which permit of its being accepted by its victims. A people is ruled by the power to which its intelligence assents; it has the government which its intelligence deserves.

The transformation which current conceptions postulate, of civilised society from an unjust usurpation and ruthless tyranny into a benevolent scheme for the benefit of mankind, constitutes moral progress. Moral progress has never been brought about by the spontaneous growth of moral sentiments in people who held power, by their bestowing the benefits of their ethical inspiration upon those whom that power used, by 'dispensing justice.' Justice has never been dispensed from above in consequence of an ethical ideal. It has been wrested from the unwilling hands of the holders of power. It represents the coercion of revolt as constituted power represents the coersion of oppression.

But the revolt of the oppressed against power no more depends solely or chiefly upon physical force than does the exercise of oppressive power. Constituted power is guarded by defences more effective than any Pretorian guard. It is protected by ideas. Those ideas are necessarily false. The power whose dominant object is to maintain the condition of things which allows of its own existence to restrain the growth of the social organism, to prevent it from developing according to natural law, cannot rest on the sanction of ideas which are in accordance with natural law, with facts. Injustice can never rest upon truth.

No resistance against unjust power can take place while the sanctioning ideas which justify that power are accepted as valid. While that first and chief line of defence is unbroken there can be no revolt. Before any injustice, any abuse or oppression can be resisted, the lie upon which it is founded must be unmasked, must be clearly recognised for what it is.

Hence every advance of justice, every step in moral progress, has been, not an abstract ethical inspiration, but a process of intellectual criticism, a victory of rational thought over irrationalism. Thus it is that whatever growth of justice and moral sense sets the modern age above the barbarism of preceding periods, has invariably gone hand in hand with the growth of rational thought.

No revolt against injustice, no resistance against oppression can take place without intellectual preparation. So long as the oppressed have remained under the influence of the irrationalism upon which the constituted power is founded, they have remained loyal to their oppressors. They have accounted it a sacred duty to toil, to fight, to lay down their lives for them. The slave may suffer and lament, but he does not dispute the authority of his master. He laments his misfortunes as he would those caused by a storm or a flood, without a thought of blasphemy. The physical force wielded by holders of power is in general that lent to them by the loyalty of their victims. It is through the power of irrational dogmas that all the iniquitous forces which have devastated Europe have exercised their mastery. The peasant armies which have slaughtered one another in the dynastic strifes of their masters have glowed with patriotism. The Vendean peasant is filled with heroic rage against those who would liberate him from his tyrants. The Russian serf worshipped his 'little father.' Nothing is more tragical and pathetic than the obstinate loyalty of the oppressed towards their oppressors.

So long as the extra-rational foundations of privilege went unquestioned, claims to justice, could not, and did not arise. So long as the divine nature of kingship was undisputed, every abuse of tyranny could exist unchallenged, so long as feudal power was looked upon as part of a superhumanly established order, every excess to which unchecked authority gives rise could proceed unquestioned. It is only when they have come to perceive that what they regarded as a sacred truth was a lie, that what they had been taught to look upon as right was iniquitous wrong, it is then only that the injured have rebelled. It is the exposure of the basic irrationality, of the justifying lie, which brings about the overthrow of the abuse. The oppressed have only revolted against tyranny or injustice, however atrocious, when they have clearly learned to perceive it as irrational, mendacious, false. The system of ideas by which unjust power is 'justified' must first be stripped of its halo of sophistry and sanctity by rational thought, must first stand out in its naked irrationality, before there can be any forces of revolt.

Revolt takes place, of course, against actual grievances, and is therefore interested. The actual motive is interest, not principles. The oppressed are in the first place driven to revolt by actual suffering, hunger, and even by mere envy and greed. The revolt of the wronged is moral, not because they are animated by any high ideal, but because their interests necessarily coincide with morality. It is out of the conflict of interests or private ends that the principle, the morality is evolved.

And since it is impossible for the utterly crushed and oppressed to revolt at all effectively, when they have done so it has usually been in alliance with other classes whose motives were frankly venal and interested. And thus that sordid element has played a conspicuous part in many of the most important emancipating movements.

The powers of an omnipotent and all-devouring Church were first curbed by needy and rapacious nobles. The power of kings and nobles, that is, power founded on privilege, has been constantly checked and sapped, and finally overthrown, by the growth of another form of power, the power of money. The opposition offered by the commercial classes, by Lombard, Florentine, Flemish, Hanseatic, English merchants, in the later Middle Ages and the Renaissance, against the exactions of imperial feudatories, nobles, and kings, was one of the main checks on tyranny, one of the chief seeds of liberty. The enormous part played by interested purposes of the most fulsome kind, by sheer covetousness, in all the movements of the Reformation, is familiar. In Germany the secession from Rome was brought about by the appetite of rulers for Church lands; in Switzerland the success of Zwingli was owing to the appropriation by Zurich and other cities of the domains of the Church. The foundation of the Anglican Church is one long story of the sordid avarice and unmitigated greed. And we find everywhere, in every emancipating movement, the same selfish, calculating, mercenary spirit at work. The American Revolution arose from the reluctance of shopkeepers to part with tax-money. Even the French Revolution was initiated, not by starving and oppressed millions, but by profiteering merchants and speculators who objected to being taxed.

But those facts are apt to be profoundly misapprehended. The exponents of economic determinism find it easy to use them in representing avarice and interest as the sole agents at work in all those movements. But those agencies have never operated until intellectual criticism had done its work.

As long as the world quailed in terror under the one paramount, exclusive thought of hell-fire, the Church could draw into its ubiquitous suckers the entire substance of Europe. There was no protest, no resistance. Not until the twelfth century when the ice began to crack, when unquestioning faith had ceased to be universal, when Europe rapidly became riddled with heresy, did the land-hunger of priests and monks begin to be opposed and curbed, and kings and barons to cry 'Hands off.' No thought of seizing Church goods, of arresting the bleeding of their domains by Rome, ever occurred to German princes till Huss, and Luther, and Zwingli had formulated clearly the outrageousness of papal pretensions. Henry VIII could do nothing but for Erasmus and Colet and the Lollardry smouldering among the people. The interests and cupidities of princes have merely been powerful auxiliaries in the battles of emancipation, auxiliaries which have often determined the victory, but were themselves the tools of the intellectual forces. The actual sufferers, the crushed and oppressed, when they have risen against barbarity and injustice, have been interested, not theoretically inspired by abstract principles; but those interested motives could not operate until the critical unmasking of irrational claims had taken place. Till then all the forces which make for justice are paralysed.

Every one is familiar with the accounts of the misery of the French people on the eve of the Revolution, the crushing exactions, feudal dues, dimes, gabels, Church tithes, which swallowed up their substance, the chronic famine and destitution which sent haggard ghosts wandering over the desolate land. It appears obvious that such a state of things could not endure; that it must inevitably result in rebellion. But things were as bad at the death of Louis XIV as at that of Louis XV, and there was no rebellion. The conditions were worse in Germany than they were in France. On the other side of the Pyrenees, a hundred years earlier, the oppression and misery of the people was even worse; the country was depopulated by famine, desolated by utter anarchy and by exactions; the people were bond-slaves, the starving population fled from the villages at the approach of the tax-gatherers, while these tore down the wretched dwellings to sell the materials;

armed crowds fought for bread before the bakers' shops more fiercely than they did in Paris; the unpaid household troops begged for food in the streets and at the doors of monasteries. And yet, beyond some demonstrations against the ministers in Madrid, nothing happened. Or rather, the most extraordinary thing continued to happen; the starving, spoliated, and tortured populace was filled with passionate loyalty towards its oppressors; it was ready to die for 'throne and altar.' A few years later, when the power of the Bourbons was being humbled by Marlborough and Prince Eugene in Germany, Flanders and Italy, when Peterborough and Stanhope scattered before them the wretched armies of Spain, the same victims of misrule rose everywhere in defence of their king, the plundered villagers scraped together all the money they could lay their hands on, and brought it to the king with tears of passionate devotion, and the peasants of Castile and Andalusia neutralised by their obstinate heroism the triumphs of Blenheim and Ramillies.

There was no rational thought, no criticism of the situation in their case, no glimmer of light whereby to discern the source of their evils in their true aspect. It is that purely intellectual process of enlightenment and criticism which is the indispensable condition of the protest of the oppressed. Until it has taken place their ethical conceptions are as immoral as those of their oppressors; their loyalty, their devotion, their endurance, their veneration, their bowing submission to the divinely appointed order, their contentment with the station in which Providence has placed them, are the counterpart of the ruthless injustice, the tyranny, the rapacity, the cruelty, the barbarity of the holders of power.

The progress of social justice is thus part of the process of intellectual development. The European world, since its awakening out of the trance of the Middle Ages, has displayed a dazzling and continuous intellectual growth and a corresponding advance in the material conditions of civilisation. Those aspects of progress it is customary to depreciate as superficial. There is a disposition to forget that hand in hand with those manifestations there has proceeded a no less conspicuous and continuous evolution which cannot be so speciously depreciated. The marvels of material civilisation at the present day, the abolishing of distance, the wonders of industry, the contrivances, the luxuries, railways and steamships, automobiles and æroplanes, ethergraphs and telegraphs, are commonly contrasted with the material civilisation of Europe, say, a hundred and fifty years ago, its lumbering conveyances, filth-strewn streets, distaffs and hand-looms, guttering candles and crude implements. But the contrast between the material conditions of today and those of the eighteenth century is not so great as that presented by the social conditions, the notion and practice of justice, the accepted sentiments of humanity of present-day Europe and those which obtained at that not very distant period. The slave-trade was in full swing; hundreds of slave-ships sailed from Liverpool; petty larceners were sold to the American colonies at five shillings a head; public executions at Tyburn, the victims often being women convicted of shoplifting, offered occasions for popular festivities; the publishers of heretical books were placed in the stocks at Charing Cross, at Temple Bar, at the Royal Exchange, and were handed over to the populace to be pelted; press-gangs scoured the country, men were seized in the street, in their homes, and sent in chains to the King's or the India Company's navy; women and children worked half-naked in the coal mines, miners and salt-workers in Scotland were legally in the position of predial slaves; the cockpit and the prize-ring offered to English gentlemen their daily amusement; the English government under the elder Pitt issued letters of marque to privateers to plunder the shipping of Holland while it was at peace with that country. On the Continent the state of things was even worse, the feudal system and all its abuses were in force, the rack and the boot were at work in Paris, *lettres de cachet* were issued, every product of independent thought was visited upon its author with persecution, the galleys were full, the Inquisition sat in Spain, and *autos-da-fé* were still alight.

Those conditions, which we have so completely outgrown that we are no longer able to conceive them distinctly, were those of comparatively recent times. They stand, I say, in far more complete contrast with the conditions of civilised European countries today, than does a modern express train to the stage-coaches in which our grandfathers journeyed.

If the material transformations wrought by the resources of the scientific age are discounted as husks and externals, the same judgment cannot be passed upon the development of social justice and humanity by which the same period is no less conspicuously marked. To what causes have those deeper changes been due? The question, when raised at all, is commonly dismissed with superficial irrelevances. The progress of refined sentiments, the humanising influences of civilisation are vaguely adduced, as if by reference to some obvious and demonstrated natural law. It is not infrequently suggested, and even asserted, that the trend towards humanity and justice in the modern age is the outcome of the Christian religion, which has, in the ages of faith, filled the world with blood, horror, and persecution. The manifestations of that trend have, in point of fact, accompanied the decay of all the influences which have been credited with fostering the moral sense, the progress of social justice has gone hand in hand with the growth of the critical and rationalistic tendencies which have been accounted damaging to the authority of moral sanctions. The last three centuries have witnessed the continuous growth of scepticism, not merely in regard to the dogmas of religions, but in regard to all things which fail to furnish a clear and rational account of themselves. Not only are dogmatic faiths today in a state of dissolution, but all traditional standards and sanctions of moral values are being subjected to unsparing criticism. Yet in spite of the extension of the critical spirit to every sphere of thought, and of the boldness with which every categorical assumption is challenged, there never was an age so moral, in the strictest sense of the term, as the present one. Whatever indictment may be brought against it, it is certain that the appeal of sentiments of justice, equity, humanity, has never been so powerful and so general, that sensitiveness to wrong, oppression, injustice have never been so keen, that the conscience of human society wherever suffering, evil, abuse exist, has never been more lively and susceptible. Abuses, injustice, social crime and vice exist today as they have done in former ages, but never have they stood so clearly arraigned and condemned at the bar of current opinion. The claims of righteousness have never, least of all in devout and puritanical periods, been so strong as in an age which rejects the authority of traditional moral sanctions and values. And more truly than in any formulated opinion or accepted sentiment, that attitude and that development are manifested in the concrete facts of human relations.

The association of moral progress with the decay of the traditional sanctions of moral values is not accidental, for no sphere of cultural tradition has been more profoundly falsified than that which has created those sanctions and assigned their claims to spurious authorities. The association of justice and humanity with the critical attitude of the modern age and with rationalistic realism is not fortuitous. It is a correlation as direct as that between that attitude and its scientific and mechanical achievements. The abolition of the horrors of feudalism, of the gross iniquity and inhumanity of social conditions in the past, is as much the direct outcome of the critical temper of thought as is the abolition of Ptolemaic astronomy or of the biology of Genesis. The intolerance of abuse and of wrong, the insistence upon justice, which place the modern age, from a moral standpoint, above its predecessors, are the fruits of the same intellectual processes which have brought about its material triumphs. The same forces which have fought irrationalism have fought oppression and abuse, have emptied the churches and filled the schools, have compassed justice and created the steam-engine and the dynamo.

XIV

EUROPEAN LIBERATIONS

THE earlier revolts against the powers which oppressed Europe have borne the aspect of religious movements. As in the theocratic East every stirring of the mind assumed the form of a 'new religion,' so in mediæval Europe, under the same incubus, social revolt wore the aspect of religious reformation. The absolutism of an unchallenged Church was the sanction on which every established power was founded; none could be resisted without attacking that foundation. Every criticism of the Church's dogma gave rise in turn to social revolt. The bold teaching of Abélard resulted in the revolution led by his pupil, Arnaldo da Brescia, and in the proclamation of a republic in Rome. Wycliff was followed by John Ball and the Lollards; John Huss by the revolt of Bohemia; and with the Lutheran Reformation all the forces of sedition were let loose. The Peasant War in Germany, the rebellion of the Netherlands were its immediate effects.

With the exception of the Netherlands' independence, revolt on the continent bore little fruit. The forces of coercion were too mighty; rebellion, extinguished in blood and fire, only tightened the fetters. Many of the most atrocious features of the feudal system date from the *Jacquerie* and the Peasant War. The plunder of the Church's wealth which supplied the main motive for the spread of the Reformation profited the princes alone. The Church of England, accounted by many the most ignoble of the two hundred and fifty-five denominations of Christendom, is in point of fact not much more sordid in its origin than most other Protestant bodies. In Germany, Switzerland, Denmark, Scandinavia, as in England, the Reformation owed its success to rapacity rather than religion. Intellectually the tyranny of Bibliolatry and the smug fanaticism of Hebraised Christianity have probably been more blighting in their effects upon the European mind than the dictatorship of the Roman Curia. The setting up of the ancient literature of the Jews as the beginning and end of wisdom and knowledge has had a more calamitous effect upon every aspect of Western civilisation than any exercised by theocratic dogmatism. But because it broke the unity of that centralised tyranny, the Protestant Reformation liberated the forces of rational revolt. So securely rooted in the fabric of European society had Catholic Christianity seemed that the most manifest indictments must recoil in impotence before its defiant power, and the timid wisdom of thinkers like Erasmus might regard as visionary any hope of breaking the spell. Like every first successful revolt, the Reformation showed that, however stable its tyranny may appear, irrational power is in truth at the mercy of human intelligence, courage and collective resolve. In the Netherlands the absorption of the country's wealth by the Church had already been checked by the Counts of Flanders and the Dukes of Burgundy; the yoke of oppression was cast off not by the nobles, but by the burghers. The United Provinces celebrated their deliverance from Spanish tyranny by founding the universities of Leyden and of Utrecht. Holland became the centre and seed-bed of all liberal thought. In the household of wealthy burghers such as that of jolly Roemer Visschen and his accomplished daughters, there gathered companies which included Vossius, the great

Grotius, author of *International Law* and *The Freedom of the Sea,* Brederoo, the comic poet, van Vondel, the dramatist, Descartes, Baruch Spinoza, Swammerdam, the first biologist, Huygens, the physicist, Rembrandt, Franz Hals. Dutch liberty prepared the way for English and all subsequent political and intellectual development.

In England the same grounds which served as the sanction of Henry Tudor's rejection of the pope's authority and of the English aristocracy's scramble for Church lands, supplied likewise the doctrinal motive for the burghers' revolt which brought royal absolutism to the scaffold and broke the power of the landowning aristocracy. Those struggles were fruitful of extended liberty not because they were religious but because they were Protestant. Catholic religious enthusiasm in France, in Spain, in England, produced not liberty, but tyranny, not Commonwealths and Declarations of Right, but St. Bartholomews, *quemaderos,* and Bloody Maries. Protestantism meant the attack of private judgment, however arrogant in its ignorance, against the constituted falsehoods which sanctioned oppression. The attitude of Protestantism, of No-Popery, whatever dogmas and ravening fanaticisms it might hug, was towards the unveracities of established authority, towards priestcraft, hocus-pocus (*hoc est corpus*), identical with that of rational criticism. The Lollards and Independents treated the holy things in the same blasphemous and sacrilegious manner as the most 'offensive' militant atheist. The throwing off of injustice and despotism, and later, as a necessary consequence, the extension of humanitarian principles, has been accomplished in England by the Protestants, and by those shades of Protestantism in particular which were farthest removed from constituted religious authority, by Dissenters, Independents, Puritans, Non-Conformists. The contemporary pietist who affirms that

England's greatness is due to the Bible is not altogether wrong; it is due to the Bible in so far as the Bible stood as the symbol of the right of private judgment as against theocratic absolutism. Owing to the inability of unarmed English rulers to enforce law and order, England's laws and England's political order became an envied example to the world, while Europe still lay sunk under the weight of mediæval absolutism. The doctrinal claims advanced by the Tudors to consolidate that absolutism inspired the Puritan burghers' choice of exile rather than submission, and drove them to Holland and thereafter to New England to redress in the New World the balance of the Old, and lay the foundations of a burgher republic which was eventually to deal the first blow to the imperialistic domination of England and to witness its decline.

But the liberating force of Protestantism which had made the Revolution of 1649 reached the term imposed by its inherent and necessary limitations. Intellectual development meanwhile did not stop at the phase which had found expression in the Protestant Reformation. The process of secularisation went on apace; no longer were the issues theological, but purely secular. From the great school of Padua, where from the fourteenth century Aristotelian tradition and that of Arabic experimental science and mathematics had commingled and struggled, and the contest had at last resulted in the triumph of the latter and a new conception of the spheres and methods of knowledge, a wave had swept over Europe on the crest of which rose Descartes and Gassendi. William Harvey had not only profited there from the lessons of Fabricius of Aquapendente, but even more perhaps from those of the professor of physics, Galilei. Pascal, prosecuting the researches of Galilei's pupil, Torricelli, had weighed the air. Seeking refuge on the Continent from the tumults of the Puritan Revolution, Bacon's secretary, Hobbes, had met

Galilei, Gassendi and Mersenne; and when the Merrie Monarch, in the reaction against puritanical tyranny, re-entered London, the first person he greeted was his old tutor, who furnished him not only with the doctrine of his own omnipotence in the *Leviathan,* but with a lively interest in the new developments of the experimental philosophy. That interest became a universal fashion; not only the king, but Buckingham, peers, prelates had their own chemical laboratories. "It was almost necessary," in the words of Macaulay, "to the character of a fine gentleman to have something to say about air-pumps and telescopes"; and the beauties of Whitehall drove to the Gresham laboratories to see experiments in static electricity and magnetism. That dilettantism was the outward manifestation of deeper and more momentous developments of the spirit of the times in Restoration England—the Royal Society, Robert Boyle, Hooke, Halley, Newton. The efflorescence of seventeenth-century English science was in turn but an aspect of the operation of the same spirit in every field of thought. One of the members of the Royal Society, Sir William Petty, created the science of *Political Arithmetic,* the precursor of political economy, and showed the agricultural labourer's wage to be fairly fixed at four shillings a week. As Puritan Protestantism had produced the Revolution of 1649, the new secular matter-of-factness produced the Whig Revolution of 1688, of which John Locke was the philosophic apologist as Milton had been that of the Commonwealth.

Those great developments of English thought, the social results already achieved by English freedom, wrought a profound influence upon the intellect of the Continent, where Montesquieu placed the English constitution, and Voltaire English science and English thought on pedestals for the admiration and emulation of all thinking men. The seed fell on fertile soil.

In the same manner as the Protestant liberation of the Northern Renaissance had settled upon its lees, while the evolution of rational thought proceeded upon its course, so the intellect of Whig-revolution England snugly ensconced itself in smiling slumbers in the beatific contemplation of its unforgettable achievements, of its Glorious Constitution, the perfection of which nothing could better; while the growth of human thought passed meanwhile on; and the seeds of its English season fructified at the new spring in France.

The French eighteenth century is one of the grand climacterics in the history of human growth. All the seeds which had been germinating in Europe since the twelfth century ripened then into fruit: a new era began, in its significance one of the epochs of most concentrated glory in the evolution of the race. Our current view and impression of it has been, and still is in a large measure, too deeply coloured by the profound detestation of all its tendencies that has poured upon it, to permit of the full magnitude of its worth being adequately appreciated. Our attention has for a hundred years been trained upon its defects and imperfections. Much in the theories of the *philosophes* (contemptuously so referred to by Carlyle, to avoid desecration of the appellation of philosopher) was crude and *a priori,* and lacking in a sufficient basis for induction; their generalisations were superficial, their shibboleths and abstractions trivial, their rhetoric declamatory. It is precisely because it was so genuinely alive and fruitful that their thought has outgrown its early form, and become 'old-fashioned.' We do not generally go to it for inspiration because it has become renewed as living thought in our own blood. It is only the traditionalism which struggles against progress which finds inspiration in unchangeable authorities. When our appetite is for fossils, we go back to the Stone Age for our text-books. When we wish to study physical science we do not go to Prévost, and Fourier, and Coulomb, or Lavoisier: we study Prévost's theory of exchanges, Fourier's theorem, Coulomb's balance, and Lavoisier's discoveries in modern scientific language and modern text-books.

As in seventeenth-century England, science expanded in eighteenth-century France, widely and eagerly cultivated, popularised in crowded lecture-rooms, and was there shaped for the first time into that organised body of knowledge and systematised enquiry which was to bear immediate fruit in the conquests of the nineteenth century. In all the intellectual activity of that active time—even the most seemingly trifling, and flippant, and superficial—a new quality, a terrible new dangerous virtue became awake. When the King's permission was requested for the performance of Beaumarchais's comedy, *The Marriage of Figaro,* he exclaimed, "But, Messieurs, if permission is granted to perform this play, one ought—to be quite consistent—to pull down the Bastille!" *Figaro* went through sixty-eight performances—and the Bastille did duly get pulled down. It was by those men, Bayle, Montesquieu, Voltaire, Diderot, D'Alembert, Volney, Holbach, Condorcet, and their contemporaries, who cast aside all conventional formulas, resolved to think for themselves, and, what is more, to speak out boldly what they thought, to own no other sanction or criterion than rational thought, that the world has been transformed. Behind them and around them stood mediævalism in all its ignorance and darkness and tyranny over life and mind, for all the superficial veneer of refinement laid over it by the Renaissance and the 'Grand Siècle.' After them is a changed world, the modern world. It was those men who threw open the portals from the one into the other.

The Revolution—the product and culmination of the gigantic intellectual battle—stands alone among the events of human history. The antagonist which it faced was unredeemed feudalism and absolutism, in the most consolidated and ugliest form of its iniquity, unadulterated and untouched by any evolution. On that one occasion in history there was no tinkering, or veiled issues, or compromises, or expedient formulas, or semi-logic, in the cry of protest and the work of reform. Only for a moment, in '89 and the Constitution of '91, was there any such genteel, mealy-mouthed, good-mannered reserve in dealing with evil. After that first moment, things were actually called by their names, and treated accordingly—*sans phrases*. With a radicalism and drastic thoroughness destined to strike everlasting horror in future ages, not only gross enormities and injustices, feudalism, Divine Right, Sacred Majesty, but the entire world-system of lies and artificialities, irrationalities, root and branch, bag and baggage, down even to stupid weights and measures and calendars, were swept away at one fell swoop. Those newly emancipated feudal vassals were not content with 'glorious constitutions,' 'ballot boxes,' 'liberal reforms within the sphere of practical politics'; they called in plain, ringing, unmeasured words for the last consequences of rational thought, for plain, uncompromising justice, for equality, for the total and final abolition, without terms or reserves, of humbug and injustice in its million forms. Nay, they called for it, not only for 'the State,' not only for France, but for the human race.

Of course they 'failed.' Every European government, England, with its Puritan and Whig liberties and 'model constitution' at the head of them, rose in arms to put down the unutterable scandal. How ragged Revolution held its ground against them all, and against priest-led peasants, and swarming traitor vermin in its midst, and humbled them to the dust, is one of the wonders of history. But in the end many of the ghosts of the Past came back to sit to this day in possession, and pour their venom on the pages of history, and turn up the whites of their eyes over 'the horrors of the French Revolution.' (More men were killed on St. Bartholomew's day by 'throne and altar' than during the whole Revolution, September massacres, Terror and all.) What those audacious hot-heads, those *enragés*, what Marat and the Hebertists aimed at, still remains in Utopia. But the world which they left behind them is a realised Utopia compared to the evil dream which they forever dispelled.

That they 'failed,' that after the close of the meteoric flight of the 'armed soldier of the Revolution,' in the course of which every throne was overturned, and the seed of 'French ideas' was scattered throughout the continent, the eighteenth-century revolution was a closed chapter of history was the naïve delusion of the mediæval phantasms whose sage heads forgathered at Vienna to reconstruct the world as if nothing had happened. Poor belated phantasms! Their venerable grey heads failed to apprehend the fact that a new age had dawned, that not revolution, but Divine Right and feudalism were a closed chapter of history. The Holy Alliance consecrated by the Russian Tzar, and founded, in the words of its preamble, "upon the sublime truths which the Holy Religion of Our Saviour teaches," set about restoring Divine Right and feudalism and employed itself in the futile task of turning back the hands of the clock. The guillotined king's brother mulcted France of forty million pounds' damages to feudal nobility, dissolved the Chamber, gagged the press, muzzled the Universities. Metternich parcelled out Italy among Austrian princes and nominees. Spanish Ferdinand brought back the Holy Inquisition with its faggots and its racks, and replenished the monasteries with monks. Terrified

Tory tyranny in England suspended the Habeas Corpus, suppressed speech, threw five hundred seditious literary gentlemen who dared give expression to 'liberal' ideas into prison, surrounded Parliament with troops while they passed the Corn Laws and the 'Gagging Acts,' and bludgeoned English thought into silence by hangings, deportations, whiffs of grape-shot, and battles of Peterloo. "The false doctrines and criminal associations that have called down upon rebellious peoples the sword of justice," as the collective wisdom of the rulers of Europe expressed it, were to be put down by armed interference in whatsoever country civilisation and the order of the universe were endangered by refusal to recognise Divine Right. Metternich's Holy Alliance, on whom lay the burden of safeguarding civilisation, was "pledged to uphold the sacred powers of legitimate monarchy." Order was restored in Piedmont and in Naples by filling the prisons and weighing down the gibbets, and French troops buttressed Sacred Majesty and Holy Inquisition at the Trocadero.

In point of fact the intelligence of the guardians of civilisation was somewhat defective. It was not revolution but Holy Alliance which ignominiously and utterly failed. Revolution had not terminated, as Metternich and the *Morning Post* supposed, in 1815; it had not terminated in 1870. Before long all Europe, from Hungary to Madrid, from Piedmont to Berlin, was aflame wtih revolution. Divine Right had hastily to pack up its carpet-bag and fly to Holyrood, and presently old iniquitous Metternich himself, pale and trembling, had to join in England the ranks of unemployed Divine Right.

Stodgy, constitutional England herself was in revolution, which was kept bloodless by the salutary memory only of the French guillotine. Birmingham armed to the teeth and provided with spiked balls for use against cavalry, was ready to march on London; the hero of

Waterloo, pelted in the streets whenever he showed his head, was dug in at Apsley House behind bullet-proof shutters; peers were perilously balancing themselves on the roofs of Mayfair mansions to elude the crowd's desire to suspend them from lamp-posts; 'Mr. Guelph's" coach had to turn back, mobbed by threatening subjects, and he and his ministers were too indisposed to attend the Lord Mayor's banquet; Queen Adelaide was under the painful impression that the fate of Marie-Antoinette was awaiting her; the plans of London barricades were ready, and the mobilisation of revolutionary troops and their officers efficiently organised; 'Sancho' Hobhouse reported from Whitehall that His Majesty's army, though their swords and bayonets had been rough-sharpened, could not be trusted. The rulers of England yielded at the last moment "after all arrangements had been completed to cut the throats of all the gentlemen in Westminster," as Carlyle put it. Anything can be obtained in England by constitutional methods.

The age of revolution was followed by the age of progress and unexampled prosperity. The wealth of the world's raw material poured into industrial England. The solid substance of English property eclipsed by its subdued opulence, its West-of-England cloth and polished mahogany, the tawdry ostentation of the courts of kings. The inevitable counterpart of that 'unexampled prosperity' was the unexampled squalor of the English slums, the warrens of poverty of the factory towns, the tenements run up by the speculative jerry-builder as slave-pens for the doubled and trebled population called upon to proliferate in order to supply 'hands' for the production of more West-of-England cloth and mahogany. Those growing millions of hopeless misery were seemingly not to be accounted a part of the unexampledly prosperous English nation.

The revolt of reason, the 'superficial' formulas of eighteenth-century French *philosophes,* had reduced the oppressors of mediæval Europe, Church, Divine Majesty, feudal nobility, to a shadow of their former power, and had brought into being the 'nation.' In the struggles which achieved those victories, the 'third estate,' the 'middle classes,' the burghers, the *bourgeois,* were identified with the people, in the same manner as barbarian kings had born the title of 'England,' or 'France,' and that identification has provided the ground of the fiction which, at the end of the nineteenth century, was to enable Rand mine-owners and Jo'burg Jews to call themselves 'the English nation.' The reaction which normally follows revolution is not caused, as it is customary to assume, by a revulsion of sentiment against the excesses of license, or by the anarchy of transition, or by the mere capricious swing of a pendulum of popular fickleness, but by the natural alliance of the victors with the older powers over which their own victory has been won. The new rulers are, as soon as that victory has been carried, eager to enlist in support of their own unconsecrated power the authority of the constituted tradition upon which the power of their former antagonists was founded. Hence their immediate alliance with the latter. The vested interests dominating the so-called democratic 'nation' become the eager defenders of the faith of feudalism against which they formerly fought.

The diminished obsolete powers see, on the other hand, in the alliance their one hope of survival. And while, accordingly, in the bourgeois age, undivine money holds the reality of power, Divine Majesty and noble aristocracy adopt democratic principles, exchange the sceptre and the crown for the umbrella and the top-hat, condescend, for the first time since the conversion of Europe, to the respectabilities of Christian ethics. Albert the Good discourses with a German accent on the welfare of the artisan, and on the refinements of art and culture.

The situation of bourgeois civilisation is the most abnormal and precarious which has yet been occupied by any phase of human society. Unlike the old absolutisms, it commands no form of loyalty. Nationalistic patriotism, the ostensible substitute for religious and feudal loyalties, is now admittedly a thinly veiled appeal to economic interests, and has therefore no effective value as a means of inspiring submission where that appeal does not apply. The social system of industrialism and capitalism possesses, therefore, no intellectual weapons of control or defence other than those which it may borrow from the very powers to whose overthrow it owes its existence. It stands in an opportunist halfway house of social logic, and is compelled to defend itself against those same mental weapons which it formerly employed, or to employ those which it formerly repelled. The strained adaptations and falsifications of thought which the protection of its interests calls for are incomparably more complex than the interests of any theocracy or autocracy demanded. A new organ has developed in response to those difficult functions. The newspaper, which originated as the seditious weapon of protest, the "vile twopenny trash," which was a hundred years ago the target of Tory fury and indignation, has become a monstrous weapon to dragoon thought, to colour every issue in the ruling interest, and, by a monopoly strenuously maintained by the millions of industrial wealth, to suppress every voice of protest and every unsuitable information. By no Inquisition, by no '*lettres de cachet*' has the tyranny of any censorship been more completely exercised. Never has the falsification of thought in the service of 'interests' assumed a baser form than in the rule of modern democracy by insanitary paper.

The 'progress,' the 'unexampled prosperity,' which

formed the theme of nineteenth-century pæans, were not merely hollow glorifications of industrial civilisation; they were indispensable conditions of its operation and existence. So long as intensive production of wealth continued, the enormous demand for labour safeguarded the system from the fatal dangers of revolt. But that safeguard is jeopardised by the slightest slackening in the intensity of wealth-production. The system can function at full speed only, a velocity which cannot be indefinitely maintained. The ancient civilisations which made no great demand upon labour enjoyed secure control of it in the form of slavery. Mediævalism, which had even less extended use for it, was equally secure in the complete subjection of the classes which supplied it. Industrial civilisation which is the offspring of democracy, and to whose competitive individualism the principles of democracy are indispensable, has multiplied beyond all precedent the supply of wage-labour over which it has no effective means of control apart from wages, and cannot therefore suffer any diminution in the demand without loosing even that control. As soon as the rate of wealth-production falls, with it falls also the power to maintain the wage-labourer and to stem, by yielding to his necessarily rising demands, his revolt against the civilisation of which he forms no part.

As invariably happens, the most signal triumphs of the system of power are, by the law of things, at the same time suicidal. The zenith of Victorian English prosperity coincided with the astute purchase by Disraeli of Khedive Mehemet Ali's Suez canal shares. By establishing her hold on Egypt, England was linked to her Indian empire by an all-English route; her scattered possessions were transfigured into a world-empire. It was the apotheosis of her power; it was also the first step in her undoing. By dishonouring her pledge in Egypt, England, whose Victorian apotheosis closed under the dark clouds of her humiliation in South Africa, was forced to pay blackmail to France at Algeciras in open defiance of Germany. While the 'Hebrew wizard' and all the world thought that he was setting a jewel in the crown of England's grandeur, he was in reality driving the first nail into her coffin. The interests of a power whose ultimate foundations are unjust cannot be advanced without at the same time hastening its decline and doom.

The Great War which dealt the fatal blow to the unstable equilibrium of European industrial civilisation was the inevitable consequence of the structure of that civilisation grafted upon the fragmented state-system of barbaric Europe. The continuous increase of speed necessary to maintain industrial society called for a constant extension of markets and sources of raw materials. Thanks to the progress of science and the marvels of industry, the effort of the contending 'nations' to save civilisation resulted in its ruin.

No gift of prophecy is needed to perceive that the phase of Western civilisation which is now striving to prolong its precarious existence is but an incidental chapter drawing to its close. Apart from all social factors, the European system of belligerent sovereign states, the legacy of the anarchy of the Dark Ages, which no concerted adjustment, however well-intentioned, can cast off without abolishing the sovereign states, assures its early destruction. The social structure of Western civilisation, whose wealth implies poverty, whose power implies slavery, renders equally impossible its prolonged existence in defiance of natural law. Every effort of the powers which rule it under shelter of the fiction that they are 'peoples' and 'nations,' and that their interests constitute the general interest of the social organism, is today expended in holding down the forces of dissolution which refuse to recognise that fiction.

That the field of vision should be clear of the illusion that the present form of Western civilisation contains any elements of finality and is the term of the evolution of social humanity is indispensable if an undistorted view of the process is to be obtained.

XV

THE MORALITY OF PROGRESS AND THE PROGRESS OF MORALS

THE conception of progress which inspired the pæans of industrial civilisation never stood more deeply discredited than it does today, in a world drifting amid dishonoured promises and disillusioned hopes towards dissolution. But it is to imaginary conceptions of human evolution, rather than to the reality of the process that the discredit attaches.

While change is a fact, progress, it has been said, is a feeling, an emotional evaluation imposed upon the stream of change, declaring it to be good. But human evolution presents objective as well as ideal values. Its course from palæolithic to modern humanity includes more than mere change. The operation of the forces which have brought about that process, and which are actively at work in the very criticism and discontent which indicts modern civilisation, are determinate forces, and not forces of indeterminate change. Progress is human evolution, and evolution is a biological process. As in any other biological process, the evolution of humanity consists in the extension of powers of control over the conditions of life. The issue is, as regards the human species, confused by the multitude of varying values by which the extension of those powers may be estimated. But any of those standards, such as growth in knowledge, in intelligence, or in material power, or in taste, or in freedom of development, is but a facet of the process.

All those particular values are, in the biological operation of the process, subject to the specific condition which distinguishes human from organic evolution. The former does not, like the latter, take place by way of the individual. The evolutionary process represented by the history of the race from Mousterian to modern culture is not the result of factors which have operated on the isolated individual; its results are not transmitted by the individual. Human evolution has no reference to the individual, but to the social organism. It is upon the structure of the latter, upon the relations which constitute its equilibrium, and not on the anatomical structure of the individual organism that it has worked. Hence all the values by which progress may be assessed count for nothing so long as they have reference to individuals only, and the social organism itself remains unadapted to the demands imposed by the conditions of human evolution. The triumphs of material control, the development of intellectual efficiency, science, industry, art, literature—those aspects of human evolution, of progress, are precious; but their value is subordinate to the fulfilment of the specific condition of adaptation in the process of human evolution. The biological value of those aspects must be, from the nature of that condition, relative to the degree of adaptation achieved in the structure of the social organism.

That primary condition of adaptation of the social organism consists in social justice. A social organism which rests upon a foundation of injustice is diseased, and, being unadapted to biological conditions, is from the first doomed to decay and destruction. It is doomed for two reasons. In the first place the victims of injustice must sooner or later revolt against it and destroy the social order. In the second place, a social order founded on unjust power can only maintain itself by lies, and by resisting every form of advance which would tend to imperil the validity of its sanctions. An unjust social order is of necessity opposed to human evolution. It is therefore doomed to elimination by the operation of natural selection.

It is usual to protest against the absence of justice in human destiny. Life does not exhibit that ideal retribution, that poetic justice which was once the theme of the moralist and dramatist. Wickedness is not punished nor virtue rewarded. Injustice, oppression, fraud do, on the contrary, commonly triumph in exultant enjoyment of the fruits of their assaults upon right, and wrong goes unrighted to the end. That injustice of the natural order, which belies the categorical validity of moral values, results from the circumstance that the operation of natural justice, that is, the factors and conditions of human evolution, has no reference to the individual. The individual goes unpunished. Not altogether, for his development, his ideals, his values, are necessarily falsified and debased. But the Nemesis of natural law does not, in general, strike the individual, but the social order in which disregard of justice is accepted and established. However much an individual or a class, or even a phase of social development, may temporarily benefit by injustice, the social organism suffers inevitable deterioration. It is unadapted to the facts of social organisation.

The social organism which chooses to set those facts aside, to disregard the conditions of human evolution, and to rely instead upon force and falsehood, upon bludgeons and intellectual chloroform, is doomed to see the result correspond with the means. That result will not be progress towards adaptation to the conditions of existence, but regress towards brutality.

The strong, ruthless rule of a powerful despotism has frequently been accounted the most effective form of social organisation. It commands the advantages which the control of men offers, it secures the achievement of its purposes. A strong government, dictatorship, Fascism, have always commended themselves as desirable resources in times of social insecurity and dissolution, as when Diocletian restored for a while the power of a tottering Roman Empire. The claims of justice, must, it is thought, yield to efficiency. But that efficiency, although it does, in the growth of every form of civilisation, compass the objects which it has in view, excludes at the same time any development beyond them or apart from them. A world of masters completely dominating a multitude of slaves would be a world of stagnation, shorn of the power of evolution, fatally and utterly emasculated. It would lead, not towards Superman, but towards Caliban man. Had such a world been perfectly realised in the Stone Age, we should still be in the Stone Age. Had the sixteenth-century pupils of Machiavelli succeeded in permanently establishing their power on Nietzschean principles, we should still be in the sixteenth century. Or rather we should be in the condition in which Spain found herself under Carlos II as a result of the perfectly successful application of those principles, when it was the proud boast of her rulers that not a single heretic or a single disloyal person was left in the realm; when in the midst of a desolate and depopulated country, sunk to the lowest depths of abject misery and degradation which any land once civilised has ever touched, the imbecile king himself was unable to obtain a sufficiency of food. Such are the ultimate fruits of efficient absolutism.

Justice in the structure of social relations is not a mere demand of self-interest, a manifestation of envy, a cry of the weak for protection; it is a condition of adaptation to the facts of human evolution. It is even the paramount condition of that process, to which, where the choice offers, all other must yield.

Democracy is the worst form of government. It is the most inefficient, the most clumsy, the most unpractical. No machinery has yet been devised that can carry out its principles in any but the most farcical manner. It reduces wisdom to impotence and secures the triumph of folly, ignorance, clap-trap and demagogy. Its critics have the easiest of tasks. Yet democracy is the only form of social order that is admissible, because it is the only one consistent with justice. Justice is of more importance than efficiencies and expediencies of the moment. The moral consideration is supreme because it is the first condition of ultimate stability and development. Justice is only possible when to every man belongs the power to resist injustice and abuse. And that is why, clumsy, inefficient, confused, and easily misguided as it is, democracy is the only form of government which is morally, and at the same time realistically, possible.

The biological requirement, as stern in its operation as any process of elimination of the unfit and inadapted, which excludes the development of one portion of the social organism at the expense of another, which requires justice as the first condition of its healthy life, has been translated into terms of moral laws, of categorical imperatives, of intuitions. It has been associated with savage tabus, with every principle employed by established power to compass the very opposite of its function. However mystical and irrational the traditional sanctions by which it has been upheld, the supremacy of ethical standards of evaluations over all others is the expression of the fundamental fact that conditions social development.

Adaptation to that paramount condition has not been promoted by discursive or dogmatic doctrines which have translated it into metaphysical or religious values, but by the resistance which injustice automatically calls forth. And that resistance has, in turn, been invariably prepared by rational criticism of the sanctions upon which the claims of unjust power have been founded.

The evolution towards higher standards of common justice, of humanity, of equity which is traceable through the centuries, and even within the span of living memory, has not been brought about by professed moral aspirations, but in conjunction with the decay of traditional moral sanctions, by the resistance to injustice offered by emancipating movements that are described as social and political. The changes which have taken place have not been moral revelations or growths of emotional sentiments, but intellectual and social changes. Irrational sanctions of power have been challenged, the assault on individual rights by prerogatives and privilege has been resisted, baseless formulas have ceased to be uncritically accepted, and injustice has been put down as a consequence. The world has grown more moral because the relations between man and man have become more just. If the present civilised world stands upon a higher plane than the weltering world of cruelty of the Middle Ages, if it has been raised above a past when constituted authority maintained itself by crushing disloyalty by means of juridic hanging, disembowelling, and quartering, and silenced heresy by fire and torture, when London was known as 'the city of gibbets,' when human rights were denied, when the infamy of injustice and oppression was sanctified by law, upheld by religion, acquiesced in by literature, when not a murmur could be uttered against it save at the price of martyrdom, it is not by the evolution of new moral principles that the advance has been brought about. No new ethical principle has been proclaimed or apprehended between the age of the Tudors and that of modern democracy. Writing in the Victorian era, Buckle could maintain the superficial fallacy that morality never changes. No new code, no new moral law, no new creed has been revealed to the world; old codes, old moral laws, old creeds have instead been shaken to their foundations, and the sanctions which were accounted absolute have lost their validity. Justice and social morality have not been promoted by ethical codes or Platonic discourses, but by the curtailment of powers established on foundations of irrationalism. To the revolt of reason and to the clinching arguments of pike and powder is due that measure of moral decency which graces modern civilisation and distinguishes Europe from Dahomey, the twentieth from the sixteenth century.

To conceal that process has been the aim of all theories, systems, and doctrines of ethics. Hence has the advance of morality gone hand in hand with the challenge of its traditional sanctions and the decay of their authority. The moral sense has been set down to divine authority, to mystic intuition, to established tradition, to humane feeling, to religious emotion, to submissiveness to consecrated authority, to the refining influences of culture—to all things except to revolt against established wrong.

Having been sedulously represented as a mystic law of supernatural origin, morality has come to be thought of as having particular reference to certain savage superstitions relating to the functions of sex. Such has been the grotesque result of the obliteration of ethical values which it has been the chief concern of falsified theories to effect. Moral judgment has been diverted from the contemplation of the atrocities of suffering inflicted by oppression and injustice, from slaughter and slavery, penury and persecution, butcheries and the brutalised lives of multitudes, and invited to concentrate its attention on the sinfulness of fornication and the immorality of nudity.

The moral tradition which reached the conclusion of its

irrationalism in that depth of inanity has successfully obscured the fact that morality is justice, that justice is the whole of morality, that to do wrong is to inflict wrong. It never occurred to the paganism of Greece and Rome in its best days to regard that manifest fact as otherwise than self-evident, and the connotation of the words δικαιοσύνη and *justitia* was with the ancients equivalent to that of our own terms, virtue, righteousness, morality. It has taken centuries of Christian ethics to obscure that simple truth.

Ethical thought suffered early from a radical confusion which stultified its operation; and that confusion still obtains. It became stultified and sterilised when its point of view became shifted from humanity to man, from human relations to the exclusive consideration of personal and individual character. When, in the first flush of their enthusiasm for rational thought, the Greek thinkers began to consider the question of right conduct, their first notion was justice, their first ideal the just man. Afterwards, when in the Mediterranean world rationalism became diluted, adulterated, and ultimately swamped by the influences of the Orient, that ideal became changed, under the Stoics and Epicureans, into that of the *wise* man, wise, that is, in contriving to protect himself by mental fences against the hardships and sufferings of life. The two actual religions of the cultivated Roman and Hellenic world, Stoicism and Epicureanism, had for their aim, not the regulation of the relations between man and man, but the formation of individual character in such a way that the individual might enjoy comparative immunity from the trials and vicissitudes of life. They produced *animas naturaliter Christianas*. The process was carried a step farther, and the ideal of the current philosophical religions, the wise man, developed into that of the Asiatic saint. The individual was further *comforted*. Thus the original purpose of ethics, the only one which possesses any meaning, the regulation of the relations between man and man, the elimination of wrong and the establishing of right, was lost sight of. It ceased to be the business of ethical thought; and in its stead the condition of the individual mind, its peace and comfort, 'a good conscience,' good intentions, became substituted as the end-all of so-called morality. As the 'just man' gave place to the saint, so for the notion of wrong and injustice was substituted that of sin, and thus mere equity, mere justice came to be thought of as an inferior order of good, and moral excellence came instead to be associated with the notion of certain exalted conditions of the feelings and emotions, and to be judged with reference to the state of the individual's mind rather than to the effects of his conduct.

That transformation by Stoical and Epicurean thought of the original Greek conception of morality constitutes the most profound perversion which the ethical ideals of men have suffered. Moral conduct between man and man, which does not result in the actual good of mankind is shorn of its function. That function is not the individual's own good, his salvation, though it is in reality the highest condition of that good, but his behaviour in relation to the vaster organism of which he is a part. Of that actual moral relation the essence and foundation is justice.

And justice is not an ethereal ideal, a constructive conception, the product of some sublime vision. It is simply the negation of wrong, of injustice. It demands that there shall be no despotic oppression, no arbitrary violence done by man to man, no gratuitous abuse and cruelty, that, in his life, his activity, his thought, man shall not be tyrannised over by man, by virtue of mere power, privilege, factitious authority. Those things are wrong, in whatever light we look at them, so long as we attach any meaning whatever to the word. In demanding immunity from them, man demands only, as he puts it, his *right*. That right, although not founded on the sanction of any contract, not demonstrable by any legal formula, although, if you will, quite an arbitrary claim—regarded as a *claim*—constitutes the fundamental demand, the root and essence of the significance of morality. The elimination of wrong is the irreducible minimum of morality. Whatever lofty superstructure of ideal ethical emotion be reared above that minimum, it counts for nothing so long as the primary essentials of right are not secured, so long as wrong is upheld. In order that a man or a society of men should have any claim to be regarded as moral, it is of no avail that they should entertain sublime emotions, that they should live in a sustained ecstasis of exalted feeling, if they do not fulfil the primary condition of forgoing wrongdoing, of ceasing to be unjust.

Not only is the prime function of morality obscured and overshadowed by the personal and ascetic ideal, but the opposite function becomes substituted for it. Not right, but renouncement is the ideal of Stoicism, not abstention from wrong, but the protection of the individual from the *effects* of wrong. The object of morality is no longer to resist evil, but to submit to it; not to advance justice, but to bow to and ignore injustice. The basal function of all morality becomes inverted; it actually behoves to 'resist *not* evil.' Through such a perversion the effect of ethical emotion instead of being to promote the development of the race, comes to be the opposite. It loses all concern for the human future, for the means of achievement, the efforts of progress. All those things it rejects and denounces as 'the world'; it comes to place its ideal precisely in the completeness of its detachment from all that which constitutes the evolutionary force and life of humanity. It not only does not contribute to them but despises them, resists, abhors them.

Thus it is that those epochs and those societies in which that ideal has been in the ascendant have, in spite of any humanitarian character they may present, not only been phases of harshness and cruelty, but of stagnation, and have promoted neither freedom nor justice.

It is a reproach commonly urged against Christianity that throughout its history it has constantly associated itself with, and supported, power and oppression, that, except in those rare instances where the cause of the oppressed happened to coincide with the political interests of the Church, the power of the latter has been inefficiently exercised in the cause of freedom, in the liberation of classes, in the rectification of intolerable wrongs, but has, on the contrary, been the consistent bulwark of privilege, despotism and established abuse. The old claim that Christianity abolished slavery can now no longer be insisted on: slavery in the ancient world disappeared owing to the failure of the supply, and Christianity had as little to do with the failure of the supply of slaves as it has to do at the present day with the failure of the supply of domestic servants. It is not altogether fair to charge Christianity with the support of Divine Right, feudalism and all established powers and abuses. Motives of policy influenced, not by the spirit of Christianity, but by human avarice and greed for power, the corruption of religious offices and ideals in hierarchical princes and powerful monks, not those ideals themselves, have been responsible for the part played by Christian churches in opposing every manifestation of liberty and progress. But, while that distinction is duly borne in mind, it must nevertheless be admitted that that characteristic attitude has been rendered possible only because the idea of justice is necessarily thrust into the background by ascetic ideals.

The notion of justice is as foreign to the spirit of Christianity as is that of intellectual honesty. It lies outside the field of its ethical vision. Christianity—I am not referring to interpretations which may be disclaimed as corruptions or applications which may be set down to frailty and error, but to the most idealised conception of its substance and the most exalted manifestations of its spirit—Christianity has offered comfort and consolation to men who suffered under injustice, but of that injustice itself it has remained absolutely incognizant. It has called upon the weary and heavy laden, upon the suffering and the afflicted, it has proclaimed to them the law of love, the duty of mercy and forgiveness, the Fatherhood of God; but in that torrent of religious and ethical emotion which has impressed men as the summit of ethical ideals, common justice, common honesty have no place. The ideal Christian, the saint, is seen descending like an angel from heaven amid the welter of human misery, among the victims of ruthless oppression and injustice, bringing to them the comfort and consolation of the Paraclete, of the Religion of Sorrow. But the cause of that misery lies outside the range of his consciousness; no glimmer of the notion of right and wrong enters into his view of it. It is the established order of things, the divinely appointed government of the world, the trial laid upon sinners by divine ordinance. St. Vincent de Paul visits the living hell of the French galleys; he proclaims the message of love and calls sinners to repentance; but to the iniquity which creates and maintains that hell, he remains absolutely indifferent. He is appointed Grand-Almoner to His Most Christian Majesty. The world might groan in misery under the despotism of oppressors, men's lives and men's minds might be enslaved, crushed and blighted; the spirit of Christianity would go forth and *comfort* them, but it would never occur to it to redress one of those wrongs. It has remained unconscious of them. To those wrongs, to men's right to be delivered from them, it was by nature blind. In respect to justice, to right and wrong, the spirit of Christianity is not so much immoral as amoral. The notion was as alien to it as was the notion of truth. Included in its code was, it might be controversially alleged, an old formula, 'the golden rule,' a commonplace of most literatures, which was popular in the East from China to Asia Minor; but that isolated precept was never interpreted in the sense of justice. It meant forgiveness, forbearing, kindness, but never mere justice, common equity; those virtues were far too unemotional in aspect to appeal to the religious enthusiast. The renunciation of life and all its 'vanities,' the casting overboard of all sordid cares for its maintenance, the suppression of desire, prodigal almsgiving, the consecration of a life the value of which had disappeared in his eyes to charity and love, non-resistance, passive obedience, the turning of the other cheek to an enemy, the whole riot of those hyperbolic ethical emotions could fire the Christian consciousness, while it remained unmoved by every form of wrong, iniquity and injustice.

In one of his most charming essays Matthew Arnold enlarges upon that favourite contrast between 'paganism' regarded as the religion of joy, and Christianity as the religion of sorrow. The point of his argument is that, since there is an enormous amount of suffering in the world, since "for the mass of mankind life is full of hardship," the religion of sorrow finds a much wider application than the religion of joy. But of that suffering, of that hardship with which the life of the mass of mankind is full, nine-tenths is the direct product of perpetrated injustice, of conduct which is wrong and immoral precisely because it produces that suffering and hardship. Comfort and consolation are admirable and blessed things, though it may be questioned how far delusive comfort is ultimately beneficial or false consolation expedient—but they are not morality. They are not morality especially while the question of right and wrong is entirely set aside and discarded. Comfort and consolation, forgiveness and loving-kindness, admirable though they be, no more constitute morality than do the opiates and narcotics sometimes administered to the victims of the Holy Office before they were stretched on the rack or sent to the stake. By all means let us have comfort and loving-kindness and mercy, but let us have justice first, let us have right.

The failure so unfortunately charged against Christianity to discriminate between established wrong and manifest right is not wholly unconnected with an incapacity it has sometimes shown of discerning between error and truth. Unconsciousness of right and wrong, of justice, of the elementary moral values, is the inevitable correlative of unconsciousness of intellectual values.

The two things, intellectual honesty and justice, are in fact directly connected aspects of one and the same mental quality. The feeling for truth and the feeling for right, the judicial attitude towards human relations and the judicial attitude towards facts and intellectual relations, are but the same condition of the mind under slightly different aspects. It is impossible for the man who is destitute of the sense of intellectual honesty, who can palter with facts, circumvent his own reason, deliberately put out his mind's eye, blink at the data of truth, manufacture and manipulate evidence, for the self-deceiver, for him who is insusceptible to the morality of truth and falsehood, to perceive aught of the distinction between right and wrong, between justice and injustice. His judgment on the moral plane is inevitably the same as his judgment on the intellectual plane. Moral rectitude is incompatible with intellectual obliquity.

In the low state of moral development in which the notion of honesty of thought is unknown, honesty in the relations of man to man is also unperceivable; justice, the rudiments of morality are unapprehensible. Honesty of thought, honesty of moral judgment—the two issues, that which we call intellectual and that which we call moral, are inextricably united, are in reality inseparable.

The ineptitude of the so-called sciences of ethics which occupy our academic chairs, stammering their feeble dogmatisms in apologetic consciousness of their invalidity, reaches its *reductio ad absurdum* when our principles of moral philosophy are confronted with the task of passing judgment upon history.

In considering the criminal acts of unenlightened ages—Richard I, say, putting out the eyes of fifteen French knights, or James I suggesting refinements of torture to extract confessions of witchcraft—we remark that those worthies would not have behaved as they did, had they lived at the present day; the turpitude of their acts was not an attribute of their personal depravity, but of the age they lived in. Whatever perversity they may have naturally possessed would, in our own day, have taken a different and less outrageous form; the atrocities which they committed are to be set down to the nature of the views, customs, and opinions current in their day. Lion-hearted Richard would, had he lived today, have proved himself a very gallant gentleman. The most high and mighty prince James, by the Grace of God Defender of the Faith, would have been a pillar of the Establishment and a zealous supporter of religious education, but he would not have hammered nails in John Fian's finger-tips. The *mores,* the public opinion of Plantagenet England, were accustomed to worse Norman atrocities than King

Richard's: a Norman king or baron who did not devise some egregious cruelty or treachery would have been an object of amazement; and King Philip Augustus of France was nothing loath to retaliate by treating fifteen English knights in the same manner as Richard had treated the French. Public opinion in England in the sixteenth century quite approved of torturing persons suspected of witchcraft.

Yet while we are thus accustomed to set down the atrocities or revolting moral judgments of men in the past to the barbarism and ignorance of the current opinions of their day, we at the same time continue to profess the dogma that moral good and moral evil are intimate personal attributes of individual 'character,' and to regard opinions and intellectual judgments as lying outside the sphere of moral values. The two views stand, of course, in flat contradiction to one another. They are the *reductio ad absurdum* of the principles which govern our moral judgments. If in one age the grossest iniquities were committed by men who would certainly not have perpetrated them had they lived in another age, the attribute of moral 'badness' belongs not to their personal character, but to their opinions. If Sir Thomas Browne, who picturesquely set his face against 'ambulatory morality,' and Sir Matthew Hale, no less fluent in ethical theorising, could assist in convicting old women of witchchaft, if Shakespeare could callously pillory the memory of Joan of Arc, it was not Sir Thomas Browne, Sir Matthew Hale, and Shakespeare who were morally perverse, but the irrational current opinions which they accepted. It was not bad men who burned women alive, but the Christianity of the sixteenth century.

You cannot have it both ways. Either the conscientious intention is bad or the opinion which justifies it; either Sir Thomas Browne was immoral or the verse of Exodus and the ignorance which accepted its authority; either evil-doers are morally reprehensible, and no generally accepted opinion can be morally condemned, or the stigma of moral evil attaches to those opinions and not to the men who act upon them.

Our current ethics are here reduced to impotent titubation. On the one hand our ethical theories justify as blameless all conduct which proceeds from good intentions, a good conscience, steadfast principles. Our traditional moral estimates are concerned with 'judging' actions with reference to punishment or reward. A bad action, in terms of those notions, means a *punishable action.* And the chief, the only relevant considerations in an assessment of punishment or reward—or their equivalent, blame or praise—are the motives of the individual, his conscience, his responsibility, his intentions. The current doctrine, on the other hand, is that opinions, pertaining as they do to the domain of the intellect, lie outside that of morality; and that no stigma of moral reprobation can attach to any opinion as such, which is held in good faith.

At one time, when rationally irresponsible dogma and authority were claimed to be the foundations of belief, the directly opposite doctrine was held. The grossest evils from which the European world has suffered have been the results of attempts to put down opinions which were regarded as wicked and immoral. The enormities of dogmatic intolerance produced a revolt to which it was found expedient to yield. The reverse doctrine thus received tacit assent—that all opinions are equally entitled to respect and consideration. In other words, when it was found no longer possible to enforce the standard of arbitrary authority superior to reason, the assumption was encouraged that no definite standard of right opinion exists. It was thus possible to elude the necessity of recognising the real standard of valid opinion—rational thought, and intellectual honesty. The mediæval doctrine of intolerance and the modern illogical doctrine of tolerance are at one in refusing to acknowledge rational thought as the sole valid sanction of opinion. Irrational authority, having lost the power of effectually exercising intolerance, claimed the benefits of tolerance; finding it impossible to maintain the absolute supremacy and universal recognition of irrational sanctions, it secured the best terms of surrender, by obtaining for them equality of status with rational sanctions. But it did more than secure the acceptance of the outrageous doctrine that irrational opinions have the same moral status as rational opinions. Since the supporters of irrational authority had treated the opinions of their opponents as morally reprehensible, it came to be professed that no opinions are morally reprehensible; thus the alternative inference was eluded, that irrational opinions are themselves morally reprehensible.

Thus it is that the modern attitude towards opinions has arisen. Rational and irrational opinions being on the same footing, no standard of valid opinion, no standard of intellectual ethics, no standard of right judgment is recognised. Opinions are inviolable individual rights. Their sanctity is as jealously protected as that of property. The grossest irrationality is secure in that protection. Every folly and patent idiocy can claim the same 'respect' as the most stringent rational conclusion. The baby-farmer is sent to gaol, but the 'Christian Scientist' is entitled to consideration and even protection for his 'honest' opinions. It would be heinous to dispute his right to propagate them and to impose them. Should any one venture to raise a doubt about the right to inflict deliberate and irremediable deformation on the defenceless mind of a child, to instil irrational prejudices, to teach falsehoods, to cripple effectually and completely his rational powers, to poison the sources of judgment, such a suggestion would raise a storm of righteous indignation. The cry would go up from the successors of the Inquisitors and High Commissioners that the sacred rights of conscience are being challenged, that it is sought to bring back persecution and intolerance, that liberty, freedom of teaching, the most indefeasible rights of the subject are being menaced and violated. It would be as scandalous to dispute the parent's right to strangle a child's mind as it would formerly have been to dispute his right to strangle his body. All sincere opinions are 'honest.' While their truth or falsehood may in proper circumstances be debated, to apply moral judgments to them is itself a turpitude and a violation of the canons of debate. Hence opinions have come to be regarded as of little or no ethical importance. We have to do with good or bad men, not with opinions. To insist on taking opinions too seriously is a mark of narrowness and intolerance. Wrong must not be tolerated, but every opinion has a sacred right to be tolerated. That anarchy of tolerance is necessarily extended to our historical judgments; we can only bestow praise or blame on 'good' or 'bad' men; opinions are morally neutral.

But, as a matter of fact, the good and the bad in human history have not proceeded from the 'goodness' or 'badness' of men, but from their views and opinions. The men who have inflicted the worst calamities upon the human race, opposed its welfare by every means in their power, obstructed its advance, betrayed its destinies, drenched the world in blood, oppressed it with injustice, the foes of humanity, have not been men of bad intentions—bad men; they have been men who have held wrong, that is, irrational opinions. Far from desiring to inflict injury, they have for the most part been actuated by a sincere and disinterested sense of duty towards mankind. Torquemada, who died "in the conviction that he had given his best—indeed, his all—to the service of God," was a 'good man';

he loved humanity, he was animated, not by any personal and selfish motives, but by a perfervid sense of duty: he roasted alive ten thousand men and women with the sincere purpose of benefiting them and the human race—and quite consistently. Calvin, who murdered Servetus in circumstances of aggravated treachery and atrocity, and John Knox, who demanded the slaughter of every Catholic in Scotland, were men whose whole lives were dedicated to an ethical ideal. Charles V, who decreed that every heretic should be beheaded, burned, or buried alive, and who put from fifty to a hundred thousand people to death in Holland alone, had as his supreme object the maintenance of true religion, and was "clement beyond example."

Read the expressions of Roman Catholic opinion in instigation and in praise of the massacres of the Huguenots, the pæans of exultation over the glorious and meritorious deed, the pious hopes that it might prove but the beginning of more extensive butcheries, and mark the awakening of Christian princes to a sense of their highest moral duty. Those men spoke as pillars of moral conviction, their language is that of conscious rectitude. One might be reading a leading article in *The Times*. We call them bloody murderers, infamous monsters; but they were in their own sight pre-eminently virtuous. The mind of Gregory XIII celebrating a *Te Deum* over the St. Bartholomew was suffused with as much righteous pride and joy as that of Thomas Clarkson on hearing of the abolition of the slave-trade. It is doubtful whether we could even call them cruel: one French bishop on being informed of the plot nearly fainted from physical horror, but yielded to a sense of moral duty.

The upholders of feudalism were inspired by what appeared to them the most noble and sacred ideals. Peruse their memoirs; see in what light their hideous cause appeared to them, with what sense of playing the *beau rôle* they fought against the liberation of humanity from the most outrageous cruelty and injustice. Their romantic young women were fired with heroic inspiration, ready to shed their blood to bring back the rack and the Bastille, the *corvée,* misery, famine, and spoliation, ready 'to die for their king.'

All the tyrants, the oppressors, the kings, the priests, the inquisitors, the reactionaries of all ages, who have striven to check human growth, to maintain the ugly past, to crush mankind, who have upheld and perpetrated every infamy and abomination, have had in their minds the loftiest sentiments, and on their lips the words which they accounted most sacred—truth, religion, morals, honour, loyalty. And the things which they fought tooth and nail bore in their language the ugliest names—error, blasphemy, sedition, disloyalty, treason, infidelity, anarchy, atheism. Those distorted terminologies were not mere rhetorical pretences and controversial tags; they, as a general rule, truly represented the point of view of those who used them. Very few men indeed have ever with any vigour espoused and defended a bad cause, knowing it to be bad. The evil which they have inflicted on the human race has been wrought with a clear and approving conscience. The most atrocious crimes in the Newgate Calendar of history are associated with good intentions and conscientious purposes. The true evil-doers, the most dangerous foes of the race, and the blackest traitors to its most vital interests have been 'good men.' And the evil which they have wrought when they have acted as the organs of wrong opinions, has been in proportion to their 'goodness,' to their zeal, sincerity and conscientiousness. The hell of human suffering, evil, and oppression is paved with good intentions.

The plain truth is that views and opinions alone are ethically significant, moral and immoral. It is not what men do, knowing and judging it to be bad and wicked, but what they do considering it to be highly moral, conscientiously believing it to be good, which is answerable for by far the largest measure of the wrongdoing and injustice in the world. The calamities which have afflicted the human race, the crimes of history, do not arise from malignant intentions, but from excellent and erroneous intentions. The true police function of morality is not to restrain bad men, but to restrain good men. The 'wicked man' of the Nicomachean ethics who "calmly does wrong," who habitually and systematically does what he apprehends to be wrong, is a rare monster. He is either a miserable weakling or a pathological pervert. He is exceptional. Conscious, intentional and self-condemned iniquity is as a drop in the ocean of conscientious, approved iniquity.

And moral wrong is conscientious and approved because it rests upon wrong opinions.

The moral reformer who attacks a glaring injustice and perversion of the moral sense invariably finds that his real adversary is not at all a false sentiment or a deformed feeling, but an irrational falsehood about a four-square matter of fact. He denounces persons for wickedness, injustice, and finds, to his embarrassment, that they are in their intentions neither wicked nor unjust, that they believe themselves to be in the right, and that the real tyrant, the real evil-doer is some opinion, some intellectual absurdity which justifies them in their own eyes.

Strictly speaking, opinions are the only indictable offences. And they are culpable to the extent that they are irrational. There is not a false opinion, an error, however theoretical it may appear, which is not chargeable with moral evil, with injustice in its consequences.

What, for instance, seemingly more inoffensive, nay, almost amiable form of idiocy than that of a saintly, devout little Catholic lady whose feminine emotionalism finds its outlet in passionate indulgence in the mysticisms and rites of her religion? What fanatical rationalist would be so tactless as to offend the feelings of the poor, sweet lady who spends the surplus of her treasures of tender emotion in sacrifice and good work? But give that inoffensive little lady power, set her on a throne, and you have Isabel and the Spanish Inquisition, Bloody Mary and the English Inquisition, Madame de Maintenon and the Revocation of the Edict, the dragonnades and the ruin of a kingdom.[1] Inoffensive! No lie in this world can contrive to be inoffensive. No lie and no error whatever. If it has power it will be bloody and murderous.

We are prone to think of intellectual enquiry, of the pursuit of truth, as amiable forms of curiosity. But in point of fact there is not an error that has not shed blood, nor a false opinion that has not been a breeder of injustice. And every freedom and immunity from wrong which we enjoy is the fruit of some intellectual truth. The supposed line of demarcation between the intellectual and the moral is a fiction. It is to intellectual products that moral values are applicable.

That is true of individual opinions, but it is even more momentously and tragically true of those opinions which are widely prevalent, which constitute the established standards of a people, of an epoch, or of a party, which constitute 'public opinion.' Morality, *mores,* is custom, in the sense that it is dependent upon the nature of acknowl-

[1] It is now customary to state that Madame de Maintenon had nothing to do with the Revocation of the Edict of Nantes. If we bear in mind the character of her influence on Louis XIV, the King's suspiciousness of being in any way led by others, the clever tactfulness of his wife in guiding him without ever appearing to do so, and the evolution of his fanaticism from his "conversion" onward under her influence, we can have little doubt as to whence his religious policy emanated.

edged and current opinions. Individual 'goodness,' good intention, deliberate righteousness, a good conscience, simply mean conformity with the constituted opinions and views of the age. And the constituted opinions of various ages have countenanced and supported every crime under the sun. If those opinions be bad, unjust, irrational, no degree of conscientiousness, of well-meaning and enthusiasm for virtue, can make an individual's conduct and attitude moral.

There are at all times evil-doers who stand condemned by the accepted standards of their age—how far their immorality is the effect of the irrational provisions and arrangements of the age, of its injustice, is another question. But the ethical measure of evil resulting from that immorality is as nothing by comparison with that which is inherent in the accepted and approved opinions of the age.

It is public morality, public opinion, accepted views and beliefs, approved standards of judgment, and not at all individual character and malignant intentions which are responsible for overwhelming the world with blood and injustice. Those are the real culprits, those are the criminals, those are the actual malefactors. The immorality which has afflicted humanity is not a matter of broken commandments, of moral insensibility; it resolves itself into irrationality which renders possible the uncritical foundations of wrong. It is in that supposedly 'intellectual' field that the real moral reform takes place; progress in morality takes place through the overthrow of some view or theory which is regarded as having nothing to do with morality. We are not under the influence of a higher ethical code than our forefathers, we are not animated by a more intense and loftier moral purpose than Sir Thomas Browne, or Melanchthon, or John Calvin, but the field of rational thought has enlarged. If Dominicans no longer burn heretics, judges no longer use the 'question,' tyrants no longer exercise fantastic forms of oppression, it is not because we have received some sublime moral enlightenment. Our morality has improved because our intellectual development and rationality have advanced.

The anarchy of our moral judgments, which renders possible the glorification of scoundrels by historians, of Frederick II, for example, by Carlyle, of Henry VIII by Froude, is most crucially exposed when the delinquent is such merely through the natural consequence of opinions to which even to this day no definite moral stigma is held to attach. Our approved and accepted opinions breed iniquity as inevitably as Sir Thomas Browne's or King James's opinions on witchcraft.

The inquisitor and the tyrant, the block, the stake, and the torture-chamber are melodramatic enormities which have become so remote that we almost fail to think of them as ever having been terrible actualities; they have become semi-fabulous, almost ridiculous in their grossness, like ogres and werewolves, and reference to such obsolete horrors is apt to leave us somewhat cold. But the psychological and logical relation is precisely the same in regard to what we consider debatable views and opinions in the actual order of the world. The tyrant and the inquisitor have changed their names and callings, they wield less sensational weapons, but they are with us still, standing in the same relations as of yore to human destinies.

And the same is true of the moral issues at stake in the present world, and of men's attitude and conduct in regard to them as of the most violent actions of oppression in the past. The determining factors of constituted immorality in the ages of darkest tyranny are the same which operate today in apparently—but only apparently—more innocuous forms. We have amongst us the same delusions of gross immorality believing itself conscientiously moral as in the days of inquisitions and witch-hunts.

Murder and torture, however validated and sanctified by existing opinion, are unmistakably recognised as evil when those opinions have lost their force. But other evils may be inflicted on humanity besides homicide and gross instant tyranny. Lord Acton, seeking a fixed standard of historical moral judgment, made homicide the criterion. But if we look at human affairs from the point of view of the actual natural laws which govern them, even human life is not the most important consideration. Even the sacrifice of many human lives is not so great an evil as the setting back of the course of evolution for centuries. The ends of the great process manifested in the development of humanity, the compassing of justice, are objects even more sacred than human life. Individuals are willing to sacrifice life for those things; the race does not hesitate to cast away lives in thousands, to sacrifice a whole generation in the cause of justice.

The conflict and struggle of which human good and human progress have been the outcome, and which is daily being waged for the same objects, is not a battle against men, but against opinions. It is not recognised immorality which needs to be combated, but recognised morality. Not what is known as wrong, but what passes for right. The task of the forces of moral progress is an intellectual one; it does not call so much for greater purity of purpose, as for more critical intellectual rectitude.

Sentiments of humanity, respect for human life, compassion for suffering are in fact forms of the spirit of justice, and all wrongs which offend against those feelings are acts of injustice countenanced in the first instance by the morality of dominant power.

It is commonly assumed that the moral condition of a

community is the result and expression of moral ideas; but the order of causation is in general the exact reverse—moral ideas are the result of moral conditions. So long as unresisted predominant power, predominant interest, are free to perpetrate wrong, the wrong is necessarily countenanced and consecrated as right. The moral life of a community is necessarily determined by the standard which, as a concrete system of ethics, upheld and sanctified by accredited opinion, is in operation. If the organisation of a society be unjust, if it be founded upon the interests of power-holding classes, it is vain to seek for absolute standards of justice, even where those dominant interests are not directly involved. The mental law which sets the seal of authoritative approval on the established order, and pronounces it moral, likewise shapes every ethical estimate under that order. Divine law always conforms to the type of established human law. Some barbarities have not been direct acts of encroachment on the part of a dominant power and subservient to its immediate interests, but they were countenanced by the character of those encroachments. And it is through the action of rational criticism that barbaric custom and inhumanity, like the abuses of legitimised power, are eliminated.

Intellectual development and moral development, far from being, as is commonly pretended, two distinct and unrelated aspects of human growth, following each its separate course irrespectively of the other, are on the contrary found everywhere indissolubly associated. Barbarism does not mean a rude material life only, a primitive fashion of clothes and dwellings, rough tools, ignorance, illiteracy, superstition, it means also inhumanity, cruelty and injustice. Culture and civilisation do not stand for arts, material comforts, knowledge, intellectual achievements only, but for a greater measure of equity, humanity and justice in the life and relations of men. The moral development of a people bears in all ages an exact proportion to its degree of intellectual competence. Wherever vigorous intellectual growth takes place, there also the conduct, the *mores,* the morals of the community stand through their fairness and mercifulness in contrast with those of their barbarous and superstitious neighbours.

The culture of the first theocratic empires was crude and sterile; so was their ethics. But it marked an advance above primal savagery as notable as the intellectual achievements of Babylon and Heliopolis. The dawn of material and intellectual culture was also that of moral ideals. Semitic and Egyptian civilisations have emerged shamefacedly from their infant phase of human sacrifice and cannibalism. In a dim and confused, but zealous and enthusiastic way they recognise and proclaim moral ideals. They have no clear principles, they are incapable of defining the nature, the why and wherefore, of right and wrong; the form of their ethical notions is still largely that of the savage, an enumeration of tabus and rituals, things to be done and things forbidden, decalogues; they are divine commands; justice and mere rites are grotesquely muddled together, abstention from murder and Sabbath observance are tabus of equal importance and authority, philanthropy and phylacteries stand on the same plane of moral obligation. But there has nevertheless arisen amongst them the concern for morality, the conception of right which finds expression in Ptah-Hotep and in the code of Hammurabi, in the Psalms of Babylon and in the various religious poetries which she inspired.

But it is to Greece, the renewer of mankind, the uplifter of human evolution to a new level, to rationalistic Greece that we must turn for the foundations of ethical development also. Of that activity which unlocked every portal of intellectual enquiry, quite the largest proportion was devoted to ethical thought, to wrestling with the problems of conduct, to the building of the conception of ideal right. As part and parcel of that mighty intellectual unfolding, infused through all its manifestations, was the ideal of man's worth, of the beauty of his purpose and conduct, matching that beauty of his body which inspired Praxiteles and Polykleitos. The ethical thought of Greece, like all else that she has put forth, has fed all that came after her. As in art and in literature, so here also the foundations and principles which she laid down have been the standards which have shaped the world's thought. Nay, to a far greater extent than in either art or literature, the results of Greek thought upon the question of right conduct, of just life, which she was the first to make the object of discussion, have remained the high-water mark of what man has been able to think upon that subject up to the coming of quite new conditions of knowledge, have indeed been in advance of his capacity for many subsequent ages.

Yet so long has European thought been under an influence committed to the depreciation of that aspect of the legacy of Greece, with a view to the extolment and glorification of what passes for the Semitic ideal, that the ethical achievement of Hellas has been prevented from towering on our horizon with the same transcendence as the other fruits of her creative power. Even a Matthew Arnold and a Seeley could, under the heavy incubus of that influence, play upon the *leit-motiv* of the superiority of Hebraic over Hellenic ethical inspiration.

Ethical thought manifesting itself in principle and precept is not the true measure of moral development. But the case is somewhat different when we have to do, not with the unctuous profession of sentiments consecrated by secular standards, but with principles for the first time propounded, which are accordingly the living expression of real growth. That Hellenic ethical thought, like her philosophic and scientific thought, was not decisive, was an inevitable consequence of the lack of scientific data and of the conditions of the ancient world. Only the modern age, with its systematised experience and its adequate perception of universal processes and relations, is in a position to approach the root of those problems. Without anthropological data, without the conception of evolution, without co-ordinated natural knowledge, it would be as futile to expect to find the Greek thinker seizing upon the essential meaning and relations of ethics, as to expect Pythagoras or Archimedes to discover cathodic rays.

But apart from extensions and reconsiderations which are only beginning to be possible, it was Greek thought which created those ideals which have up to the present constituted the moral sense of Europe. And it went indeed far beyond even the professed and theoretical expression of European morality for many centuries. We are apt to fail in appreciating the evolution of what is to us trite and commonplace, and in realising what an achievement lay in its birth into the world. Greece not only enounced the paramountcy of moral right over all human goods, but in a world which implicitly acknowledged the *lex talionis,* an eye for an eye, and a tooth for a tooth, affirmed that "it is wrong to requite injustice with injustice, to inflict evil upon any man, whatever we may have suffered at his hand." The dying Perikles rejoiced above all his claims to honour "that no Athenian had ever mourned on his account," and the dying Sokrates that he felt no anger against those who had voted for his death. And consider, for example, the attitude of Greek thought towards the notion of punishment—that since all evil proceeds from ignorance and folly it calls, like a disease, for the healing hand of the moral physician and not for senseless retribution; to punish is in the Greek speech 'to make just'—δικαιοῦν, 'to make temperate'—σωφρονίζειν. It has taken twenty centuries for Christian Europe to catch up to that plane of judgment. And those conceptions founded themselves upon faith in the natural excellence of man, "for no man is naturally wicked," and sought no external sanction but only the honour of that manhood—"self-reverence, self-knowledge, self-control."

Like all her products, the ethical thought of Greece suffered from over-abstraction, from a too detached intellectualism. It was first and foremost as thought pure and simple, rather than as thought struck out from the sharp contact with experience and life, that it took shape. It was only later, in the world-contacts of the concrete Roman mind, that it attained the full glow and fertility of its ripeness. Yet originally, as the Greek was the intellectual superior of the Roman, so was he his ethical superior also. The hardness of Rome, her coarse tastes, her gladiatorial shows, never could acclimatise themselves on Hellenic soil. Intellect told inevitably on the moral nature of the Greek, even though it was essentially an abstract fruit of thought rather than of life that his ethical spirit developed. The moral philosopher, the representative Greek, a Sokrates, a Perikles, a Euripides, with all their thought-detachment, do not present themselves to us as pious blackguards like a David or a Solomon. With the effulgent growth of the Greek mind, there went a quiet, and real moral redemption; the Drakonian Code was but a softened redaction of the usage, the morality of the primitive Greek tribes, and to full-grown Greece it became a proverbial by-word of ferocious brutality.

It is under the influence of Greece that both intellectual culture and humanitarian spirit grew on Latin soil. The one accompanied the other from the day when Karneades, in the interval of a diplomatic mission, lectured on justice, and initiated the Greek conquest of Rome. The aboriginal *virtus* of Rome, whose energy was absorbed in struggle, domination, and organisation, was valour and patriotism, filial and civic discipline, and issued forth in a certain grand punctilio of honour in her dealings with foes and conquered people, as, for instance, in the rule never to attack without previous declaration of war, in the strict and at times heroic keeping of faith. It was as Hellenic influence became more and more complete, as all the mental culture and inspiration of Rome became Greek, ceased to be antagonised by the native sternness of the fighter, and was felicitously combined with her native orderly genius for organisation, government, law, her natural seriousness and stoicism, and her long habit of balancing conflicting claims, that the great and glorious growth of Roman morality, humanitarian thought and legislation proceeded to develop. From that influence and combination resulted the most important fructification of ethical ideals which the world has seen, ideals which were in many respects false, which suffered at their very root from an original and irremediable deflection, but which have served nevertheless the world for ages as the guiding and guarding lodestar of moral authority. For in truth those fixed and accepted standards of moral law, the spirit which has stood for the categorical ethical imperative throughout the development of Europe, are particularly the product of Rome. The foundations and fertilising impulse came from Greece, and, both through Greece and directly, from the old religious spirit of the East; but in the final form and character which it assumed and in which it has been handed down to the modern world, the 'eternal and absolute' laws of righteousness, and those which stand for the equity of just dealing, the entire ambit of traditional European moral ideas is Roman.

To the intellectual culture of Islam, which has been fraught with consequences of such moment, corresponded an ethical development no less notable in the influence which it has exercised. The fierce intolerance of Christian Europe was indeed more enraged than humiliated by the spectacle of the broad tolerance which made no distinction of creed and bestowed honour and position on Christian and Jew alike, and whose principles are symbolised in the well-known apologue of the Three Rings popularised by Boccaccio and Lessing. It was, however, not without far-reaching influence on the more thoughtful minds of those who came in contact with Moorish civilisation. But barbaric Europe confessed itself impressed and was stung to emulation by the lofty magnanimity and the ideals of chivalrous honour presented to it by the knights of Spain, by *gentlemen* like the fierce soldier Al-Mansûr who claimed that, though he had slain many enemies in battle, he had never offered an insult to any—an ideal of knightly demeanour and dignity which twentieth-century England might with profit perpend. The ruffianly Crusaders were shamed by the grandeur of conduct and generosity of Saladin and his chivalry.[1] The ideal of knightly virtue was

[1] Of that contrast, which might be so amply illustrated, one instance shall suffice. I give it in the words of Professor Palmer from Besant and Palmer's *Jerusalem:* "It was agreed that the lives and property of the defenders of Acre should be spared on condition of their paying two hundred thousand dínárs, releasing five hundred captives, and giving up possession of the True Cross. . . . The first instalment of a hundred thousand dínárs was given up, but Saladin refused to pay the rest, or to hand over the captives until he had received some guarantee that the Christians would perform their part of the contract, and allow the prisoners of Acre to go free. . . . The money was weighed out and placed before Saladin, the captives were ready to be given up, and the 'True Cross' was also displayed. Richard (Cœur de Lion) was encamped close by the Merj 'Ayún, and had caused the Acre captives to be ranged behind him on the neighbouring hillside. Suddenly, at a signal from the King, the Christian soldiers turned upon the unhappy and helpless captives, and massacred them all in cold blood. Even at such a moment as this Saladin did not forget his humane disposition and his princely character. The proud Saladin disdained to sully his honour by making reprisals upon the unarmed prisoners at his side; he simply refused to give up the money or the cross, and sent the prisoners to Damascus. Which was the Paynim, and which the Christian, then?"

adopted, the tradition of *noblesse oblige* was established. Poetry and romances deeply tinged with Arabian ideas formed the only secular literature which circulated and appealed to popular imagination; and a new conception of the place and dignity of woman passed into Europe through the courts of Provence from the Moorish world, where she shared the intellectual interests and pleasures of man.

There never was an 'age of chivalry.' Like the golden age it has only existed as a mirage dimly located in the vague distances of an imaginary past. Poetic imagination has associated it with the brutal and barbaric times of Charlemagne, or with the legendary figures of a King Arthur or a Parsifal. But the ideal of knightliness, of courtesy and honour was throughout the iniquities and abominations of feudal and tyrannic Europe the one source of substantial, concrete moral qualities. That *gran bontà de' cavalieri antichi* forced by the sheer moral superiority of the Moors upon the brigand nobility of Europe, became the sole redeeming ethical grace of Christendom; and the tradition has been handed down to our own day in the notion so dear to the English mind of a 'gentleman.' Thus, shocking as the paradox may be to our traditional notions, it would probably be no more than strictly true to say that Muhâmmadan culture has contributed as largely to the actual, practical, concrete morality of Europe as many a more sublimated ethical doctrine.

That 'refining,' humanising influence which men have always ascribed to culture is not a mystic, obscure, and vague effect of elegant taste and æsthetic effeminacy, but the direct result of intelligence, knowledge, and rationality of thought, upon the foundations of all ethical estimates. Where people are ignorant, uncritical, and irrational, they are unjust, cruel, ready to perpetrate and to tolerate abuses of unscrupulous and unchecked power. Those abuses, those injustices, those cruelties become, when their minds are enlightened, as intolerable and impossible to accept as the puerile conceptions and crude world-theories of the barbarian and the savage.

XVI

WHAT IS PROGRESS?

PROGRESSIVE development is most unmistakably apparent in two aspects of the career of mankind, namely, in the advance of material culture and of social justice. Of those two aspects the former is that which inspired the hawking eloquence of nineteenth-century glorifications of industrial civilisation, and the connotation of the term 'progress' having become chiefly applied to that aspect, the superficial nature of the conception has become a commonplace which is, in turn, taken perhaps too readily for granted. Humanity does not necessarily stand upon a higher plane of being when riding above the clouds, nor does a hundred miles an hour constitute progress. But although modern man's intrinsic worth is not increased by his driving a motor-car or listening to jazz-music over the radio, his opportunities of development in other directions are undoubtedly greater than when he had to hunt for his breakfast and to listen to the roar of wild beasts round his cave. If the material aspects of human progress are apt to be dismissed as husks and externals, the same cannot be so readily done as regards the advance in the conditions of social justice, which, however imperfectly achieved, has been no less continuous than that of human control over material conditions.

Those two aspects of human development where progress has indisputably taken place are those which are most directly subject to the operation of rational intelligence.

Material progress is the product of rational intelligence and of it alone. It is the only field of human activity in which the honest use of that power does not admit of being trifled with. The gentle arts of sophistry and self-deception cannot be introduced into a mechanical device. A machine is impervious to the helpful influence of fine interpretations, and high, consecrated sentiments. The subtle misrepresentations, the conspiracies of silence, the eloquent appeals to prejudice, the plausible formulas, the bland casuistry, which in every other field of human thought have such fine scope are rudely and inexorably excluded from the field of mechanics. Your machine is an irreclaimable rationalist. It is obdurately and shockingly indifferent to conventional distinctions. It refuses to be bamboozled. There is no orthodoxy or heterodoxy in mechanics; there is no conscience clause; there is an utter disregard of the sacred rights of sincere opinions to be respected, of the susceptibilities of the non-conformist conscience. Hence the horror which mere mechanism commonly inspires, and the opprobrious connotations attached to the words 'material' and 'mechanical.' If you desire to obtain a given mechanical result, you must strictly and absolutely, with no saving phrases or polite reservations, conform to facts as they are. If you do not it is your own loss: your machine will not work.

As I have endeavoured to show, the advance of social justice has been brought about by exactly the same methods of intelligence which have created the steam-engine and the dynamo. The connection of the moral progress that marks the modern age with its scientific and material achievements is not accidental. Both changes, the material and the moral, are effects of the same causes. The abolition of the horrors of feudalism, of the ferocities and inhumanities of theocratic and absolutist despotisms, are the result of the same critical attitude of human reason to which is due the abolition of the Ptolemaic system of astronomy, or the creation theory of biology, or the phlogistic theory of chemistry, or the degeneration theory of anthropology.

Progress, where it is manifest and indisputable, has not taken place through the influence of any of the substitutes for rational intelligence which have been recommended, through sublime intuitions, or categorical imperatives, or refinements of sentiment, but through the operation of that specific means of development by which the human animal first obtained biological predominance. It has been brought about by the honest use of his intelligence.

That this and no other has been the means by which human progress has been achieved is confirmed by the circumstance that where that action is not directly applicable, or rigorously enforced by circumstances, no continuous progressive development, such as is conspicuously presented in the growth of material culture and of social justice, is discernible. In the sphere of art, for example, continuity of development is not definitely perceptible. The art of palæolithic societies of twenty thousand years ago need not fear comparison with that of any other age, although the cave-dwellings which it adorns excite the compassion of the dweller in a modern city, and the savage manners of the Magdalenian artist would probably cause him to be promptly locked up as a dangerous animal. So likewise the art of Greece has not, within the order of its ideals, been matched, far less surpassed, by any effort of subsequent generations in the same direction.

Similarly many more intangible and less readily definable aspects of various past periods appear to have presented in different degrees the realisation of ideals on which succeeding ages have looked back with wistful regret. Human progress is not, any more than is organic evolution, a form of predestination urging towards a fore-ordained type; it is simply the operation of the means of adaptation at the disposal of the race. The continuous advance of that adaptive development is therefore manifest where the pressure of circumstances renders that operation imperative. It is not so clear and so continuous where that pressure is not urgent and where the influence of man's specific powers is accordingly more indirect. To conquer its physical environment is a matter of urgent necessity to humanity; to resist unjust oppression is equally urgent; to achieve good taste and to judge life by adequate values is not a necessity which imposes itself with the same stern imperiousness.

But much has to be taken into account before the type of any past culture can be pronounced a high-water mark of development from which the human race has subsequently declined. That it did not maintain itself is presumptive evidence that it was wanting in matters of greater importance than those in which it may be thought to have succeeded. Like individual memory, the laudation of the enacted past tricks it out in the hues of a wistful optimism, filtering away its unsightly and unpleasant elements, and preserving only its mellow glamour and charm.

Many have thought that in Athens during the fifth and fourth centuries human life attained a degree of balanced harmony which has never since been matched. And there is much to render the estimate plausible. Yet there is a large part of illusion even in the most valid grounds of that estimate. The Athens of Perikles is presented to us in the chosen thought, in the literature, which was an expression of the culture of a few. True, that culture has determined not only the outlook of the civilisation of which it was contemporary, but the whole course of

Western culture, the subsequent evolution of the race. But in that inestimable determining influence rather, much rather, than in what it actually won for itself lies the achievement of Greece. It may be doubted whether the most fervid worship of the Hellenic spirit would not suffer some disillusion from prolonged contact with the actual conditions of Hellenic life. Could he be transported to the Athens of Perikles the modern disciple who enjoys the priceless gift of her inspiration would enter an extremely dirty little Levantine town. As he picked his way along the unpaved lanes over scattered refuse he would be blinded with dust, his gorge would rise at the smells wafted to his nostrils from dingy booths adorned with fly-soiled strings of onions hanging in the sun. In the square, low hovels, with the dunghill heaped by the fig-tree at the side, he would find no home, no comfort. Old Euripides, who lives like a troglodyte in his cave at Salamis, fuming there with disgust at a desolating world, is considerably better housed than most Athenians. It is not to the material conditions alone that our Hellenist would need to become acclimatised. Existence is by no means a state of peaceful contemplation in the groves of Akademe. Those immortal products of Greece, those Platonic dialogues, those Aeschylean plays, that Parthenon, those Pheidian figures, that thought, that art, that poetry, whose pacifying serenity seems to breathe the spirit of a divine calm, were wrought under conditions which we should regard as a Reign of Terror. War was ever at the gates. And even the nightmare of modern war and of its volcanic forces of devastation does not include the imminent possibilities which were ordinary features of Greek warfare. No 'Hun' has contemplated 'andropodising' a conquered city. That meant putting every man to the sword, and selling the women and children to be scattered in the markets of Delos and the brothels of the Levant.

That is the way in which the Athenians treated Melos and Skione, Histiaia and other Greek cities; that is the way in which, under the shadow of the Akropolis, the fellow-citizens of Perikles and of Plato calmly contemplated dealing with Mytilene. We are the grateful heirs of the rationalism, the thought, the art of Greece; but in that which, over and above these, humanity has won, may it not be claimed that there has been progress?

And if that be true of the culture which has with greater justification been regarded as the high-water mark of man's adjustment to life, what other phase in human evolution may claim to have stood higher than the present? The Middle Ages have their lovers. To Carlyle, feeling keenly as do all generous spirits, the faults and follies of the world about him, the notion of progress, of the "perfectibility of the species," was the butt of his most scornful sarcasms; but the past period which he held up as an exemplar for the emulation of the Present was the thirteenth century! Some yearn for the mental repose of the abdication of reason, and the ages of faith. But if the conditions which obtained in the Middle Ages were reproduced today, even they would probably rise with the whole world in revolt and indignation against the unspeakable horror of barbarism and iniquity. Neither the Florence of Dante, nor the Rome of Cellini, nor the Paris of the Valois and the St. Bartholomew, nor Tudor London, where the shadow of the Tower and the block lay over the life of every great one, and that of the gallows across that of every poor, nor the century of the Roi Soleil when every light of free intelligence was imprisoned in the dungeons of omnipotent Ignorance and Intolerance, or hiding in Holland, appears to offer a more desirable abode to the human spirit that chafes at the follies and injustices of the present day and levels cheap scoffs at the conception of 'progress.' How many would consent to step back even into that prim and fettered mid-Victorian world that lies almost within our memories?

It does not, of course, follow that because the course of artistic development, of individual culture, of the general attitude of individual taste towards life, does not exhibit the progressive continuity which is presented by the advance of material culture and of social justice, those aspects are not therefore subject to the progressive determination of rational factors. What is proved by the indeterminate fluctuations of those features of human civilisation is that the culture of the individual yields in every instance, as a character of the validity and viability of any phase of civilisation, to the major demand of adaptation in the social organism as a whole, that is, to justice. What is proved is the supremacy of ethics. What is proved is the fallacy of the constant aim of culture to produce individual culture, individual satisfaction, individual well-being, individual realisation. To produce the superman at the expense of the subman may be a very attractive program. But it definitely does not work. Because human evolution operates on humanity, and not on the individual, the superman is ruthlessly ruled out of court by the unchangeable laws of the process. The successive failures of civilisation, the 'cycles' of history are chiefly the outcome of tragically fallacious attempts to create the superman, with the result of creating instead the chaos of yahoo humanity and the necessity of starting all over again.

Strictly speaking, humanity has never started all over again. Nothing of the achieved results of human development is ever lost. Time does not devour its children. That which is unadapted perishes, that which is adapted is preserved. Trample out Minoan culture, it shoots up again in thousandfold splendour in the glory of Greece; crush down Greece, the whole world is fertilised; give the

Roman world up to the fury of barbarian hordes, and the ultimate outcome is Western civilisation. Civilisations, not civilisation, are destroyed. Every treading down of the seed results in a harvest richer than the last. Chaldæan, Egyptian, Greek, Roman, European, bear the torch in turn; but the lampadophoria of human evolution is continuous. Modern civilisation benefits by the products of phases of civilisation which were intolerable atrocities.

The very feeling which causes the ideal atmosphere of some past period to be regarded with wistful attachment is, like the wholesome sense of revolt against the ugliness, vulgarity, and folly, the abuses which offend in the present, a proof that what was of value in that which the past has created is still vital and active. The one feeling is like the other the surest token of the reality of the forces of progress. That modern man is discontented constitutes the most concrete assurance that humanity is on the march. Its case would be indeed desperate if it were content with things as they are. Modern man is confronted with difficulties and problems far more distracting and formidable than ever troubled his predecessors, because mankind has transcended the conditions of the world in which they moved, and the field of its endeavours has become transferred to new and enormously enlarged spheres.

Human beings are chiefly concerned with being happy, whatever notion they may form of what constitutes that state of adaptation to the conditions of existence. The peculiar biological conditions of the human species, however, make it impossible for that adaptation to be achieved by the single individual. The human individual as such has made no advance whatsoever, either in control over material conditions, or in intelligence, or in æsthetic appreciation since the Stone Age. That is why progress and civilisation are spoken of as veneers superinduced upon a foundation of savage human nature. That is also why mankind is concerned with progress, that is to say, with the advance of social conditions as a whole. The adaptation of the conditions of life to the individual's desire for happiness can only be brought about by the adaptation of the social organism to that purpose. Civilised society has been an attempt to promote the happiness of a small number of individuals by sacrificing the happiness of the larger number. But—and that is the moral of the history of civilised society—that attempted compromise is a blundering mistake by which the laws governing human evolution have vainly been defied in the endeavour to circumvent them.

Civilised mankind is for the first time beginning to learn—not through the sharpening of its intelligence, but through the insistent hammering of hard facts—that the interests of individuals cannot be served in any secure and permanent manner without taking into account the interests of the whole of mankind. Civilisation was not set up with that object, but with a view to reaping the advantages of power, leisure, and property for a small number of individuals, and the problem of its organisation has hitherto appeared to be how to govern the mass of mankind so as to induce them to acquiesce in that arrangement. The power, the leisure, and the property of the few who have benefited by that conception of civilisation have produced invaluable achievements, all, in fact, which is of any value in the heritage of civilisation that has been handed down to existing generations. But the conclusion is, nevertheless, being forced upon human intelligence that the arrangement will not work. It will not work not only because it has become increasingly difficult to persuade the bulk of humanity that it is satisfactory, but because it has also become apparent that the civilisation of the few who benefit by the arrangement, invaluable though much of it is, suffers radically from the necessity of adapting itself to the precarious and exacting conditions which that arrangement involves.

The one clear general fact which our elaborate 'philosophies of history' have contrived to extract from their survey of human affairs is that civilisation is subject to 'cycles,' that civilisations rise, mature, decay, and die. It has been customary since the days of Vico to apply to the phenomenon the analogy of the individual life, and to describe the rapid expansion of a civilisation as a manifestation of youthful vitality and the process of decay as one of exhaustion and senility. But there is not the slightest ground for the analogy. Animal races do not perish through senility, but because they fail to adapt themselves to changing conditions. Civilisations decay because the interests which brought them into being require that they shall not grow and change, and because concern with the maintenance of the authority of a tradition is a worse form of decrepitude than any to which the mere bodily organism is subject.

The privileged individuals in whose interests civilisation is run, have themselves come to perceive that it is not conducive to those interests that the bulk of mankind should protest against the iniquity of the arrangement. Their position is made uncomfortable and insecure by the same causes which make the position of those they rule by the pressure of economic facts and the persuasions of intellectual sophistry intolerable. It is to the interests of those who seek to derive reasonable happiness from this condition that it should as far as possible be made tolerable. The sanctions of power have, of course, under the pressure of rational thought become liberalised. They are today less homicidal than formerly. The reactionary would, in consequence of the concern which the present condition of the world compels him to feel for his position, have a hundred years ago been hanged and quartered as a raving revolutionary. The policy which Disraeli called "dishing the Whigs," that is to say, forestalling disruptive reform instead of waiting stupidly to have it thrust upon one, has become a commonplace of self-preservation. Our Tories are the loudest advocates of reform, our obscurantists of 'enlightenment.'

The lesson is being learned, in short, that individual interests cannot be efficiently promoted by ignoring those of all other people. Thus is the present world by way of becoming altruistic. Not, observe, because it has meditated to better purpose on the Sermon on the Mount; not because individualism has developed some new mysterious faculty of 'super-individualism,' as some unconscious humorist was trying to tell us the other day; but because it is deeply interested in not being blown up by the Bolshevists.

Civilisations which provide for the wealth, power, leisure of a few individuals only are always in danger of being destroyed by the Bolshevists, or the Christians, or other Barbarians. And that is one of the reasons for the successive 'cycles' which the history of civilisations presents. But it is not the only one. The necessity of maintaining such a civilisation, which can be done only by an increasing perversion of the mind, a growing intellectual dishonesty, a consolidation of prejudices, corrupts the intelligence which has given rise to it, until it ceases to be capable of civilisation, ceases to inspire respect, and ceases to be worth preserving.

Western civilisation suffers at the present moment more acutely and more profoundly from those fatal causes of decay and dissolution than any civilisation of the past in its most moribund phase ever did. It is more abundantly pervaded with anachronisms, with convicted stupidities, with obsolete superstitions than Egypt or Babylon when their mummified corpses were falling into dust; it is rent with parochialisms more suicidal than was Greece when it fell to pieces from internecine strife; it is more riddled with revolt and protest, and more futile inefficiency and blindness than was Rome when it crumbled to ruin under Christianity and barbarism. If Western civilisation has so far survived what no previous civilisation could have survived, it is because its rational resources are immeasurably greater than those of any previous phase. The power of Western civilisation does not consist, as is frequently represented, in more efficient means of maintaining itself, but in more efficient means of mending itself. Unlike any other civilisation it possesses sufficient rational resources not to be wiped out by Christians or Barbarians, but to be more efficiently operated on by rational agencies.

In the ages of faith the disorder of human society was seriously believed to correspond to the order of the universe, and people blamed God for abominations for which only the Church of God was responsible, and themselves for putting up with it. At the present day it is still declared by the apologists of capitalistic civilisation that its structure is identical with the natural order of economic facts. An even more widely spread delusion is that the follies and perversities which run riot in the anarchy of current opinions are parts of human nature. The fact that current opinions are transmitted by social and cultural tradition and not by human nature is ignored and set aside. Only a few years ago the doctrine was loudly proclaimed that the wars into which peoples have to be dragooned by every means available to political propaganda are inevitable owing to the combative disposition of human nature. That blatant and absurd falsehood is now pretty well exploded, but by an exactly analogous reasoning human nature is held to be afflicted with ineradicable prejudices. That, however, is stupidly untrue. People are not born with prejudices, they are taught them. And the artificial deformation of men's minds is no more unavoidable and necessary than is the artificial deformation of Chinese ladies' feet. There is in the nature of things no reason whatsoever why prejudices should not be eliminated from the world; there is nothing more visionary in the conception of a world free from prejudices than in that of a world free from typhoid fever or small-pox. It is quite conceivable that a stop might be put to the teaching of prejudices.

And the chief obstacle which stands in the way of cleaning up the world is not, as the misconceptions fostered by traditional prejudices lead most people to suppose, human nature, or even the dilemmas presented by economic problems, but the falsification of human thought by inoculated prejudices. Man's world is the product of his mind. What he has achieved is the product of his rational intelligence. The problems with which he is confronted are not primarily dependent upon the conditions of his social environment, but on the degree of intellectual honesty which he is capable of bringing to bear upon those conditions.

The economic problems of labour and leisure are, as is natural in a social order which is disinclined to solve them, grossly exaggerated. Two-thirds of the world's labour is utterly useless and wasted. If the labour expended on armaments and on other things which nobody wants, for which markets have to be created, were to be scrapped, half the labour now employed to keep the world in poverty could keep it in luxury. The social problem is not what to do with the useless leisured classes, but what to do with the useless workers.

The chief delusion, however, from which Western civilisation suffers is that progress depends on economic facts, whereas it, in reality, depends upon rational intelligence. Economic systems, which pass as economic facts, are the creation of intelligence. If those economic systems result in prospective ruin instead of progressive prosperity, it is for the same reason that theocratic systems or feudal systems resulted in cyclic disaster, namely, that, though extremely cunning, they were insufficiently rational, and, in their naïve inexperience, imagined that the wealth, power, and leisure of a few individuals could be permanently secured by the poverty, slavery, and degradation of the majority of human beings. The civilised world is learning to know better, not, as I said, because it is Christian, but because it is ceasing to be Christian and becoming more rational.

We are living in a phase of evolution which is known as the twentieth century and stands for a certain achieved growth of the human mind. But the enormous majority of the human race do not belong to that phase at all. Every phase of evolution from the Stone Age onward is represented in the population of the twentieth-century world. Victorians, Tudorians, ghosts surviving from the Middle Ages, and multitudes whose minds properly belong to palæolithic times far outnumber the people who truly appertain to the twentieth century. When the civilisation of the twentieth century is spoken of as being a superficial veneer, that veneer is not laid on a substratum of irremediable 'human nature,' or primal savagery and stupidity, but on a foundation quite as artificial of carefully inculcated prejudices belonging, not to human nature or primal savagery, but to a very deliberately organised 'education' intended to produce men of the Victorian age or of the ages of faith. The aim of the educational institution of England, for example, is avowedly to produce human beings who shall be effectively prevented from belonging to the twentieth century. The mental deformities by which the blunders of existing civilisations are strenuously upheld have nothing whatever to do with human nature. They are not natural facts, but artifacts, and therefore neither inevitable nor incurable.

If twentieth-century civilisation is cluttered up with living fossils surviving from every barbaric phase of the past, and masquerading as twentieth-century people, it is because no attempt has yet been made to ensure that human beings shall wear modern minds as well as modern clothes, and every care has, on the contrary, been taken to provide them with superannuated misfits. The only carrier of the products of human evolution, social tradition, social education, transmits railways and aëroplanes, instead of stage-coaches, for the material comfort of modern generations, but there exists no provision to ensure against its transmitting sedan-chairs and ox-waggons for their mental equipment. Is it to be wondered at that civilisation is but a 'veneer'? It is; but not on human nature. It is a veneer on the mediævalism sedulously manufactured at Eton and at Oxford, on the troglodytism secured by provisions for the miseducation of the race in defence of vested interests to whom the survival of troglodytism and mediævalism is vital.

Fortunately history shows that the policies of vested interests are effective in bringing about their demise.

Like every step of moment in the past development of the race the successful consummation of present and coming efforts is conditional upon the mental equipment of humanity. Problems, whether economic, or emotional, or moral, can be effectually confronted by no other means than by honesty or rational thought. Humanity must insist upon refusing all substitutes. Failing such a provision troglodytism and mediævalism must continue with us, and all attempts to shake off the dead hand of unburied evil must remain essentially ineffectual. And by that provision alone more than half the goals to which humanity is distractedly reaching out will *ipso facto* have been attained.

INDEX